ENHANCED DISPUTE RESOLUTION THROUGH THE USE OF INFORMATION TECHNOLOGY

Alternative Dispute Resolution has now supplanted litigation as the principal method of dispute resolution. This overview of dispute resolution addresses practical developments in areas such as family law, plea-bargaining, industrial relations and torts. The authors elaborate on the necessary legal safeguards that should be taken into account when developing technology-enhanced dispute resolution and explore a wide range of potential applications for new information technologies in dispute resolution.

ARNO R. LODDER is an associate professor at the Computer/Law Institute of the Vrije Universiteit Amsterdam, and is director of the Centre for Electronic Dispute Resolution.

JOHN ZELEZNIKOW is a professor and researcher at Victoria University's Laboratory of Decision Support and Dispute Management.

ENHANCED DISPUTE RESOLUTION THROUGH THE USE OF INFORMATION TECHNOLOGY

ARNO R. LODDER

*Computer/Law Institute, VU University Amsterdam and
CEDIRE – Centre for Electronic Dispute Resolution,
The Netherlands*

JOHN ZELEZNIKOW

*Laboratory of Decision Support and Dispute Management,
School of Management and Information Systems, Victoria University,
Australia*

CAMBRIDGE UNIVERSITY PRESS

Cambridge, New York, Melbourne, Madrid, Cape Town, Singapore,
São Paulo, Delhi, Dubai, Tokyo

Cambridge University Press
The Edinburgh Building, Cambridge CB2 8RU, UK

Published in the United States of America by Cambridge University Press, New York

www.cambridge.org
Information on this title: www.cambridge.org/9780521515429

First published 2010

Printed in the United Kingdom at the University Press, Cambridge

A catalogue record for this publication is available from the British Library

Library of Congress Cataloguing in Publication data
Lodder, Arno R.
Enhanced dispute resolution through the use of information
technology / Arno R. Lodder, John Zeleznikow
p.   cm.
Includes bibliographical references and index.
ISBN 978-0-521-51542-9
1. Dispute resolution (Law)–Automation.   2. Dispute resolution (Law)
I. Zeleznikow, J.   II. Title.
K2390.L63 2000
347′.09–dc22
2010008752

ISBN 978-0-521-51542-9 Hardback

CONTENTS

Preface   *page* ix

1 **Introduction**   1

  1.1 Fundamentals of dispute resolution   1

    1.1.1 Negotiation   2

    1.1.2 Mediation   3

    1.1.3 Arbitration   4

    1.1.4 Litigation   5

  1.2 Fairness and justice in Alternative Dispute
Resolution   6

  1.3 How information technology can support
dispute resolution   12

  1.4 The benefits of using information technology to
support dispute resolution   13

  1.5 Who should read this book   14

  1.6 Outline of the book   15

2 **Norms for the use of technology in dispute resolution**   18

  2.1 Introduction   18

  2.2 Literature on norms for Online Dispute
Resolution   19

  2.3 Very general: fair-trial principle   20

  2.4 Norms for Alternative Dispute Resolution
providers   22

    2.4.1 The European Union 1998 Recommendation
on Arbitration   23

    2.4.2 The European Union 2001 Recommendation
on Mediation   26

    2.4.3 The European Union 2008 Mediation Directive   29

  2.5 General legal requirements relating to online
services   31

2.5.1 European Union Directive 2000/31/EC
          on electronic commerce   32
  2.5.2 European Directive 97/7/EC on distance selling   34
2.6 Requirements specifically drafted for
     ODR providers   35
2.7 Conclusion   38

3 Developing dispute resolution processes   39
  3.1 Principles and theory of negotiation   39
    3.1.1 Negotiation analysis   39
    3.1.2 Principled Negotiation   41
    3.1.3 Developing BATNAs   42
    3.1.4 Using BATNAs to minimise optimistic
           overconfidence and reactive devaluation   43
    3.1.5 A checklist for negotiators   47
  3.2 Using bargaining and game theory to provide
       negotiation decision support   48
    3.2.1 Game theory and utility functions   49
    3.2.2 Cake-cutting and fair division   51
  3.3 Negotiation and risk management   52
  3.4 Interest, justice and power-based negotiation   53
  3.5 Developing negotiation decision support systems
       that promote constructive relationships
       following disputes   55
  3.6 Negotiation planning – developing decision support
       systems that help avoid rather than settle disputes 58
  3.7 Examples of negotiation decision support   59
    3.7.1 Australian family law and mediation   59
    3.7.2 Damages claims   64
    3.7.3 Business–consumer disputes   64
    3.7.4 Industrial relations   65
    3.7.5 Bargaining about charges and pleas   66
    3.7.6 Condominium disputes   70

4 Technologies for supporting dispute resolution   72
  4.1 Introduction   72
  4.2 Basic technology: synchronous and asynchronous   73
  4.3 The major Online Dispute Resolution providers   74
    4.3.1 The ICANN UDRP   74

	4.3.2 Cybersettle	75
	4.3.3 SquareTrade and eBay	76
4.4	The fourth party – the technology	77
4.5	The fifth party – the provider of the information technology	79
4.6	The nature of the technology used	79
4.7	When the third, fourth and fifth parties coincide	82
4.8	Matching technology with the process	84

5 Advanced intelligent technologies for dispute resolution — 86

5.1	Intelligent decision support	86
5.2	Template-based negotiation support systems	88
5.3	Negotiation support systems based upon bargaining and game theory	91
	5.3.1 Adjusted Winner	91
	5.3.2 Smartsettle	94
	5.3.3 Family_Winner	97
5.4	Artificial intelligence and negotiation support systems	108
	5.4.1 The Split-Up system	111
	5.4.2 Split-Up as a negotiation support system	114
5.5	Extending interest-based bargaining	115
	5.5.1 The Family_Mediator system	115
	5.5.2 The AssetDivider system	118
	5.5.3 The Australian Telephone Dispute Resolution Service	121
	5.5.4 The Australian Online Family Dispute Resolution Service	124
5.6	The BEST-project: BATNA establishment using semantic web technology	125
5.7	InterNeg/INSPIRE	127
5.8	GearBi	132
5.9	Plea-bargaining	139

6 A three-step model for Online Dispute Resolution — 146

6.1	The three-step model	146
6.2	BATNA establishment	147
6.3	Rational communication	148
	6.3.1 Lodder's approach to argumentation and negotiation	149

6.3.2 Using the argument tool: an example
involving family law   152

6.4 Game theoretic decision support   154

6.5 The integrated system   156

6.5.1 Resolving disputes through dialogues   158

6.5.2 Negotiation support through the use of
compensation strategies and trade-offs   159

6.5.3 The outcome of the dispute resolution process   159

6.6 Principles of fair negotiation   161

6.6.1 Transparency   161

6.6.2 Using bargaining in the shadow of the law in negotiation   165

6.6.3 The negatives in using transparency and bargaining
in the shadow of the law for negotiation support   166

7 Future prospects   168

Glossary   171
Bibliography   186
Index   203

PREFACE

Having authors in the Netherlands and Australia collaborate on a book, despite the presence of the Internet, is always difficult. Fortunately VU University Amsterdam is close to Schiphol Airport, and John Zeleznikow regularly visited whenever he was in Europe for a conference. So Amsterdam was always en route from Australia: whether it was via Boston, Lisbon or Tel Aviv. We are grateful to the Australian Research Council and Victoria University for providing the funding for Professor Zeleznikow to visit Dr Lodder.

As with any worthwhile venture, this book relied upon the efforts of many to reach fruition. We are thankful to the countless individuals who contributed in a variety of ways.

Almost a decade ago, while Arno Lodder was just beginning his exploration of the field of technology-enhanced dispute resolution, he held an instructive discussion with two leading, ground-breaking figures in the field: Ethan Katsh and Colin Rule, who were then visiting The Hague. The discussions were invaluable and Dr Lodder and Professor Zeleznikow are very thankful for the regular dialogues they have held since then.

It is not possible to mention all those who collaborated on projects relevant to this book. However, important contributions to Dr Lodder's work (listed in random order) are: Gerard Vreeswijk, Berry Zondag, Stephanie Bol, Frank van Harmelen, Michel Klein and Paul Huygen. His colleagues at VU Amsterdam University provided a rich and pleasant working environment, and in particular he had numerous stimulating discussions with Rob van den Hoven van Genderen.

Even though he passed away a decade before this book was envisaged, it was Don Berman's sagacious advice and unbridled enthusiasm about the role of artificial intelligence to support the legal system that educated and encouraged John Zeleznikow to use information technology to support dispute resolution. Domenico Calabro at Victoria Legal Aid and Shane

Klintworth at Relationships Australia (Queensland) provided much legal and negotiation advice.

John's Victoria University PhD students, Peter Condliffe, Deborah MacFarlane and Andrew Vincent, postdoctoral fellow Brooke Abrahams and collaborators Emilia Bellucci and Tania Sourdin provided invaluable advice and assisted in constructing negotiation support systems.

Without the loving dedication and patience of his parents Masha and Abram Zeleznikow, John would never have commenced his research career thirty-seven years ago.

But most of all John owes his successful completion of the book to his wonderful family. Eight-year-old Joseph looks lovingly over John's New Inventors trophy and wants to emulate him. Whilst driving Ashley, Annie and Eva to cycling, lacrosse, water polo, athletics and theatrical performances, many negotiation strategies were developed and practised. Sarah was always available to give legal advice.

But John's primary support for this project, as well as over the last eighteen years, was his gorgeous wife, Lisa. Without her generosity love, patience and warmth he would not have envisaged undertaking this monumental task. Without her, his life would be infinitely poorer.

Introduction

1.1 Fundamentals of dispute resolution

One can argue that the resolution of disputes is one of the earliest forms of human endeavour. For example, Moses supposedly descended from Mount Sinai with the Ten Commandments and the 613 laws that can be found in the Torah. In addition to providing a framework in which Jews were to lead their life, these laws also gave guidance on how Jews should resolve disputes. But the resolution of disputes and disagreements occurred well before any biblical tracts existed. One such example is the admittedly very informal, but taken from the Torah, dialogue (or negotiation) between Abraham and God regarding criteria for the destruction of Sodom and Gomorrah. Obviously, people realised the importance of resolving disputes long before state-organised litigation originated.

Litigation has a long tradition, and is characterised by its formality and legal safeguards. Judges should be impartial and independent, and legal procedural law should guarantee the processes to be fair (cf., for example, fair-trial principle of Article 8 European Convention on Human Rights). In particular businesses often need faster outcomes than litigation can provide, and want the procedures to be confidential, whereas one of the principles underlying litigation is public hearing. Therefore, for more than a century arbitration has been used to resolve (international) disputes.

More recently, modern alternatives to litigation were heavily influenced by the National Conference on the Causes of Popular Dissatisfaction with the Administration of Justice, which took place in Minneapolis, Minnesota, from 7–9 April 1976. At this conference, then US Chief Justice Warren Burger encouraged the exploration and use of informal dispute resolution processes. Sander (1976) introduced the idea of the *Multi-door Courthouse*.[1]

---

[1] According to the United States Department of Justice, the term multi-door courthouse describes courts that offer an array of dispute resolution options or screen cases and then

Over twenty-five years later Frank Sander (2002) argued that an important evolution has been the development of the field of Dispute Systems Design, which has encouraged the exploration of systematic dispute processing ex ante. Our research on information technology to support Enhanced Dispute Resolution supports this process. Whilst there has been significant work on the use of information technology to support litigation and in the courts,[2] we discuss the use of information technology to support dispute resolution in general, as well as all its forms. However, we do not take into account specific legal particularities stemming from relevant Acts or case law, but focus upon alternative forms (to litigation) of dispute resolution.

In this book we wish to provide support for people to improve their performance in resolving disputes. Whilst we shall be focusing upon information technology tools, it is important to stress that to build such tools it is essential to master the process; namely of dispute resolution. Thus we commence with a brief discussion of four of the fundamental processes of dispute resolution: negotiation, mediation, arbitration and litigation.

1.1.1   Negotiation

Negotiation is a process where the parties involved modify their demands to achieve a mutually acceptable compromise (Kennedy et al. 1984). The essence of negotiation is that there is no third party whose role is to act as facilitator or umpire in the communications between the parties as they attempt to resolve their dispute (Astor and Chinkin 2002). It is the most cost-effective and efficient method of resolving disputes between parties, but it is a process that is not without problems.

People are likely to engage in positional bargaining and face several cognitive (psychological) biases, such as the tendency to be overly optimistic about their positions (Kahneman and Tversky 1995) and the tendency to devalue proposals made by adversaries (Ross 1995; Neale and Bazerman 1991).

Positional bargaining and these biases may result in the failure of a negotiation, leaving parties with the options, in a legal dispute, of going to court, opting for another Alternative Dispute Resolution procedure or not resolving the dispute at all. A facilitative negotiation process focuses

channel them to particular alternative dispute resolution processes. See www.usdoj.gov/adr/manual/Part3_Chap1.pdf (last accessed 24 June 2008).
[2] See, for example, Oskamp et al. (2004).

on the management and conduct of bargaining between the parties while the content is about the issues – the facts and substance in dispute.

1.1.2   Mediation

Folberg and Taylor (1984) define mediation as 'a process by which the participants, together with the assistance of a neutral person or persons, systematically isolate disputed issues in order to develop options, consider alternatives, and reach a consensual settlement that will accommodate their needs'. Mediation emphasises the separation of issues of the dispute and develops options for the disputants.

This is also reflected in the definition by Brown and Marriott (1999: 127):

> Mediation is a facilitative process in which disputing parties engage the assistance of an impartial third party, the mediator, who helps them to try to arrive at an agreed resolution of their dispute. The mediator has no authority to make any decisions that are binding on them, but uses certain techniques and skills to help them to negotiate an agreed resolution of their dispute without adjudication.

A mediator has no advisory or determinative role in regard to the content of the dispute or the outcome of its resolution, but may advise on or determine the mediation process, that is the steps and stages involved in the process, whereby resolution is attempted (Charlton 2000). In recent years it is argued that mediators, although they primarily facilitate the negotiation between the parties, may evaluate the content of the dispute (e.g. Riskin 1996; Brown and Marriott 1999).

Mediation is a non-binding process and most often voluntary. A third-party neutral, known as the mediator, assists the parties in formulating their own resolution of the dispute. It is a confidential process in which the confidentiality is protected by an agreement between the parties and the mediator or by statute (such as in Australia). The fundamental difference between negotiation and mediation is the presence of an impartial, neutral third party who is not a partisan for one of the disputants but rather assists both or all the parties towards reaching an agreement (Astor and Chinkin 2002).

Mediation is not suitable for all disputes or for all parties. The parties must be willing to do, and capable of doing, what the process requires of them. Astor and Chinkin (2002) explain that willingness, in the sense that the parties are volunteers, is often cited as one of the great strengths of mediation. It also implies that the parties are prepared to make a good faith attempt to negotiate an outcome to their dispute. Capacity implies that the parties have an ability to express and negotiate for their own needs and interests.

According to Pryles (2002) mediation may be mandatory (for example in Belgium, several states in the United States, and many Australian jurisdictions), discretionary (in the sense that it may be undertaken at the discretion of a particular person) or voluntary (the parties to a dispute may voluntarily decide to attempt settlement through mediation).

1.1.3   Arbitration

Arbitration is an adversarial process whereby an independent third party, after hearing submissions from the disputants, makes an award binding upon the parties. An arbitrator can be part of a court-annexed scheme, or the parties may choose an arbitrator who is not necessarily legally qualified. In some jurisdictions, such as France and India, arbiters need to have a legal background. The choice of arbitrator may be based on his or her particular expert knowledge of the subject matter, for example an engineer or accountant. The arbitration process could be as close to judicial determination as one can get (Charlton 2000).

The English Arbitration Act 1697 provided a procedure whereby parties to a civil action could refer their matter to arbitration and have the ensuring award enforced as a judgment of the court. The establishment of the Institute of Arbitrators Australia in 1975 provided a professional organisation for the development of an arbitral identity and for the training of arbitrators (Astor and Chinkin 2002). The process includes many elements of courtroom trials: a formal hearing, examination and cross-examination of witnesses, the use of experts and the submission of evidence (Solovay and Reed 2003). Arbitration is an enforceable process and often subject to the governance of law enforcement (Astor and Chinkin 2002). Australia law on arbitration is based on international conventions, legislation (both federal and state) and the common law.

Mediation and arbitration are both Alternative Dispute Resolution (ADR) processes,[3] but have distinct purposes and hence distinct

---

[3] It actually depends on how one qualifies the term 'Alternative'. The process can be considered an alternative to public dispute resolution (e.g. litigation), in which case all private dispute resolution processes are considered ADR. This is how we see it, so arbitration is part of ADR. The term ADR is also used to denote an alternative approach to dispute resolution, hence a non-adversarial process that is not about winning and losing. Under that definition of ADR, arbitration is not part of it.

moralities. Astor and Chinkin (2002) argue that the morality of mediation lies in optimum settlement in which each party gives up what she values less, in return for what she values more. The morality of arbitration lies in a decision according to the law of contract. In most jurisdictions a court may not set aside or remit an award on the ground of error of fact or laws on the face of the award. One could say that arbitral awards are also binding for the judiciary. The New York Convention even guarantees that awards from arbitration processes abiding to the arbitration law of a state that signed the Convention (over 100 states) can be executed in any other state that signed the Convention. This is one reason why arbitration is popular for US companies. The United States does not have any treaties on the execution of foreign verdicts, but has signed the New York Convention.

1.1.4 Litigation

Black (1990) views litigation 'as a contest in a court of law for the purpose of enforcing a right or seeking a remedy'. ADR is commonly recognised as applying to processes that are alternatives to the traditional legal methods of solving disputes (Charlton 2000).

ADR and litigation are fundamentally different approaches for resolving disputes. Most ADR processes are concerned with bargaining and trade-offs, whereas litigation is primarily concerned with justice. Even arbitration, the most rigid ADR process, differs from court proceedings in that the rules of substantive and procedural law are relaxed, they can be adapted to the specific needs of the forum and institutionalised within the formal justice system (Solovay and Reed 2003).

It should be pointed out that in addition to negotiation, mediation, arbitration and litigation there are numerous other dispute resolution processes, as well as combined or hybrid dispute resolution processes. These are processes in which the dispute resolution practitioner plays multiple roles. For example, in conciliation and in conferencing, the dispute resolution practitioner may facilitate discussions, as well as provide advice on the merits of the dispute. In hybrid processes, such as med-arb, the practitioner first uses one process (mediation) and then a different one (arbitration).

Goldberg *et al.* (1985: 3) claim that:

> the 1960s were characterised by considerable strife and conflict. An apparent legacy of those times was a lessened tolerance for grievances and a greater tendency to turn them into lawsuits ... One factor was the waning role of some of society's traditional mediating institutions – the

family, the church and the community … The net result was an increased volume of legal claims, many of which had not been previously recognised. Courts began to find themselves inundated with new filings, triggering cries of alarm from the judicial administration establishment. At the same time, judicial congestion, with its concomitant delay, led to claims of denial of access to justice. One response to these problems was a demand for more judges and more courtrooms: another was a search for alternatives to the courts … The supporters of the alternative movement had four separate goals:

(1) to relieve court congestion as well as undue cost and delay;
(2) to enhance community involvement in the dispute resolution process;
(3) to facilitate access to justice;
(4) to provide more 'effective' dispute resolution.

This observation is particularly interesting for it explains that mediation as introduced in the 1970s and 1980s was not primarily a new movement but a way to compensate for the loss of the traditional mediators (family, church, community).

1.2   Fairness and justice in Alternative Dispute Resolution

Walton and McKersie (1965) propose that negotiation processes can be classified as distributive or integrative. In distributive approaches, the problems are seen as *zero-sum* and resources are imagined as fixed: *divide the pie*. In integrative approaches, problems are seen as having more potential solutions than are immediately obvious and the goal is to *expand the pie* before dividing it. Parties attempt to accommodate as many interests of each of the parties as possible, leading to the so-called *win–win* or *all gain* approach. Although Walton and McKersie did not suggest one type of negotiation being superior to the other, Kersten (2001) notes that, over the years, it has become conventional wisdom that the integrative type allows for *better compromises, win–win solutions, value creation* and *expanding the pie*. Fisher and Ury (1981), Fisher *et al.* (1994) and Lax and Sebenius (1986) discuss these issues in detail.

Traditional negotiation decision support has focused upon providing users with decision support on how they might best obtain their goals. Such advice is often based on Nash's principles of optimal negotiation or bargaining (Nash 1953). Game theory, as opposed to behavioural and descriptive studies, provides formal and normative approaches to model bargaining. One of the distinctive key features of game theory is the consideration of zero-sum and non-zero-sum games. These concepts were adopted to distinguish between distributive and integrative processes.

Limitations of game theory in providing prescriptive advice sought by disputants and their advisers on one hand, and the developments in multi-criteria decision-making and interactive methods on the other, provided the groundwork for negotiation analysis as discussed in Holsapple and Whinston (1996), Howard and Matheson (1981), Saaty (1980) and Raiffa (1982). Game theory has been used as the basis for the Adjusted Winner algorithm (Brams and Taylor 1996) and the negotiation support systems Smartsettle (Thiessen and McMahon 2000) and Family_Winner (Bellucci and Zeleznikow 2006).

Much negotiation outside the legal domain focuses upon interest-based negotiation. Expanding on the notion of integrative or inter-est-based negotiation, Fisher and Ury (1981) developed the notion of principled negotiation. Principled negotiation promotes deciding issues on their merits rather than through a haggling process focused on what each side says it will and will not do. Amongst the features of principled negotiation are:

(1) separating the people from the problem;
(2) focusing upon interests rather than positions;
(3) insisting upon objective criteria; and
(4) knowing your *BATNA* (*Best Alternative To a Negotiated Agreement*).

In the domain of legal negotiation, Mnookin and Kornhauser (1979) introduced the notion of bargaining in the shadow of the trial (or law). By examining the case of divorce law, they contended that the legal rights of each party could be understood as bargaining chips that can affect settlement outcomes. Bibas (2004) has claimed that some scholars (but not himself) treat plea-bargaining as simply another case of bargaining in the shadow of a trial. He notes that 'the conventional wisdom is that litigants bargain towards settlement in the shadow of expected trial out-comes. In this model, rational parties forecast the expected trial outcome and strike bargains that leave both sides better off by splitting the saved costs of trial ... This shadow of trial model now dominates the literature on civil settlements'.

But does Alternative Dispute Resolution *provide more 'effective' dis-pute resolution*? Commentators such as Alexander (1997) and Raines and Conley Tyler (2007) have questioned whether such developments have always taken into account notions of justice and fairness. In particular, they worry whether this trend has led to certain parties being unjustly treated. McEwen *et al.* (1995), Phegan (1995) and Zeleznikow (2009) examine these issues in the context of family law. Mack and Roach Anleu (1997 and 1998) consider issues of fairness in plea-bargaining.

For example, are accused persons disadvantaged in guilty plea negotiations because of a lack of available information on sentencing precedents? Are some parties before the Family Court accepting outcomes which are unjust to both themselves and/or their children? In addition to the standard problems associated with the use of information technology and decision support systems (such as usability), how can we ensure that the advice tendered by decision support systems providing negotiation advice is 'reasonable', 'consistent' and 'based upon publicly acceptable principles'?

Essentially, bargaining in the shadow of the law and the provision of BATNAs add notions of justice to interest-based negotiation. Druckman (2005: 276) postulates whether fairer negotiations are more endurable. To even approach this question we must develop techniques for deciding what is a 'fair' or 'just' negotiation. And when we can define a negotiation to have 'endured'. And it is equally important to make trade-offs between fairness and endurance and cost and speed. After all, if we complicate our processes by focusing upon fairness, we may escalate the cost and decrease the speed of systems to the extent that there are limited benefits for using information technology to support dispute resolution.

In his masterpiece, *Animal Farm*, the British novelist George Orwell (1945) developed the mantra 'four legs good, two legs bad'.[4] Similarly many governments have promoted the principle that 'negotiation is good and conflict is bad'.[5] This is not surprising, since most conflicts are destructive and normally solutions to conflicts contribute better to society than conflicts do.

In Australia, both the federal and state governments have strongly promoted Alternative Dispute Resolution as a preferred option to litigation. They have emphasised the benefits of greater speed; more flexibility in outcomes; that it is more informal and that it is solution- rather than blame-oriented. However there is little doubt that they view the major benefit to be the reduced cost in the provision of court and legal services. Prior to being allowed to appear before the Family Court of Australia, disputants must engage in compulsory mediation. In commercial disputes,

---

[4] Here Orwell was implying humans were evil whilst farm animals were kind.
[5] Significantly, in the final scene of *Animal Farm*, once the pigs have taken over the farm, they take on human features: 'four legs good, two legs better'.

Australian judges regularly suggest litigants undertake some form of mediation prior to the court further hearing the case. But is undertaking the process of negotiation desirable in all instances?

Consider for example the situation of the British Prime Minister, Neville Chamberlain, on returning from Munich in August 1938. Chamberlain claimed that we have 'peace in our time'. Yet within a little over twelve months:

(1) Kristallnacht in Germany and Austria on 9 and 10 November 1938 led to the destruction of Jewish property and synagogues as well as numerous deaths. Whilst this was not the commencement of Nazi anti-Semitism it was a significant escalation and milestone towards the 'Final Solution'.

(2) The Molotov–Ribbentrop Pact of June 1939 divided Poland into German (Western Poland) and Soviet (Eastern Poland) sectors.

(3) On 1 September 1939 Germany invaded Western Poland leading to the commencement of the Second World War.

Was Chamberlain correct in his views to accept the negotiations concluded in the Treaty of Munich? Were his negotiations successful? Most people would answer no, and that by acceding to Hitler's wishes Chamberlain encouraged German belligerence.

But even seventy years later, supporters (or apologists, depending upon one's viewpoint) of Chamberlain rationalise that he was correct in accepting the treaty, and won the United Kingdom vital time to prosecute the war.[6]

It is important that we develop measures for when to negotiate and when to continue conflicts. Mnookin (2003) considers the issue of when to negotiate. He develops a framework of six issues that should be considered in making a decision about whether to conduct a negotiation:

(1) identify your interests and those of the other parties;
(2) think about all sides' BATNAs;
(3) try to imagine options that might better serve the negotiators' interests than their BATNAs;
(4) ensure that the commitments made in any negotiated deal have a reasonable prospect of actually being implemented;

---

[6] As did the former Australian Prime Minister Sir Robert Gordon Menzies in the twenty-second Sir Richard Stawell Oration, 'Churchill and his Contemporaries', delivered at the University of Melbourne on 8 October 1955 – see www.menziesvirtualmuseum.org. au/transcripts/Speech_is_of_Time/202_ChurchillContemp.html (last accessed 23 July 2008).

(5) consider the expected costs – both direct and indirect (such as damage to reputation and setting adverse precedents) – of engaging in the negotiation process;
(6) consider issues of legitimacy and morality – the mere process of negotiating with a counterpart confers some recognition and legitimacy on them.

Alternative Dispute Resolution has many implications that are not immediately clear, and that could be undesirable. For example, in Australia and the United States bargaining about charges and pleas occurs. Because such bargaining is an alternative to judicial decision-making, we view it as a form of Alternative Dispute Resolution.

Under plea-bargaining practices, which is not the case in litigation, a participant cannot challenge a decision. Consider the case of an Australian resident, but Croatian citizen, who is offered a non-custodial sentence for a crime he did not commit, but of which he has been advised he is likely to be convicted. Whilst he may receive a charge or plea bargain that keeps him out of jail, he does not realise he will never be allowed to visit his family in the United States and will be deported to Croatia.

When using information technology to support dispute resolution we must focus upon the issue of providing 'fair' and 'just' negotiation support. But what do we mean by '*fair*'? Unlike most users of the word '*fair*' in relation to negotiation, we do not mean 'fairness' in meeting the interests of the disputants. We mean '*fair*' in meeting the concept of '*justice*'.

Brams and Taylor (1996) and Raith (2000) also examine fair-division in negotiation. However, their notion of 'fairness' is not related to the fairness of outcomes respective to societal values. Rather, they are concerned that their algorithms are equitable in distributing issues in dispute equally to both parties in a two-party dispute. Raith (2000) argues that:

> in contrast to 'normative' mathematical models of bargaining or 'descriptive' analyses of actual negotiations, negotiation analysis is a practically oriented field of research that can be characterized as 'prescriptive', meaning that the objective is to give procedural advice on how negotiators can reach a mutually beneficial outcome.

According to Brams and Taylor (1996):

> bargaining theories have proved inapplicable to the settlement of real-life disputes because of their divorce from theories of fair division. They show that, by viewing negotiation problems as problems of fair division, one can apply intuitive procedures to a variety of complex conflicts.

Lowenstein *et al.* (1993) note that:

> concerns about fairness and unfairness affect bargaining. The classical example is ultimatum bargaining: one person divides an amount between herself and another person. If the other person rejects the proposed division, both people get nothing. Self-interested bargainers who are neither altruistic nor envious should offer the smallest possible amount and the offer should be accepted. Nevertheless, in most studies, people keep an amount of 60% for themselves and 40% to the other person. When less than 20% is offered, the offer is typically rejected.

Druckman and Albin (2008) explore the relationship between principles of justice and the durability of negotiated agreements. Focusing primarily on peace agreements negotiated during the early 1990s, the study provides evidence for a positive relationship between a negotiation being just and that negotiation enduring over time.

In current research,[7] we believe that if the following principles are applied, '*fairness*' in the development of negotiation support systems will improve:

(1) The provision of transparency: by promoting transparency we will know how the process worked. This is important for ensuring procedural justice. We will be able to recreate past decisions and rectify those decisions that were unfair (this is especially important in bargaining about charges and pleas).

(2) Bargaining in the shadow of the law: through the appropriate use of bargaining in the shadow of the law we will develop standards for adhering to *legally just* and *fair* norms. By using bargaining in the shadow of the law, we can use facilitative mediation (as in Family_ Mediator) to ensure mediation is fair.

There are, however, certain dangers in promoting transparency and bargaining in the shadow of the law for negotiation support:

(1) disputants might be reluctant to be frank if they feel their opinions might be circulated;

(2) disputants may worry that the negotiated agreement might encourage others to pursue similar future settlements;

---

[7] In a keynote address to the Group Decision and Negotiation Conference, *Incorporating Interests and Fairness in the Development of Negotiation Support Systems*, at the University of Coimbra, Portugal, 20 June 2008. A revised version of the paper has been submitted to the *Group Decision and Negotiation* journal.

(3) by advocating advice upon bargaining in the shadow of the law, mediators might be seen to be biased (such as in evaluative mediation);
(4) developing systems might be more complex and costly.

In Chapter 3 we shall investigate how bargaining and other theories can provide negotiation decision support.

1.3   How information technology can support dispute resolution

Until now, we have discussed dispute resolution, but not information technology. The reason for this is that once the processes have been developed, the appropriate systems will follow. The main task in knowledge management[8] and software engineering[9] is the development of accurate and effective processes.

Further, our goal is to assist dispute resolution rather than to merely create information systems. Information technology is one of many useful tools for supporting dispute resolution. But to use information technology appropriately, we need to have a good understanding of dispute resolution. Our goal is not to develop computing paradigms but to use appropriately information technology to support dispute resolution. Hence we must have a good understanding of the principles behind Alternative Dispute Resolution.

In Chapter 4 we will investigate existing technologies for dispute resolution. Following our paper published in the *Harvard Negotiation Law Review* (Lodder and Zeleznikow 2005), we will view negotiation decision support in law as a three-step process:

receiving advice about BATNAs;
allowing the disputants to conduct dialogues and arguments amongst each other;
providing negotiation decision analysis advice to the disputants.

Information systems that provide exactly one of (1), (2) or (3) have been developed and will be discussed in Chapter 4. The authors, both separately

---

[8] Knowledge management involves a variety of techniques used by individuals and organisations to create, distribute, identify and represent knowledge.
[9] Software engineering is the application of a systematic, disciplined, quantifiable approach to the development, operation and maintenance of software. 'IEEE Standard Glossary of Software Engineering Terminology', IEEE std 610.12–1990, 1990.

and jointly, are currently conducting research to develop negotiation support systems that incorporate (1), (2) and (3).

1.4 The benefits of using information technology to support dispute resolution

Katsh and Rifkin (2001) state that compared to litigation, Alternative Dispute Resolution has the following advantages:

(1) lower cost;
(2) greater speed;
(3) more flexibility in outcomes;
(4) less adversarial;
(5) more informal;
(6) solution- rather than blame-oriented;
(7) private.

Online Dispute Resolution has additional benefits including:

(8) disputants do not have to meet face to face: an important factor if there has been a history of violence; and
(9) mediation can occur at any time, with participants located in different countries.

The use of information technology can further promote many of the benefits of Alternative Dispute Resolution. Receiving advice online, with the potential benefits of decision support systems, will reduce costs due to a lower reliance on support from lawyers and mediators. Further, because this advice will be available online, or at least through the use of computer systems, such advice will be timely. The backlog in seeing lawyers or mediators will be less critical. Anecdotal evidence shows that the time taken to hear a dispute is often a factor in the successful resolution of that dispute. The sooner disputants are able to have their views heard, the more likely is the prospect of a successful resolution.

A further advantage of using negotiation support systems is the ability for disputants and mediators to conduct hypotheticals. Rather than mandate solutions, systems such as Family_Winner offer advice. If users of the system are not happy with the advice given by the system, they can alter their inputs. This forces the disputants to reconsider their priorities.

Systems such as Adjusted Winner, Smartsettle and Family_Winner, discussed in detail in Chapter 5, use bargaining and game theory to provide win–win solutions to participants in disputes. Because of their ability

to efficiently search through a wide variety of solutions and meet disputants' needs, they can provide more flexibility in providing a useful range
of outcomes.

The use of information technology can also enhance the ability of
citizens to access justice: whether by filing online complaints or receiving online advice. Such advice is generally given quickly and cheaply.
Further, such systems provide for the effective use of e-government and
e-commerce.

According to Colin Rule,[10] Director of Dispute Resolution at eBay,
thirty-five million disputes were filed with eBay in 2006. eBay has developed many resources for supporting Online Dispute Resolution. eBay
develops such resources not because it wishes to be seen as a good corporate company developing principles of fairness, but because it believes that
doing so is good commercial practice. Without secure and fair Online
Dispute Resolution processes, consumers would be reluctant to purchase
products over the Internet: whether from eBay, Amazon, low-cost airlines
or a multitude of other companies.

1.5 Who should read this book

This book focuses upon how information technology (IT) can help support dispute resolution. It attempts to solve the following problems:

(1) How to cope with the rapidly escalating number of disputes: both offline and on the Internet.[11]
(2) How to harness the increasing availability of IT to support decision-
making.
(3) How to employ IT to support the resolution of conflicts.

In doing so, we attempt to clarify the confusions held by many computer
scientists, who argue that IT can only be used to make decisions. They
thus develop automated negotiation systems. We argue that IT is most
appropriately used to advise humans how to improve their negotiation

---

[10] Talk given at the Fourth International Conference on Online Dispute Resolution, held in
conjunction with the Tenth International Conference on Artificial Intelligence and Law,
Palo Alto, 8 June 2007, see http://odrworkshop.info.
[11] The number of transactions occurring over the Internet is rising rapidly, and so is the
number of disputes. Whilst the number of judicial decisions occurring in US civil and
criminal couts is declining, the amount of litigation is decreasing. The litigation is being
resolved through alternative (to litigation) methods of dispute resolution (Stipanowich
2004). This article provides empirical data that most conflicts are being settled via ADR
rather than by trial judgments.

performance. Thus IT is a decision support tool. It does not make decisions. IT can also be used to enhance communication between parties to a dispute.

This book is unique in that it proposes solutions for using IT to provide negotiation support, rather than merely indicating the need for Online Dispute Resolution (ODR).[12] With the growing prevalence of electronic and non-electronic disputes, it is important to provide electronic advice regarding dispute resolution for the benefit of the judiciary, lawyers, litigants, businesses and the general public.[13]

The book is hence of interest to the following categories of readers:

(1) Dispute resolution professionals, such as lawyers, mediators, businessmen, paralegals and students.
(2) Developers of automated or semi-automated ODR systems who are interested in knowing not only about relevant technologies, but also about ADR and ODR principles.
(3) The book is written for a general audience interested in dispute resolution and how IT can support the resolution of disputes.[14]
(4) It will prove invaluable to both undergraduate and postgraduate students studying ADR, law, economics and business.
(5) The book will serve as an introduction to how IT can support dispute resolution for many professionals, such as accountants, arbitrators and mediators, the judiciary, lawyers, paralegals and businessmen.
(6) The technology and all other material will be explained at a level understandable to any high-school graduate.

1.6   Outline of the book

Following this introductory chapter, in Chapter 2 we examine benefits and barriers to the use of information technology to support dispute resolution. Issues discussed include animosity between parties, convenience, costs and distance. Whilst examining norms for the use of IT in

---

[12] Books such as *Cross-border Internet Disputes* write about the fundamental laws required for ODR to work effectively, whilst this book is about the fundamental technical and organisational mechanisms necessary for ODR to work without too much human input.
[13] Further, we argue that disputes that arose online can most appropriately be resolved online.
[14] In the text, we will try to limit any mathematical formalisms, so that it can be understood by dispute resolution practitioners. Thus those not interested in formalisms can avoid this material, whilst those who are comforted by the notion that the ideas presented are soundly based can peruse the relevant mathematics.

dispute resolution, we consider both online and offline disputes, how to ensure that parties are treated equally, confidentiality, trust that the process is fair and enforceability of the outcome. The structure of the chapter reflects the types of norm that are addressed. We start with the most general norm for dispute resolution, the fair-trial principle, and continue with norms for ADR, norms for online providers, and conclude the chapter by discussing disclosure details for online ADR providers.

In Chapter 3 we examine the management of negotiation knowledge. We commence by examining principles and theories of negotiation including principled negotiation and the determination of BATNAs, reactive devaluation,[15] bargaining in the shadow of the law, and interest, justice and power-based negotiation. We then examine how bargaining and game theory have been used to provide decision support for negotiation. Often the goal of such decision support is to conduct effective risk management. We conclude the chapter by examining how negotiation decision support has been provided in diverse legal domains such as bargaining about charges and pleas, business-to-consumer disputes, damages and family law.

Our next chapter looks at current technologies for supporting dispute resolution. We commence by discussing the difference between asynchronous and synchronous communication. We next consider the provision of current Online Dispute Resolution Services, in particular WIPO (World Intellectual Property Organization),[16] Cybersettle and SquareTrade/eBay. A detailed examination of supporting communication amongst disputants follows. We consider e-mail, SMS, chat, video conferencing, discussion groups, telephones and fax, and explain what is meant by the concept commonly used to refer to the technology in Online Dispute Resolution, hence the fourth party. We present an additional concept, labelled the fifth party, that represents the provider of the technology in dispute resolution. The chapter concludes with observations to match technology to a specific dispute resolution process.

In Chapter 5 we conduct a detailed examination of intelligent negotiation support systems. Examples examined include Split-Up, the

---

[15] Reactive devaluation in a negotiation refers to the fact that the very offer of a particular proposal or concession – especially if the offer comes from an *adversary* – may diminish its apparent value or attractiveness in the eyes of the recipient.

[16] The World Intellectual Property Organization (WIPO) is a specialised agency of the United Nations. It is dedicated to developing a balanced and accessible international intellectual property system, which rewards creativity, stimulates innovation and contributes to economic development while safeguarding the public interest.

BEST-project, Smartsettle, Family_Winner and Family_Mediator, INSPIRE, GearBi and charge and plea-bargaining.

In Chapter 6 we discuss our model for Online Dispute Resolution. We expand upon a lengthy paper that appeared in the autumn 2005 edition of the *Harvard Negotiation Law Review* (Lodder and Zeleznikow 2005). Our model contains three stages:

Step 1: BATNA establishment.
Step 2: Rational communication.
Step 3: Game theoretic decision support.

Chapter 7 provides a conclusion to our discussion of Enhanced Dispute Resolution through the use of information technology, and offers some observations on the prospects of technology-enhanced dispute resolution. We have also provided an extensive list of references and a glossary of key terms used in the book.

Norms for the use of technology in dispute resolution

2.1 Introduction

Dispute resolution enhanced by technology can be approached from both a technical angle and from a legal angle. At first sight there seems to be a clear distinction between these approaches. For instance, design decisions seem typical for the technical angle, whereas disclosure of specific information appears to be a legal issue. However, design decisions can be influenced by legal norms, and fulfilling information requirements can have consequences for the design. This illustrates that law and technology cannot be fully separated, but are better approached in combination (Lodder and Oskamp 2006).

In this chapter, our starting point is the law and legal norms, but our discussions are also relevant from a technology perspective. We specifically concentrate on norms applicable to online forms of dispute resolution.

The best-known general sources for norms and Online Dispute Resolution are the European Union recommendations on online arbitration (1998) and online mediation (2001)[1] and *ABA's Recommended Best Practices for Online Dispute Resolution Service Providers.*[2] We will discuss these three initiatives. We discuss what we consider are the pivotal norms that providers of technology-enhanced dispute resolution should follow.

In this chapter our approach is to address a very general norm first (Section 2.3), and then discuss norms on Alternative Dispute Resolution (Section 2.4), online activities (Section 2.5) and Online Dispute Resolution

---

[1] Recommendation 98/257/CE of the Commission on the Principles Applicable to the Bodies Responsible for Out-of-Court Settlement of Consumer Disputes 1998 *Official Journal*, L. 115, and Recommendation 2001/310/EC of 4 April 2001 on Principles for Out-of-Court Bodies Involved in Consensual Resolution of Consumer Disputes 2001 *Official Journal*, L. 109.

[2] See the final version of the American Bar Association Recommended Best Practices, www.abanet.org/dispute/documents/BestPracticesFinal102802.pdf (last accessed 31 July 2009).

(Section 2.6). We start, however, with an overview of existing work on the topic.

2.2   Literature on norms for Online Dispute Resolution

In recent years, several doctoral dissertations have appeared on the topic of norms for Online Dispute Resolution. Thomas Schultz (2005) and Julia Hörnle[3] focused primarily on online arbitration, whereas Stephanie Bol (2007) developed a normative framework for online mediation. Coincidently, in October 2008 two dissertations were defended on the very topic of this chapter. Pablo Cortes defended successfully his doctoral dissertation entitled 'Developing Online Dispute Resolution for Consumers in the European Union' at the University of Cork (Ireland) on 3 October 2008.[4] The motivation for Cortes' research was derived from his firm belief in the benefits of Online Dispute Resolution, and the legal role norms should play:

> This PhD thesis evaluates how the introduction of ADR when complemented with ICT can assist in resolving consumer disputes that arise from e-commerce. ADR laws and principles as well as flexible judicial processes, such as the small claims process, will be evaluated as most of these principles also apply to ODR. The aim of this thesis is to explore the current use and potential of ODR in the B2C context and to identify obstacles to a more widespread use of ODR for consumer transactions. The final objective will be to identify the legal responses, if any, required in the EU to accelerate the expansion of ODR in the resolution of B2C disputes.

Susan Schiavetta defended her doctoral dissertation entitled 'Electronic Alternative Dispute Resolution – Increasing Access To Justice Via Procedural Protections' at the University of Oslo (Norway) on 23 and 24 October 2008.[5] Schiavetta (2008: 7) takes as point of departure the fair-trial principle of Article 6 of the European Convention on Human Rights (ECHR, see also Section 2.3 below):

> It is suggested that disputants will only opt for out-of-court forms of dispute resolution like e-ADR where they will also be in receipt of procedural safeguards equivalent to those given in court. This is particularly true

---

[3] Her 2007 dissertation has been published in Hörnle (2009).
[4] The supervisor was Professor Steve Hedley. Professor Lodder chaired the evaluation committee.
[5] Supervisors were Professors Ola Mestad and Lee Bygrave. Professors Lodder and Elizabeth Thornburg participated in the adjudication committee.

where the e-ADR procedure chosen is binding and disputants lose their right to go to court de novo (i.e., prevented from starting proceedings afresh in a court of law). Naturally, disputants may be willing to accept the weakening of certain procedural safeguards so long as this is compensated for by other benefits accruing from the use of e-ADR, such as a cheap and fast resolution process. The extent to which disputants accept this corrosion of their rights will vary from disputant to disputant.

Schiavetta elaborates upon the principles entailed in the fair-trial principle:

(1) Adverserial hearing;
(2) independence and impartiality;
(3) public hearing;
(4) efficiency;
(5) accessibility.

Although the approaches of Schiavetta and Cortes differ, they both developed a normative framework for Online Dispute Resolution. Cortes proposed drafting a European Union Directive on the topic, whilst Schiavetta proposed a European Union regulation.[6]

2.3   Very general: fair-trial principle

Independent of the type of dispute resolution process we will consider, fairness is the basic assumption underlying all processes. Whilst the degree of fairness varies from process to process, all dispute resolution processes possess a minimal standard of fairness.

Elizabeth Thornburg starts her dispute resolution classes with an illustration from the game of Tic-Tac-Toe.[7] This game has no winning strategy. If parties pursue an optimal strategy, each game ends in a draw. Only if a player makes a mistake, can the other party win. But what if you change the rules? If you blindfold one of the players and then let him randomly point at the spot where he wants to put his cross (or circle), then the blindfolded player will probably lose. Similarly, if you allow one of the players to have two consecutive moves, she would normally win. We would normally consider both of these examples to be unfair. This illustrates that at

---

[6] A regulation is directly binding without need for further action from the member states, whilst a Directive needs to be transposed (but is also binding, indirectly).

[7] Also known as noughts and crosses. See http://en.wikipedia.org/wiki/Tic-tac-toe (last accessed 31 July 2009) for a description.

some point procedural rules can become unfair, although it is not easy to indicate exactly when this is case.

Within Europe, a very general principle on fair trial can be found in Article 6 (1) of the European Convention on Human Rights (ECHR). It states:

> in the determination of his civil rights and obligations ... everyone is enti-
> tled to a fair and public hearing within a reasonable time by an independ-
> ent and impartial tribunal established by law.

This is the basic norm on dispute resolution with regards to primarily state-organised processes, such as litigation. Alternatives such as mediation and arbitration do not entail all the procedural safeguards of litigation, but in exchange offer basically faster and cheaper dispute resolution. The central and challenging question is: to what level are we willing to lower procedural fairness in order to have cheaper and quicker dispute resolution?

An interesting example from practice concerning the concept of *reasonable time*[8] comes from the Online Dispute Resolution practice of PayPal. Colin Rule[9] indicated that users of PayPal dispute resolution consider the time the process takes as more important than the outcome. They would rather lose after a few days, than win after a few weeks. Even three or four weeks is considered in this respect as a long period. So, PayPal tries to make the process as short as possible. There is obviously a point where shortening of the process no longer has a positive effect. For instance, if PayPal would just throw a dice for each dispute, they could resolve it almost instantly. However, outcomes would then be too arbitrary, and the users would not accept such a process. The challenge is to have a process that is effective, but still fair. You can loosen some safeguards, but not all and not too much.

A complication is the enforcement of the norms. The norms of state-organised dispute resolution can be found in the code, and the enforcement of the norms is an integral part of the process. The public character allows anyone to 'check' the process, whereas most private dispute resolution processes have a confidential nature. This makes it more difficult to enforce procedural norms. Closely related to this issue is the question of

---

[8] See Article 6 ECHR.
[9] At a meeting in Brussels of the CEN standardisation of ODR committee on 20 October 2008, Colin Rule, director of mediation at eBay, gave a presentation remotely (by phone).

how one can force the dispute resolution providers to follow procedural norms.

Most of the norms discussed in the remainder of this chapter are not compulsory for the dispute resolution providers, so their intrinsic, self-evident value is important.

2.4   Norms for Alternative Dispute Resolution providers

In several jurisdictions legislation has been enacted regarding Alternative Dispute Resolution. During the twentieth century many countries have enacted Arbitration Acts, and over the past decade much legislation on mediation has been drafted (e.g. in Belgium and Hungary).

In many civil procedural codes a number of norms can be found that regulate the arbitration process. Arbitration is an important dispute mechanism in international business conflicts, in particular for US companies. The reason for this is not only because of high litigation costs, but also because the United States does not have treaties with other countries regarding the execution of foreign verdicts. As a consequence, a foreign verdict is not easily executed in the United States, and US verdicts are not easily executed in other countries. The United States is, however, party to the New York Convention that facilitates the execution of cross-border arbitral awards. In case of international conflicts a US company will therefore mostly rely on arbitration. Arbitral awards can be executed in another country if the arbitration process complies with some minimum standards described in the New York Convention. These standards should be incorporated in the law of the states that are party to the Convention (over 100).

On the level of the European Union, several regulative initiatives on Alternative Dispute Resolution have been taken over the years, in particular Recommendation 98/257 on arbitration and Recommendation 2001/310 on mediation. In 2008, a Directive on mediation was enacted. The proposal for a European Union Directive on Consumer Rights from December 2008 mentions dispute resolution in several places.[10] Notably at p. 2:

> The fragmentation and the related uneven level of consumer protection make it difficult to … carry out alternative dispute resolution mechanisms.

This indicates that the resolution of consumer disputes is considered important. In Article 9 it states:

[10] Proposal for a Directive of the European Parliament and of the Council on consumer rights, 8.10.2008, COM(2008) 614 final.

As regards distance or off-premises contracts, the trader shall provide the following information which shall form an integral part of the contract:

(e) the possibility of having recourse to an amicable dispute settlement, where applicable.

Thus the use of ADR should form an integrated part of the contract.

In the remainder of this section we will discuss the main European Union initiatives: the recommendations on arbitration (1998) and mediation (2001), as well as the mediation directive (2008). This European Union law applies within the European Union, but because of its general nature the norms are applicable to other jurisdictions as well and therefore are valuable also for countries outside the European Union.

2.4.1 The European Union 1998 Recommendation on Arbitration

The 1998 Recommendation on Arbitration is officially called the 'Recommendation on the principles applicable to the bodies responsible for out-of-court settlement of consumer disputes'.[11] The Commission expects that money and time can be saved through Alternative Dispute Resolution (cf. recitals):

> Whereas the experience gained by several Member States shows that alternative mechanisms for the out-of-court settlement of consumer disputes – provided certain essential principles are respected – have had good results, both for consumers and firms, by reducing the cost of settling consumer disputes and the duration of the procedure.

The reason for drafting the principles is also clearly indicated in the recitals:

> Whereas the adoption of such principles at European level would facilitate the implementation of out-of-court procedures for settling consumer disputes.

If ADR providers follow the principles, we can be confident that their processes meet certain basic standards. So, building trust is specifically mentioned:

> in the case of cross-border conflicts, this would enhance mutual confidence between existing out-of-court bodies in the different Member States and strengthen consumer confidence in the existing national procedures.

---

[11] *Official Journal* L 115, 17/04/1998 pp. 31–34.

The recommendation does not specifically mention arbitration, probably because in the legal sense this term is normally used to refer to processes that comply with existing arbitration laws. It is clear, however, that the recommendation applies to arbitration in the broad sense, that is, dispute resolution in which a third party resolves the conflict by a decision:

> Whereas this recommendation must be limited to procedures which, no matter what they are called, lead to the settling of a dispute through the active intervention of a third party, who proposes or imposes a solution.

The term 'decision' should not be taken literally, for any suggestion for a solution falls within the scope of the recommendation:

> Whereas the decisions ... may be mere recommendations or may constitute settlement proposals which have to be accepted by the parties; whereas for the purposes of this recommendation these various cases are covered by the term 'decision'.

The aforementioned Article 6 of the European Human Rights Convention is recognised in this recommendation, which states that consumers may not be deprived of their right to have their case decided by a court:

> Article 6 of the European Human Rights Convention, access to the courts is a fundamental right that knows no exceptions ... out-of-court procedures cannot be designed to replace court procedures ... may not deprive consumers of their right to bring the matter before the courts unless they expressly agree to do so, in full awareness of the facts and only after the dispute has materialised.

Pre-dispute clauses are invalid under European law. This is not the case in other countries, for example in the United States.

The recommendation lays down seven principles:

(1) principle of independence;
(2) principle of transparency;
(3) adversarial principle;
(4) principle of effectiveness;
(5) principle of legality;
(6) principle of liberty;
(7) principle of representation.

We will shortly discuss each principle.

Fundamental to any dispute resolution process is the notion that the process should be decided by a third party who has no interest in the outcome, nor is his revenue dependent on the nature of the decision. The recommendation indicates that the third decision-maker should possess the necessary abilities, experience and competence, particularly in the field of law. Just as is the case for judges, who are appointed for a substantial period or for lifetime, these third parties should be granted a period of office of sufficient duration to ensure the independence of their action and shall not be liable to be relieved of their duties without just cause. In case of a panel, the members should equally represent consumers and professionals.

Disclosure of relevant information, or transparency as it is called in the recommendation, is the second principle. The competent body should publish an annual report setting out the decisions taken, enabling the results obtained to be assessed and the nature of the disputes referred to it to be identified. ODR providers are not always willing to publish such annual reports, since many starting providers only resolve a few cases during the first year(s) of operation. Once the service has taken off, the ODR provider will have fewer problems with publishing the necessary data, although from a perspective of competition the providers may still want to keep the information to themselves. We are not aware of any ODR provider that publishes the requested information each year.

A list of information requirements completes the transparency principle. Information should be provided on the types of disputes the provider resolves, including information on eventual territorial or monetary restrictions. Also, the procedural rules should be disclosed, and the costs of the procedure. It is important for participants to know what norms apply, and how the process is conducted. On the basis of this information they can decide if they want to use a specific ODR provider. As for all e-commerce transactions, accurate and clear pricing information is essential. An information requirement typical for ADR is about the possible legal enforcement of the decision taken.

The adversarial principle briefly indicates that both parties should be heard.

The principle of effectiveness is the first principle that is typical solely for ADR. In the case of litigation, principles of independence, transparency, and the adversarial nature of the dispute are applicable as well. But the ADR process distinguishes itself from litigation in terms of being concerned about effectiveness.

So, a consumer may choose someone to represent him in the dispute resolution process, for effectiveness; it is not necessary for him to be to be represented. Plus the procedure should be free, or of moderate costs, for consumers. This is an understandable requirement, because the monetary value of the consumer disputes is often low and the process cannot be called effective if a consumer has to pay more for the process than what is at stake. It does, however, raise a question of funding. Who pays for the process? If none of the participating businesses, a business association or the government funds the process, it is very unlikely that a profitable business plan for Online Dispute Resolution will exist. The process should be fast (there should be a short period between referral of the case to the third party and a decision being made) and the third party should be active (she should consider all factors conducive to a settlement).

The principle of legality is concerned with the consumer not being deprived of mandatory legal provisions. It also states that decisions should be communicated to the parties concerned as soon as possible, stating the grounds on which they are based.

The principle of liberty stresses the voluntary nature of ADR. Decisions can only be binding if the parties were informed in advance of the binding nature and explicitly agree to this requirement. Consumers can only be deprived of access to a court if they agree with this procedure prior to the dispute resolution process commencing.

The principle of representation is partly a mirror of the effectiveness principle (that there is no obligatory representation). This principle simply states that a consumer always has a right to be represented.

2.4.2   The European Union 2001 Recommendation on Mediation

Three years after the Recommendation on Arbitration, the mediation recommendation was issued by the Commission. It is officially called 'Recommendation on the principles for out-of-court bodies involved in the consensual resolution of consumer disputes'. This recommendation supplements the just discussed 1998 recommendation. In the opening recitals it indicated:

> The continuing development of new forms of commercial practices involving consumers such as electronic commerce, and the expected increase in cross-border transactions, require that particular attention be paid to generating the confidence of consumers, in particular by ensuring easy access to practical, effective and inexpensive means of redress, including access by electronic means.

Whereas the online element was practically absent in the 1998 recommendation, the increase of cross-border e-commerce was the main reason for drafting the 2001 recommendation. The recital also explicitly refers to ODR:

> access to practical, effective and inexpensive means of redress … by electronic means.

The need for addressing mediation became apparent during the launch of a European Union-wide network of national bodies for the extra-judicial settlement of consumer disputes.[12] The Council noted that mediation could be very effective for consumer disputes. However, the topic was not covered in the 1998 recommendation. Therefore, the 2001 recommendation covered mediation and defined standards guaranteeing quality, fairness and effectiveness.

Recital 6 clearly illustrates the high expectation existing concerning Online Dispute Resolution:

> New technology can contribute to the development of electronic dispute settlement systems, providing a mechanism to effectively settle disputes across different jurisdictions without the need for face-to-face contact, and therefore should be encouraged through principles ensuring consistent and reliable standards to give all users confidence.

In recital 8 it is:

> stressed that in general it is in the interest of consumers and undertakings to try to settle their disputes amicably before resorting to the courts and reiterated the importance of continuing the work on alternative methods of dispute settlement at European Community level.

Mediation is not used as a term in the recommendation, but the dispute resolution mechanisms falling under the scope of the recommendation are defined as (recital 9):

> third party procedures, no matter what they are called, which facilitate the resolution of a consumer dispute by bringing the parties together and assisting them, for example by making informal suggestions on settlement options, in reaching a solution by common consent.

The recommendation is built around four principles:

(1) impartiality;
(2) transparency;
(3) effectiveness; and
(4) fairness.

---

[12] *Official Journal* C 155, 6.6.2000, p. 1.

These principles are largely the same as those of the 1998 recommendation. 'Impartiality' and 'independence' are similar terms, 'transparency' and 'effectiveness' were also included in the 1998 recommendation, and the fairness principle generally covers what was referred to as Liberty, Legality and Representation. Obviously, the adversarial principle is missing, simply because mediation is not an adversarial process. We will briefly indicate some small but relevant differences between the two recommendations.

Under the effectiveness principle the 2001 recommendation refers to ODR, thus:

> It should be easily accessible and available to both parties, for instance by electronic means, irrespective of where the parties are situated.

Under the fairness principle, the voluntary nature of mediation is expressed:

> the parties should be informed of their right to refuse to participate or to withdraw from the procedure at any time.

This is considered an important characteristic of mediation, because if parties know they can leave the process at any time, they may be more willing to communicate. The confidentiality requirement guarantees that in case they leave the procedure, not that much is lost (of course, time and money is always lost). The confidentiality and voluntary nature of the mediation directive, in combination, guarantee that what parties declare during mediation cannot be used against them if litigation eventually ensues.

In line with these observations, the recommendation states that:

> both parties should be encouraged to fully cooperate with the procedure, in particular by providing any information necessary for a fair resolution of the dispute.

Finally, and somewhat controversially, the following fairness principle appears in the directive:

> The consumer should be informed in clear und understandable language, before agreeing to a suggested solution, of the following points … (b) the suggested solution may be less favourable than an outcome determined by a court applying legal rules.

Normally, one would consider such options (a BATNA) before commencing mediation. If a solution is reached then, for most cases, it is too late to refer the case to court, even if one of the parties might achieve a more favourable decision. It is also questionable whether a court procedure following a successful mediation can ever be favourable. Substantially it might appear more favourable (e.g. a party gets 1,000 euro during mediation, whilst he would normally receive 1,500–2,000 euro in court), but from a procedural point of view it would not be advantageous to recommence litigation.

2.4.3   The European Union 2008 Mediation Directive

The European Union Directive on Mediation dates from 21 May 2008. The principles laid down in the recommendations discussed above will be followed by ADR or ODR providers. But they cannot be forced to comply with them. This is different with a Directive, which is binding. The member states should transpose the articles of the Directive (cf. Article 12):

> bring into force the laws, regulations, and administrative provisions necessary to comply with this Directive.

The benefits of mediation, as the European Union sees it, are clearly described in recital 6:

> Mediation can provide a cost-effective and quick extrajudicial resolution of disputes in civil and commercial matters through processes tailored to the needs of the parties. Agreements resulting from mediation are more likely to be complied with voluntarily and are more likely to preserve an amicable and sustainable relationship between the parties. These benefits become even more pronounced in situations displaying cross-border elements.

The aim of the Directive is put forth in recital 7:

> In order to promote further the use of mediation and ensure that parties having recourse to mediation can rely on a predictable legal framework, it is necessary to introduce framework legislation addressing, in particular, key aspects of civil procedure.

The link to ODR could have been more positively defined than does the Directive in recital 9:

> This Directive should not in any way prevent the use of modern communication technologies in the mediation process.

The objective of the Directive, as described in Article 1, is to:

> facilitate access to alternative dispute resolution and to promote the amicable settlement of disputes by encouraging the use of mediation

and by ensuring a balanced relationship between mediation and judicial proceedings.

Mediation is defined in Article 3 in a commonly accepted way:

> [as] a structured process, however named or referred to, whereby two or more parties to a dispute attempt by themselves, on a voluntary basis, to reach an agreement on the settlement of their dispute with the assistance of a mediator. This process may be initiated by the parties or suggested or ordered by a court or prescribed by the law of a Member State.

The Directive is an important initiative, since it brings mediation to the attention of member states. The remaining Articles of the Directive do not have that much impact. This is due to the fact that the Directive is a compromise between member states, who did not want to give up too much of their sovereignty.

Article 4 is on the quality of mediation, but is phrased mildly. It says that member states should *encourage* a Code of Conducts on mediation, control mechanisms, and the training of mediators.

Article 5 indicates that the judiciary can direct cases to mediation. Because of the fact that mediation is still not that widely known, a court may also invite the parties to attend an information session on the use of mediation.

Article 6 is probably the most interesting norm, for it deals with the enforceability of outcomes of mediation. The outcome of litigation is a verdict, in arbitration an award, but in all other forms of (alternative) dispute resolution, the outcome is a contract between the parties. This makes the outcome difficult to enforce. Article 6(2) indicates that an agreement:

> may be made enforceable by a court or other competent authority in a judgment or decision or in an authentic instrument in accordance with the law of the Member State where the request is made.

The enforceability of ODR outcomes has always been seen as a major concern and drawback. For the European Union this concern is now remedied by the Directive.

Article 7 deals with one of the central concepts of mediation, namely confidentiality. An important difference between alternative forms of dispute resolution and the processes organised by the state is confidentiality. Litigation is public; ADR is not. This has consequences for the development of information technology for dispute resolution.

Confidentiality of mediation is generally recognised, but in some court cases judges forced the mediator or parties to the mediation to be witnesses about what took place during the mediation. The general principle is that the parties, mediators or those involved in the administration of the mediation process (e.g. providers of the technology) shall not be compelled to give evidence in civil and commercial judicial proceedings or arbitration regarding information arising out of or in connection with a mediation process. There are two exceptions. The grounds for the first one are quite severe:

> for overriding considerations of public policy … in particular when required to ensure the protection of the best interests of children or to prevent harm to the physical or psychological integrity of a person.

Family mediation is one example where this exception may apply. The second exception deals with disclosure necessary in order to implement or enforce the mediation agreement. Under this exception the breach of confidentiality is not that severe, since the process has already ended with an agreement.

Article 8 guarantees that parties commencing mediation should not be deprived of access to courts due to the expiration of the time normally allowed to commence a law suit. This would also mean that if mediation is started directly after a court ruled in the first instance, the period for appeal will be much longer than would normally be the case.

Finally, Article 9 is again softly phrased:

> Member States shall encourage, by any means which they consider appropriate, the availability to the general public, in particular on the Internet, of information on how to contact mediators and organisations providing mediation services.

This is an important action that governments need to undertake, for there exists a general consensus that lack of awareness is a major reason for the limited uptake of mediation in Online Dispute Resolution.

2.5   General legal requirements relating to online services

Regardless of what process is used to resolve the conflict, by nature the ODR process is conducted online, and at a distance. Therefore, the regulation of distance and online services in general applies to Online Dispute Resolution. Within the European Union several directives deal with aspects of online trade, most notably Directive 2000/31/EC on electronic commerce, which will be discussed below. Directive 97/7/EC on distance contracts overlaps in part, but deserves to be addressed separately.

2.5.1   European Union Directive 2000/31/EC on electronic commerce

The Directive 2000/31/EC is usually called the e-commerce Directive, or the Directive on e-commerce. Whilst several other Directives deal solely, or at least for the greater part, with e-commerce topics, Directive 2000/31/EC regulates central issues regarding electronic commerce, e.g. commercial communications, formation of online contracts, and liability of intermediaries. The Directive deals with key issues of e-commerce, and for this reason the Directive is also known as the legal framework Directive.[13]

Directives are one of the regulative instruments of the European Union. Directives do not have direct effect in the European Union member states. Directives should be implemented into national law within a fixed period of time (normally between one and three years). National legislatures need to adapt their law in order to comply with a Directive. The Directive 2000/31/EC on electronic commerce applies to what is called information society services, defined as:

(1) *Any service normally provided for remuneration.* It is not necessary that a service is paid for by the recipient. The costs of a service can also be covered by advertisement. For instance, free Internet providers fall under the scope of the Directive. The decisive criterion is that the service can be considered an economic activity. The threshold is quite low, so most websites are considered to be normally provided for remuneration. So, Online Dispute Resolution services, even if offered for free to the user, will always meet this condition.

(2) *At a distance.* The service should be provided without the parties being simultaneously present (see also Directive 97/7/EC on distance selling). The rationale for the criterion is that parties at a distance cannot communicate face to face. So, the actual criterion should be whether face-to-face contact is possible. If parties are not at a distance and face-to-face contact is possible, the service should not be considered an information society service; in all other cases, it is one. Online Dispute Resolution is normally carried out at a distance. Only in the case that the parties are in the same room, and use online technology to facilitate their offline process, is the ODR service not considered an information society service.

---

[13] See recital 7: 'this Directive must lay down a clear and general framework to cover certain legal aspects of electronic commerce in the internal market', and recital 8: 'the objective of this Directive is to create a legal framework'.

(3) *By electronic means.* The service should be sent and received using electronic equipment. Traditional distance selling methods, like mailorder firms, are not information society services. Online Dispute Resolution by definition uses electronic equipment to carry out the process.

(4) *At the individual request of a recipient of services.* The service should be delivered on demand. A visit to a website is always a service on demand, since the recipient 'requests' the website by typing in the URL or by following a link. One could argue that if one party initiates the ODR process and invites the other party to join, the ODR service is not at the individual request of this latter party. However, during the ODR process also this latter party will have to individually request the service. So even in this case, ODR is an information society service for both parties.

As the discussion of the four conditions illustrates, all Online Dispute Resolution services fall under this definition. Of particular relevance are the information requirements that have to be complied with. Included, amongst others, is Article 5(1):

> that the service provider shall render easily, directly and permanently accessible to the recipients of the service and competent authorities, at least the following information:
>
> (a) the name of the service provider;
> (b) the geographic address at which the service provider is established;
> (c) the details of the service provider, including his electronic mail address, which allow him to be contacted rapidly and communicated with in a direct and effective manner.

We will not discuss all applicable norms that follow from this qualification, but refer to general literature on this topic (e.g. Lodder 2002a). A point worth mentioning is the special position Online Dispute Resolution services take in this Directive. As we have seen, ODR services can be qualified as information society services and do therefore fall under the scope of the Directive. On the other hand, the Directive sees ODR also as a means to enhance trust in these very same information society services. Article 17 is about out-of-court settlement.

> Article 17
> Out-of-court dispute settlement
>
> 1. Member States shall ensure that, in the event of disagreement between an information society service provider and the recipient of

the service, their legislation does not hamper the use of out-of-court schemes, available under national law, for dispute settlement, including appropriate electronic means.

2. Member States shall encourage bodies responsible for the out-of-court settlement of, in particular, consumer disputes to operate in a way which provides adequate procedural guarantees for the parties concerned.

3. Member States shall encourage bodies responsible for out-of-court dispute settlement to inform the Commission of the significant decisions they take regarding information society services and to transmit any other information on the practices, usages or customs relating to electronic commerce.

Similarly, recital 51 states:

Each Member State should be required, where necessary, to amend any legislation which is liable to hamper the use of schemes for the out-of-court settlement of disputes through electronic channels; the result of this amendment must be to make the functioning of such schemes genuinely and effectively possible in law and in practice, even across borders.

So, ODR is itself an online service but also one of the means to enhance trust in these same online services (cf. Directive 2000/31/EC on e-commerce), namely, if people expect eventual conflicts to be handled satisfactorily they will be more willing to use online services.

2.5.2   European Directive 97/7/EC on distance selling

Another EU Directive that is particularly relevant for ODR providers within the European Union is the Directive on distance selling. This directive has been drafted in order to protect consumers buying products and ordering services at a distance. Electronic commerce is the main area of application, so the Directive is relevant for Online Dispute Resolution. Basically, the Directive requires distance sellers (including distance service providers) to provide information necessary to make an informed decision. This information partly overlaps with, and partly supplements the e-commerce directive. Article 4 requires amongst others:

(1) the supplier's name (and in the case of advance payment also their address), (Article 4(1)(a));
(2) the main characteristics of the goods or services, i.e. essentially a description of the goods or services (Article 4(1)(b));
(3) the price including all taxes (VAT) and all delivery costs (Article 4(1) (c) and (d));

(4) the existence of a right of withdrawal, unless the sale is exempted from that right (Article 4(1)(f));

(5) how long the offer or the price remains valid (Article 4(1)(h)).

It is important to mention the legal right of withdrawal within seven working days after conclusion of the contract. This could be relevant in cases where one of the parties involved in ODR is a consumer, and the other is a professional party. For some processes this withdrawal right will not add much, since they are voluntary in the sense that parties are allowed to leave the process at any time. Mediation is an example of such a process. In the case of online arbitration this clause may be relevant though, especially in the case where a consumer has second thoughts after deciding to engage in this form of ODR with a company. One should realise that often arbitration is based on a contractual arbitration clause, and pre-dispute contracts are invalid under most European jurisdictions but allowed in the United States. So the practical effect of this legal withdrawal right is very limited, but EU-based providers should at least consider that this situation of withdrawal might occur.

2.6 Requirements specifically drafted for ODR providers

There have been several recommendations on Online Dispute Resolution by international bodies, particularly addressing the question of best practice in ODR. These include:[14]

(1) US Federal Trade Commission and Department of Commerce;[15]
(2) Canadian Working Group on Electronic Commerce and Consumers;[16]
(3) Australian National Alternative Dispute Resolution Advisory Council (NADRAC);[17]

---

[14] Overview is taken from *CEN/ISS [Draft] Workshop Agreement on Standardisation of Online Dispute Resolution Tools* 2009, authored by B. Hutchinson, V. Tilman, A.R. Lodder, A. Borri and J. Gouimenou.

[15] Conference held in Washington, DC on B2C ODR, June 2000 – see www.ftc.gov/bcp/altdisresolution/summary.pdf (last accessed 3 August 2009).

[16] Canadian Working Group on Electronic Commerce and Consumers, 'Principles of Consumer Protection for Electronic Commerce, A Canadian Framework', strategis.ic.gc.ca (last accessed 3 August 2009).

[17] NADRAC, 'Online ADR: Background Paper', www.nadrac.gov.au/www/nadrac/rwpattach.nsf/VAP/(960DF944D2AF105D4B7573C11018CFB4)~ADR.rtf/$file/ADR.rtf (last accessed 3 August 2009).

(4) Alliance for Global Business; [18]
(5) Global Business Dialogue on Electronic Commerce;[19]
(6) Transatlantic Consumer Dialogue;[20]
(7) Consumers International;[21]
(8) European Consumers' Organisation (BEUC);[22]
(9) International Chamber of Commerce (ICC);[23]
(10) American Bar Association.[24]

The most influential is the last one mentioned, the 'Recommended Best Practices for ODR Providers' from 2002, drafted by the American Bar Association (ABA) Task Force on E-commerce and ADR.[25] The principles defined therein are intended to assist ODR providers, neutrals, users of these services, in particular consumers, and online merchants and marketplaces. According to the ABA taskforce, compliance with the principles can either follow from codes of conduct that take them into account, or follow from the way ODR providers operate. So, although parties other than ODR providers can profit from the principles, the ODR providers should implement them.

The role of online merchants and marketplaces is to disclose:

(1) the existence of pre-dispute ADR/ODR clauses;
(2) the nature of the online merchant's dispute resolution process;
(3) any contractual relationships with ADR/ODR providers; and
(4) information to educate their customers about ADR/ODR methods.

---

[18] Alliance for Global Business, 'A Global Action Plan for Electronic Business', www.iccwbo. org/home/e_business/word_documents/3rd%20Edition%20Global%20Action%20Plan. pdf (last accessed 3 August 2009).

[19] Global Business Dialogue on Electronic Commerce, Consumer Confidence Working Group, 'Alternative Dispute Resolution – The Tokyo 2001 Recommendations', www. gbd-e.org/pubs/Tokyo_Recommendations_2001.pdf (last accessed 3 August 2009).

[20] Transatlantic Consumer Dialogue, 'Alternative Dispute Resolution in the Context of Electronic Commerce', February 2000.

[21] Consumers International, 'Disputes in Cyberspace' (2001), www.consumersinternational.org/Shared_ASP_Files/UploadedFiles/DD330597–5945–4B5A-A8BD-4A6573F3F9AF_ADRReport2001.pdf (last accessed 3 August 2009).

[22] 'Alternative Dispute Resolution – BEUC's Position on the Commission's Green Paper', BEUC/X/048/2002.

[23] ICC, 'Resolving Disputes Online: Best Practices for Online Dispute Resolution (ODR) in B2C and C2C Transactions' (2003).

[24] American Bar Association Task Force on E-Commerce and ADR, 'Addressing Disputes in Electronic Commerce. Final Report and Recommendations'.

[25] American Bar Association Task Force on E-Commerce and ADR, 'Recommended Best Practices for Online Dispute Resolution Service Providers'.

The approach of the Recommended Best Practices Group is based mainly on the use of disclosure: it does not aim to set minimum substantive standards. Just as in the European Union recommendations, regular periodic statistical reports are required, under the condition that the ODR provider handles a substantial number of B2C (business to consumer) disputes.

After (I) the scope and (II) Transparency and Adequate Means of Providing Information and Disclosure, the further principles laid down are:

III. Minimum Basic Disclosures;
IV. Use of Technology and the Online Environment for Dispute Resolution;
V. Costs and Funding;
VI. Impartiality;
VII. Confidentiality, Privacy and Information Security;
VIII. Qualifications and Responsibilities of Neutrals;
IX. Accountability for ODR Providers and Neutrals;
X. Enforcement;
XI. Jurisdiction and Choice of Law.

Most of the principles were discussed in the previous section (2.4) on European Union regulation. We will not repeat this here, but concentrate on some noteworthy distinctive parts of the ABA recommendations.

Principle IV introduces some new points. Disclosure about system requirements now seems somewhat outdated. Whilst it was not the case in 2002, today's computers can generally run most web-based applications. Thus, such information is rarely presented by existing ODR providers. Information on the limitations on accessibility to ODR systems seems inappropriate, in particular with reference to hours of operation. Whilst the Internet is available twenty-four hours a day, seven days a week (24/7), this is not true for human mediators. For assisted negotiation, one can use systems such as Cybersettle which are available 24/7. But information on the availability of humans involved in the ODR process is needed.

The requirement under IV(4) is to provide information on 'Any specific electronic techniques offered to enhance the efficacy of ODR and, if so, what these are and how they function'. This refers to non-standard techniques, in which some information about their operation is very welcome.

Information about 'If they provide training in adapting the neutrals' skills to the online environment' may, over time, become unnecessary, but even in 2010 it is wise to train neutrals about the platform and using the technologies that the platform applies. If users know the neutrals are trained, they will be more confident in using ODR.

In part VII (c) 2–3, information security is addressed. This topic is very relevant for ODR services. The ODR provider should apply adequate security technology. This is a clear example of a disclosure duty that affects the operation of the ODR provider. If the information provided under information security measures does not meet minimum standards, users will not confidently use the ODR service. Therefore, the ODR provider should disclose what forms of security are applied for all online processes, and what kinds of security mechanisms have been put in place to safeguard participant information.

Finally the jurisdiction principle under X is probably different from what one would initially expect:

> ODR Providers should disclose the jurisdiction where complaints against the ODR Provider can be brought, and any relevant jurisdictional limitations.

One might expect that complaints about ODR providers would be resolved by other ODR providers, not by courts. Why this principle was chosen is not clear from the commentaries, because this principle is the only one without comments. Whilst this principle might be self-evident, some consideration about why complaints should be filed with specific courts would have been welcome.

2.7   Conclusion

From the discussion of the various regulative initiatives for technology-based dispute resolution, it becomes clear that independence/impartiality, confidentiality and enforcement are the key concepts. Information about the outcomes in yearly reports is a recurring theme in several initiatives. What is also clear is that most initiatives do not have a binding status. The only exceptions are the European Union Mediation Directive and the general EU Directives related to e-commerce. Regardless of the voluntary nature of most of the norms discussed in this chapter, any ODR provider taking itself seriously will comply with the initiatives.

Developing dispute resolution processes

3.1 Principles and theory of negotiation

Numerous models have been developed from detailed studies of how people negotiate. Formal models, such as game theory, rely upon a mathematical concept of optimal convergence. But do such models realistically simulate human behaviour?

3.1.1 Negotiation analysis

Sebenius (2007) describes the emergent field of *negotiation analysis*. He claims that it is conceptually located between decision analysis[1] and game theory[2] and seeks to develop prescriptive theory and useful advice for negotiators and third parties. It generally emphasises assessment of the parties' underlying interests, alternatives to negotiated agreement, approaches to productively manage the inherent tension between competitive actions to 'claim' value individually and cooperative ones to 'create' value jointly, as well as efforts to change perceptions of the negotiation itself. Since advice to one side does not necessarily presume the full (game theoretic) rationality of the other side(s), negotiation analysts often draw on the findings of behavioural scientists and experimental economists.

Sebenius further claims that this approach does not generally assume that all the elements of the negotiation or 'game' are common knowledge. The theory tends to de-emphasise the application of game theoretic solution concepts or efforts to find unique equilibrium outcomes.

---

[1] Decision analysis (Senger 2004), generated from statistical decision theory, is a methodology typically used to support decision-makers actively in assessing alternative courses of action.

[2] Game theory is a branch of applied mathematics that provides advice about the optimal distribution of resources. In the case of a negotiation, the goal of game theory is to develop the best outcome related to the choices each person has made.

Instead, it evaluates possible strategies and tactics. Negotiation analysts generally focus on changes in perceptions of the *zone of possible agreement*[3] and the (subjective) distribution of possible negotiated outcomes conditional on various actions. It has been used to develop prescriptive advice for the simplest bilateral negotiations between monolithic parties, for negotiations through agents or with linked 'internal' and 'external' aspects, for negotiations in hierarchies and networks, for more complex coalitional interactions, as well as moves 'away from the table' to change the perceived negotiation itself, including the challenge of 'negotiation design' to enhance the likelihood of desirable outcomes.

Simon (1957) introduced the notion of *satisficing* as a decision-making strategy of selecting the first alternative discovered that happens to be sufficient with respect to some minimal criteria. While conventional economists maintained that people make rational choices to obtain the best commodity at the best price, Simon argued that inevitable limits on knowledge and analytical ability force people to choose the first option that satisfices or is good enough for them, whether they are buying a loaf or bread or choosing a spouse. Because they make these choices from a limited number of possibilities, Simon viewed human decision-making as being of bounded rationality.[4]

Kalai and Stanford (1998) note that humans are more correctly modelled as having bounded rationality, that is choosing strategies from less-than-complete considerations and striving for satisfactory rather than optimal levels of utility.[5] Sycara (1993) notes that bargainers are constantly asked if they prefer one set of outcomes to another. She suggests that negotiators should consider two issues at a time, assuming all other issues remain fixed. Sycara (1998) notes that in developing real-world negotiation support systems one must assume bounded rationality and the presence of incomplete information.

---

[3] The *zone of possible agreement* (ZOPA), in a negotiation, indicates the joint area or range where an agreement can be met to which both parties can agree. Within this zone, an agreement is possible. Outside of the zone, no amount of negotiation will yield an agreement (Lewicki *et al.* 1999).

[4] Bounded rationality involves choosing strategies from less-than-complete considerations and striving for satisfactory rather than optimal levels of utility.

[5] For example, to conduct trade-offs during negotiations, disputants need to be aware of their utility functions. In current economics and in decision theory, the utility of outcomes and attributes refers to their weight in decisions: utility is inferred from observed choices and is in turn used to explain these choices. Thus utility is a measure of the relative satisfaction gained by consuming different bundles of goods and services (Zeleznikow *et al.* 2007a).

Game theory, for example, seems to ignore satisfaction as an underlying requirement of ensuring a mutually acceptable outcome. It supports a win–lose approach rather than promoting cooperation among the parties.

3.1.2   Principled Negotiation

Principled Negotiation was developed by the Harvard Negotiation Project[6] (Fisher and Ury 1981), and essentially it emphasises the notion that parties look for mutual gains. When interests conflict, Principled Negotiation advocates that parties arrive at a ruling that is independent of the beliefs of either side. The essential features of Principled Negotiation as a problem-solving task are as follows:

(1) *Separate the people from the problem* – this is to ensure that persons with stronger personalities cannot influence others into a decision that is biased towards a party or group of parties. This aspect is perhaps most relevant in disputes between people who are involved in an ongoing relationship, for example in family law disputes that concern the welfare of children.

(2) *Focus on interests, not on positions* – participants must distinguish and make known their underlying values in order to justify their position. In most negotiations, each party will have interests that they would like satisfied by settlement, and it is important that these be understood as separate from their positions. By isolating the reasons why a position is most appealing, participants in a negotiation will increase the chance of achieving agreement.

(3) *Invent options for mutual gain* – even if the parties' interests differ, there may be bargaining outcomes that will advance the interests of both parties. Once interests have been ranked to determine the relative importance of each, a range of options is discussed before deciding on an outcome. Next, the negotiators need to invent options for mutual gain.

(4) *Insist on objective criteria* – some negotiations are not susceptible to a win–win situation. The most obvious of these is haggling over the price of an item: since the more money one side negotiates, the less their opponent receives. In these cases, unbiased independent evaluations of an item will guide a price for the item that both parties will agree on.

---

[6] See www.pon.harvard.edu (last accessed 25 May 2008).

(5) *Know your best alternative to a negotiated agreement – BATNA* (*Best Alternative To a Negotiated Agreement*). The reason you negotiate with someone is to produce better results than would otherwise occur. If you are unaware of what results you could obtain if the negotiations are unsuccessful, you run the risk of:

    (a) Entering into an agreement that you would be better off rejecting; or

    (b) Rejecting an agreement you would be better off entering into.

For example, when a person wishes to buy a used car, they will usually refer to a commonly accepted set of approximate automotive prices. Using this initial figure and considering other variables such as new components, the distance travelled by the car and its current condition, the buyer then decides the value they wish to place on a car. If the seller is not willing to sell the car at this price, then you can argue the merits of your valuation, in an attempt to persuade the seller to accept your BATNA. BATNAs can be used to form a basis from which fair agreements can be obtained.

Developing BATNAs is an important step for disputants to engage in when they are reality-checking.

3.1.3   *Developing BATNAs*

As De Vries *et al.* (2005) claim, if negotiators do take account of their options outside a negotiation, they are better protected against agreements that should be rejected. It also helps them to reach agreements that better satisfy their interests. In order to assess whether an offer should be rejected, a party in a dispute has to establish what can be accomplished in alternative procedures to the one currently being conducted.

In a legal conflict, this may include exiting the procedure altogether, or handing over the case to a court. Once the alternatives are known, these can be compared to what one expects to win by accepting an offer in the current procedure. If the proposal is worse than the (best) alternative outside the procedure, it should be rejected; if it is better it should be considered for acceptance. In this respect each party's BATNA serves as a point of reference or a value with which to compare offers (Raiffa *et al.* 2002: 112).

Knowing one's BATNA is important because it influences negotiation power. Parties who are aware of their alternatives will be more confident about trying to negotiate a solution that better serves their interests. For example, when trying to sell one's car to a second-hand car dealer, knowing what other car sales people (or even individuals) offer or have offered for your (or a similar) car helps in obtaining a reasonable price for your vehicle.

The BATNA concept is a useful metaphor in all dispute resolution procedures where parties have the option to exit the process, such as negotiation and mediation. A BATNA in this sense is a way to put pressure on the other party. If terminating the process has advantages over accepting the other party's offer, it should be an incentive to continue the negotiation, just as if the other party is unwilling to reconsider the offer, walking out is a very sensible option.

BATNAs not only serve a purpose in evaluating offers in the dispute, but can also play a role in determining whether or not to accept a certain dispute resolution method. Mnookin (2003) claimed that having an accurate BATNA is part of the armoury one should use to evaluate whether or not to agree to enter a negotiation. This holds for many dispute resolution methods, including arbitration and mediation, but also for tools and techniques within these methods, such as (blind) bidding, persuasion dialogues, and final-offer arbitration. Comparing the possible (range of) outcomes with alternative options encourages parties to accept methods that are in the interests of disputants and enables them to identify those that are not. It is likely that most parties, to some extent, test the values of their BATNAs when assessing whether or not to opt for a certain dispute resolution method.

Although BATNAs are an important aspect of the dispute resolution process, there is reason to believe that parties engaged in actual disputes are not very good at determining their BATNAs. In particular we need to address issues of over-optimistic confidence and reactive devaluation.

3.1.4   Using BATNAs to minimise optimistic overconfidence and reactive devaluation

Research shows that people have a tendency to develop an overly optimistic view about their chances of success in disputes (see, for example, Neale and Bazerman 1991: 53–55; Kahneman and Tversky 1995: 46–50). This process is referred to as 'optimistic overconfidence', because disputants have unrealistic optimistic expectations about the validity of their judgments (Lewicki et al. 2003: 157).

Neale and Bazerman (1983) showed this effect in a (laboratory) experiment, where both parties were asked to submit a final offer to an arbitrator.[7] The participants were told that the arbitrator had to choose one of the offers. The experiment showed that the disputants, on average, believed they had a 65.4 per cent chance of getting their final offer accepted, while on average their real chance of success was only 50 per cent. This experiment suggests that people systematically overestimate their probability of success in dispute resolution.

This effect of overestimating one's position is present with respect to predicting outcomes of current situations as well as outcomes of future events. These valuations and predictions influence how disputants calculate their BATNAs. The consequence of overly optimistic BATNAs is that a generous offer in a negotiation, or an offer to start a procedure that is in the interest of a party, is prone to be rejected.

One of the likely sources of the overconfidence effect is that people find it hard to move from earlier positions (Pruitt and Carnevale 1993: 33). They strongly adhere to positions taken and are more likely to actively collect information that confirms the validity of their position, and they downplay or ignore information that refutes their choice. Raiffa *et al.* (2002: 36) call this the '*Confirming Evidence Trap*'. Phenomena, such as optimistic overconfidence, are rooted in the psychological make-up of people, and should be taken into account when trying to build dispute resolution tools.

The consequence of the optimistic overconfidence effect is that people regularly support positions or options that are incorrect (Lewicki *et al.* 2003: 157). People with overoptimistic BATNAs may reject procedures and proposals that might actually be in their interest. The effect on proposals is rather straightforward (tough luck, you ignored an excellent bargain), but the effect of not accepting certain procedures needs some explanation.

An obvious alternative to accepting an offer to opt for an Alternative Dispute Resolution method, such as arbitration or mediation, is to resort to a court proceeding. Many people think court proceedings have an all-or-nothing outcome. Hence, an overly optimistic disputant may conclude that he or she is better off in court than opting for a more cooperative procedure such as mediation or negotiation. The cooperative procedure in this case is perceived as less attractive, because in such a procedure it

---

[7] This is an existing dispute resolution method called Final-offer Arbitration (Brown and Marriot 1999: 63).

is normal that both parties make concessions (see also Barendrecht and De Vries 2004: 23–24). An over-optimistic disputant will be reluctant to make concessions if she thinks she will surely be able to obtain everything she desires in court.

To limit the chances of optimistic overconfidence causing poor decision-making, it may be useful to provide the disputing parties with something one may call a 'reality test' of their BATNA. There are not that many possible sources for a reality check on BATNAs. Obviously, the opponent appears not to be a suitable candidate as she has a vested interest in her own position or offer. Alternatively, actors sympathising with the person seeking advice may also not be too suited as they may fall into the same, or similar, traps as the information seeker. This leaves only a neutral party as a candidate.[8]

Neutrality is an important value in any dispute resolution system. This has to do with the notion of fairness. In a court proceeding, the parties should be able to express their side of their case, and the judge should assess the arguments in an unbiased manner. This same lack of bias is the reason why neutrality is also of importance in other dispute resolution systems such as ADR and ODR.

But fairness is not the only reason for providing advice on the realism of BATNAs provided by a neutral party. From a cognitive psychology perspective, neutrality is valuable. People have the tendency to devalue information given by parties or organisations they perceive as adversaries. In the literature this psychological process is called '*reactive devaluation*' and is supported by several empirical studies (Ross 1995: 29–38). One of the explanations for this phenomenon is that parties lack information about the interests and intentions of the other party. This lack of insight in the interests of others induces a kind of distrust in their opinions (we are talking of parties that are already in a dispute and hence a lack of trust in the opponent's statements is inevitable) and the proposals the opponent presents. The idea that a proposal made by the opponent naturally benefits this person is easily accepted.

The effect of the reactive devaluation process is that advice given by the opponent is not judged as 'neutral' advice. Therefore it is useful that someone or something that is perceived as neutral to both parties provides negotiation advice about BATNAs.

---

[8] This, of course, is not a new idea. Korobkin (2006: 14), for instance, discusses the option of a mediator offering direct evaluation of possible chances in litigation to the parties in a dispute.

As mentioned above, one of Fisher and Ury's (1981) criteria for principled negotiation was to invent options for mutual gain. They suggest that before seeking to reach agreement on solutions for the future, multiple solution options should be developed prior to evaluation of those options. The typical way of doing this is called *brainstorming*. In brainstorming, the parties, with or without the mediator's participation, generate many possible solutions before deciding which of those best fulfil the parties' joint interests. Wertheim *et al.* (1992: 130–135) insist that brainstorming is one way of encouraging cooperative decision-making.

Other approaches for inventing options for mutual gain include *expanding the pie*, *awarding compensation* and *logrolling*.

Expanding or enlarging the pie involves the parties in a dispute creating additional resources so that both sides can maintain their major goals. For example, Peterson mentions the story, frequently repeated, of a claim involving the death of a child. The settlement included a public monument in a park in honour of the child. In another negotiation, one condition of the settlement was for the defendant company to incorporate specific safety measures to avoid similar accidents in the future. The plaintiffs had stated repeatedly that they wanted to see that nothing like what happened to them was repeated. In these two instances, emotional needs (generally overlooked) had to be addressed to reach agreement (Peterson 2008).

Compensation in negotiation involves one side receiving what it desires and the other side being compensated by being awarded another issue as compensation. Logrolling is a process in which participants look collectively at multiple issues to find issues that one party considers more important than does the opposing party. Logrolling is successful if the parties concede issues to which they give low importance values.

Bellucci and Zeleznikow (2006) claim that compensation and logrolling are similar techniques. They argue that both seek to resolve differences between disputants in their interests and preferences. An interest is defined as what a person truly desires from a situation, consisting of a person's wants, needs, concerns and fears. An agreement is far more likely if at least some of these interests are satisfied in the final agreement. Compensation allows for parties to be rewarded as a method to promote fairness in the final settlement. Logrolling does not assume compensation, entirely resting on considering priorities (and the differences between them) to form an agreement.

3.1.5   A checklist for negotiators

In his treatise on the art and science of negotiation, Raiffa (1982) provides a checklist for negotiators. These are questions disputants should ask each other before engaging in a negotiation.

A) *Preparing for negotiation*:
   1) *Know yourself* – consider what you want. Search carefully for and analyse alternatives.
   2) *Know your adversaries* – consider what they want. Search carefully for and analyse alternatives.
   3) *Consider the negotiation conventions in each context* – how open should you be? Can you trust your adversaries?
   4) *Consider the logistics of the situation* – who should negotiate? Do you need professional assistance? When and where should negotiations take place?
   5) *Simulate role playing* – software can be very useful for performing this task.
   6) *Iterate and set your aspiration levels*.

B) *Opening gambits*:
   1) *Who should make the first offer* – it should not be so conservative as to fall in your opponent's ZOPA[9] or so extreme that it will destroy any possibility of a negotiated settlement.
   2) *Protect your integrity* – avoid disclosing information.

C) *The negotiation dance*:
   1) *The pattern of concessions* – your concessions should be paced and linked to those of your adversary.
   2) *Reassessing perceptions* – reassess your perceptions about your adversaries' desires and your aspiration levels.

D) *End play*:
   1) *Making commitments* – you might want to signal how far you will go.
   2) *Breaking commitments gracefully* – how can you disengage from a commitment that did not work?
   3) *Helping your adversaries to break commitments gracefully*.

---

[9] Since, if this occurs, there will be immediate agreement, you will meet your opponent's needs and miss the opportunity to negotiate a better deal.

4) *Introducing an intervenor* – such as using an arbitrator or mediator, to whom both you and your adversary might be willing to disclose more confidential information.
5) *Broadening the domain of negotiation* – in the end, there may be no ZOPA. But if the domain of negotiation is enlarged to include more complicated exchanges or to include additional issues, then a mutually profitable contract may be possible and desirable for both parties.

Bellucci and Zeleznikow (2005a and 2005b) and Zeleznikow (2006) investigate the management of negotiation knowledge. This extends the work of Rusanow (2003) on knowledge management in law. In this book we will not explicitly develop new negotiation strategies. However, in Chapter 5 we will discuss our strategy for supporting trade-offs and decision analysis in negotiation and in Chapter 6 we will introduce a strategy for supporting the resolution of online disputes.

3.2   Using bargaining and game theory to provide negotiation decision support

Decision analysis, behavioural decision-making and game theory are basic approaches for providing decision support for the negotiation process. Decision analysis and game theory have their foundations in the domains of information systems and mathematics whereas behavioural decision-making is grounded in psychology.

Senger (2004) discusses decision analysis in negotiation. He uses decision trees[10] and probability theory to look at likely outcomes resulting from following certain strategies. His goal is to minimise the risks inherent in international conflicts.

The issue of minimising risk in dispute resolution is discussed in Section 3.3. Senger (2004: 733) notes that:

> Decision analysis is not a perfect tool. The probabilities that parties place on the likelihood of various events are not magically accurate. The final result of an analysis is only as reliable as the data that parties use to create it, and the data are usually uncertain and subjective. Indeed, the figure that results from a decision analysis can appear artificially precise. Parties must recognize that it represents only an estimate based on the information available at the time.

---

[10] A decision tree is an explicit representation of all scenarios that can result from a given decision. The root of the tree represents the initial situation, whilst each path from the root corresponds to one possible scenario.

> Nonetheless, decision analysis can be a valuable tool to enable parties to make more accurate predictions in negotiation. Assessing the future outcomes is uncertain and subjective no matter what method is used. Predictions based on hunches or intuition are no more accurate than those based on decision analysis, and they may be less so. The advantage of decision analysis is that it allows parties to combine several individual hunches in a rigorous, mathematical manner.

Senger quotes Raiffa (1968) in saying:

> The spirit of decision analysis is divide and conquer: Decompose a complex problem into simpler problems, get one's thinking straight in these simpler problems, paste these analyses together with a logical glue, and come out with a program for action for the complex problem.

Decision analysis can also help parties overcome the human tendency to be overconfident, as mentioned by Mnookin and Ross (1995).

3.2.1   Game theory and utility functions

The mathematical theory of games was invented by von Neumann and Morgenstern (1947). It is a branch of applied mathematics that provides advice about the optimal distribution of resources. In the case of a negotiation, the goal of game theory is to develop the best outcome related to the choices each person has made.

Game theory is widely used in many fields including economics, finance, philosophy and political science. In industrial relations, for example, it can be used for bargaining between workers and employers, and in finance to help analyse stockmarkets.

An agent is, by definition, an entity with *preferences*. In a negotiation, each party to the negotiation is considered to be an agent. Sycara (1998) notes that in developing real-world negotiation support systems one must assume bounded rationality and the presence of incomplete information. In such decision-making, we assume each agent has a *utility*. An agent's utility refers to the amount of 'welfare' an agent derives from an object or an event. By 'welfare' we refer to some normative index of relative well-being, justified by reference to some background framework. In game theory, the objective is to optimise utility functions.

The concept of utility functions is derived from the notion of utilitarianism, which was propounded by Jeremy Bentham and his followers. The principle of utility or 'greatest happiness' mandates actions which produce the greatest sum of happiness (or pleasure or preference-satisfaction) as added up for the citizenry in the aggregate (Bentham 1988 (1789)). The concept of utilitarianism as advocated by Bentham is in fact the basis of integrative or interest-based negotiation as proposed by Walton and McKersie (1965).[11] It is distinct from the zero-sum games (or indeed often lose–lose games once the cost of litigation is taken into account) of litigation.

In game theory and economic theory, *zero-sum* describes a situation in which a participant's gain or loss is exactly balanced by the losses or gains of the other participant(s). If the total gains and losses of the participants are summed, then the sum will be zero. Cutting a cake is zero-sum, because taking a larger piece reduces the amount of cake available for others. The zero-sum property (if one gains, another loses) means that any result of a zero-sum situation is Pareto-optimal.[12]

Von Wright (1972) claims that preferences are an important object of study in economic theory. Modern decision theory has developed the new conceptions of utility functions and personal probabilities. In current economics and in decision theory, the utility of outcomes and attributes refers to their weight in decisions: utility is inferred from observed choices and is in turn used to explain these choices. Thus utility is a measure of the relative satisfaction gained by consuming different bundles of goods and services.

More specifically, as defined in the INSPIRE negotiation project (Kersten 2001), a utility function is a subjective measurement that expresses the relative value of different packages by using a numerical scale. The minimum number expresses the least desirable and least preferred package. The highest number represents the most desirable and preferred package.

Wright (1999) states there is no independent weight given in the utilitarian theory to the distribution of happiness (or wealth or power) or to the promotion of individuals' equal (positive and negative) freedom. Raiffa (1982) argues that there are very few researchers who prefer to trust the recommendations of formal utility theory rather their own intuition. We do not argue that utility theory is the panacea for building interest-based

---

[11] Whereas Walton and McKersie (1965) and Raiffa (1982) focus upon techniques for obtaining your goals in a negotiation, Fisher and Ury (1981) concentrate on how to conduct fair and successful negotiations. Fisher and Ury hence focus upon legal principles whilst Raiffa and, to a lesser extent, Walton and McKersie focus upon optimal strategies.

[12] Given a set of alternative allocations for a set of agents, a movement from one allocation to another that can make at least one agent better off without making any other agent worse off is called a Pareto improvement. An allocation is Pareto-optimal when no further Pareto improvements can be made.

negotiation support systems. However, models that use utility theory can provide useful negotiation advice.

In our discussion of utility functions, we focus upon the interests (in terms of optimising their utility function) of the disputants, rather than being concerned with the interests of society.

3.2.2 Cake-cutting and fair division

In Section 5.3.1 we shall discuss the Adjusted Winner algorithm for the fair distribution of assets in a dispute.

Game theoretic techniques and decision theory were the basis for Adjusted Winner (Brams and Taylor 1996). It is a two-party point allocation procedure that distributes items or issues to people on the premise of whoever values the item or issue more.

The two disputants are required to indicate explicitly how much they value each of the different issues by distributing 100 points across the range of issues in dispute. In this paradigm, it is assumed there are k discrete issues in dispute, each of which is divisible. Brams and Taylor (1996) claim the Adjusted Winner paradigm is a fair and equitable procedure because, at the end of allocation, each party will have accrued the same number of points.

Adjusted Winner's architecture is governed by a simple formula to calculate the division of issues or items. Brams and Taylor (1996) define the procedure as the allocation of k goods between parties A and B.

It allocates items so that Party A initially obtains all goods she desires more than Party B, and Party B is allocated the rest. In the next step the algorithm attempts to achieve equitability – that is to ensure the point totals of the two players are equal. The equitability adjustment formula aims to equalise the number of points both players have been allocated. Once the program has finished the calculation, it alerts the users to the items/issues the parties have been allocated and if appropriate will indicate the percentage to be given to both parties of an item that requires further division.

As Bellucci and Zeleznikow (2006) indicate, whilst the Adjusted Winner system suggests an allocation of items, it is up to human negotiators to finalise an agreement acceptable to real-world disputants. For example, if a couple are disputing the custody of children it is impossible to give 75 per cent to the wife and 25 per cent to the husband. However it could be suggested that the wife have custody with generous access for the husband. If the system recommended that the wife have 75 per cent of the house, this could be achieved by selling the house and giving the wife 75 per cent of the profit.

Bellucci and Zeleznikow (2006) extended the principles developed by Brams and Taylor (1996) into their Family_Winner system. The Family_ Winner software develops a strategy to decide which of the parties in a divorce gains particular items that have been valued by each party. The program uses game theory and a system of underlying rules (for instance, choose as the first item to distribute the one where there is the greatest difference in perceived value).

There is a dynamic rating of issues based on who wins the item and who loses. The program will distribute items to the party who values them the most and compensates the other by giving them extra points for the next item.

3.3   Negotiation and risk management

Zeleznikow and Stranieri (1998) stress that software such as the Split-Up system[13] can help with legal interpretation, but cannot make decisions about facts. They noted that only a human can make decisions with regard to facts and that humans will disregard information they find inconceivable.

In building legal decision support systems, it is thus better to focus upon interpreting the law rather than making decisions upon facts. Because of the *beyond reasonable doubt* onus in criminal law, very few decision support systems have been built in criminal law. The exceptions are in the domain of sentencing (see Schild 1998, Zeleznikow 2000 and Schild and Zeleznikow 2008 for a discussion of discretion and sentencing information systems). The burden of proof in civil law is *on the balance of probabilities*. Hence it easier to provide decision support systems in civil-law domains.

One of the major benefits of decision support systems that advise upon risk assessment is that they help avoid litigation. To avoid the risks of extra costs and an unfavourable outcome, disputants often prefer to negotiate rather than litigate. Whilst investigating how disputants evaluate the risks of litigation, researchers are faced with a basic hurdle – outcomes of negotiations are often, indeed usually, kept secret. If the case is litigated, it could be used as a precedent for future cases, which may be a disincentive for one or more of the litigants (Goldring 1976). Publicity of cases and the

---

[13] The Split-Up system proffers advice about property distribution following divorce in Australia.

norms resulting from cases makes the public aware of the changing attitudes towards legal issues.[14] The adjudication decision not only leads to the resolution of the dispute between the parties, but also provides norms for changing community standards (Eisenberg 1976). This latter facet is lost in negotiated settlements.

The secrecy behind negotiated settlements is one of the reasons for the paucity of published material on legal decision support systems dealing with risk. WIRE IQ (Wire Intelligent Quantum) is an Internet-delivered decision support system which allows lawyers, insurers and re-insurers access to up-to-the-minute quantitative analysis of current claims settlement values for a wide range of personal injuries (Douglas and Toulson 1999). Douglas and Toulson (1999) state that analysis and price discovery of tort in un-settled personal injury claims has been conducted using rule-based systems. In such systems, the details of the claim (injury type, claimant's age, sex, earnings, etc.) are entered into the system. The system then applies predefined rules to determine the settlement value of the claim.

WIRE IQ uses a database with thousands of records of settled claims and court awards for a range of personal injury claims. It then provides the following analysis services based on the data: trend analysis, comparative analysis, precedent search and forecasts. The forecasts are performed using neural networks.

JNANA (www.jnana.com) was founded in 1995 as Counselware, with the aim of building decision support systems for lawyers. The company very quickly realised that there was a large commercial need for decision support systems that advise upon risk assessment. Such systems are not made available to the public. JNANA currently focuses upon building a software platform to enable advice to be deployed over the Internet and Intranet. JNANA software is now being used broadly in many industries, such as financial services, healthcare, customer-relationship management, legal, and regulatory compliance.

3.4 Interest, justice and power-based negotiation

Fisher and Ury (1981:42) and Ury *et al.* (1988) describe three modes of negotiation: *interest-based negotiation*; *justice-* or rights-*based negotiation*; and

---

[14] In common-law countries, changing community values towards issues such as abortion, euthanasia and rape within marriage have been enacted in the legal system through landmark precedents, rather than parliamentary legislation.

power-based negotiation. In an interest-based orientation, the disputants attempt to reconcile their underlying interests. A rights- or justice-based orientation relies upon a determination of who is right in accordance with some accepted guidelines for behaviour.[15] A power-based orientation often takes the form of a power contest where each side strives to force the other to concede.

As Jameson (2001) says, rights-based strategies include processes such as fact-finding or *discovery, internal adjudication* and, for cases that might otherwise lead to litigation, *arbitration.* These formal rights-based strategies may be carried out by an ombudsperson or other designated person, a peer review board (if available) or an arbitrator (Ewing 1989). It is expected that these formal, rights-based approaches are used when there is considerable ongoing conflict.

Jameson says that because the goal of Alternative Dispute Resolution is to offer less adversarial approaches to conflict management than are found in the courts, it is not surprising that the Alternative Dispute Resolution research emphasises interest- and rights-based models. Yet in the organisational context, power-based approaches may be used by a variety of organisational members. Managers and other internal third parties may act *autocratically*, either by imposing a solution or *restructuring* work assignments to minimise interdependence of the disputants.

Disputants may also use a power-based approach to conflict management. They may appeal to a higher level of authority, for example, to overturn a supervisor's decision. Disputants may also use *threats* to coerce another party to submit to their will (Ury *et al.* 1988). Employees may also build a *coalition* to influence a variety of group or organisational decisions (Murninghan 1986) or in an attempt to coerce an employer to change organisational practices (Clegg 1994).

The concept of power in international disputes is a vital one. Despite the existence of the United Nations and the International Court of Justice, weaker countries often need to abide by the desires of stronger countries in times of conflict. Likewise, a large multinational company has the financial resources to undertake a lengthy litigation against a consumer with limited resources.

Through their research on the dispute-handling processes used in the coal-mining industry, Ury *et al.* (1988) found that interest-based strategies had the best long-term outcomes (such as improved relationship between

---

[15] These guidelines for appropriate behaviour often come from legislation or cases, but can in fact be derived from community practice.

the parties, greater perception of fairness and satisfaction, and greater commitment to solutions). Rights- and power-based strategies tended to produce adversarial relationships and continued workplace dissatisfaction.

These findings led the authors to conclude that the most effective dispute system design should rely on an interest-based approach to conflict management most often, moving to a rights- or power-based approach (in that order) only if an interest-based approach is ineffective.

Much research on third-party intervention in the past decade has echoed this sentiment, suggesting that conflict management approaches that encourage disputants to take an active role in the problem-solving process (such as mediation) produce more positive outcomes than strategies that leave the final decision in the hands of a third party, such as arbitration (Shapiro and Brett 1993).

While many negotiations involve two or three modes, most negotiation decision support has focused upon interest-based or integrative negotiation. The focus upon integrative bargaining is quite natural in areas such as online auctions or e-commerce, where logical consumers will only engage in actions that are beneficial (Zeleznikow and Vincent 2007).[16] But in other domains, issues of power and justice must be taken into account. For example, in Australian family law, judges have the power to impose justice- or fairness-based principles over the interests of the parents.

3.5 Developing negotiation decision support systems that promote constructive relationships following disputes

Negotiation support systems ordinarily focus upon transactional negotiation rather than forms of negotiation that are used in disputes where a continuing relationship is present. In addition, few systems focus

(1) on achieving a wise agreement – that is an agreement that meets the legitimate interests of each side to the extent possible, resolves conflicting interests fairly, is durable, and takes community interests into account (Fisher and Ury 1981); and
(2) upon improving or maintaining the relationship between the disputing parties.

In the case of both body corporate[17] and family disputes involving children, negotiations must meet these criteria, as the disputants inevitably need to deal with each other once the conflict has abated.

---

[16] In terms of their utility function.   [17] Also known as condominiums.

Both Relationships Australia (which operates in the domain of family mediation)[18] and Victoria Body Corporate Services (which amongst other things handles body corporate disputes)[19] provide dispute resolution services for clients who need to have constructive relationships following the cessation of the conflict.

Mr Shane Klintworth, director of the Queensland branch of Relationships Australia became aware of the interest-based negotiation support system Family_Winner when it won the section of the Australian Broadcasting Commission television show *The New Inventors*, screened on 16 November 2005.[20] Mr Klintworth saw the benefits to Relationships Australia (Queensland branch) of a system that could enhance interest-based negotiation. However, he also saw the need to emphasise the paramount interests of the children in any system. While meeting parental desires is important, meeting children's needs is paramount. Further, especially in cases where the divorcing couple have children, it is vital to encourage a harmonious ongoing relationship between the parents.

Similarly, because the disputants living in a body corporate are in close proximity to each other, it is important that disputes be resolved so that the body corporate members can continue with harmonious relationships. With this in mind, Mr Herman Klein, director of Victoria Body Corporate Services, wants to develop software that can help his managers quickly and amicably resolve disputes. Mr Klein also believes that the innovative application of negotiation support systems will give him a marketing advantage over other body corporate companies.

The project proposal was suggested to Professors Zeleznikow and Sourdin[21] by the industry partners, who wanted to develop *just* and

---

[18] Relationships Australia is one of Australia's primary providers of family counselling and family mediation services. Its Queensland branch (www.relationships.com.au/who-we-are/state-and-territory-organisations/qld, last accessed 11 September 2008) runs some national Family Relationship Centres. These centres provide information and advice on 1) building and strengthening existing relationships; 2) early intervention and prevention services for couples thinking of separating; 3) child-friendly services for families in conflict; 4) family dispute resolution services; and 5) parenting plans.

[19] Victoria Body Corporate Services (www.vbcs.com.au, last accessed 11 September 2008) is a medium size company offering personalised management services to bodies corporate, strata title units and company share properties. A major facet of its role is the successful resolution of disputes amongst body corporate members. Because, in general, the disputants live in the body corporate (and hence in close proximity to each other) it is important that disputes be resolved so that the body corporate members can continue with harmonious relationships.

[20] www.abc.net.au/tv/newinventors/txt/s1504763.htm (last accessed 11 September 2008).

[21] Professor of Conflict Resolution at the Australian Centre for Peace and Conflict Studies; see www.uq.edu.au/acpacs/professor-tania-sourdin (last accessed 11 September 2008).

usable negotiation support systems that help their managers and mediators advocate solutions that allow for the continuation of constructive relationships following disputes.

The Queensland branch of Relationships Australia wants to use a modified version of Family_Winner (Bellucci and Zeleznikow 2006) to provide decision support for their clients. The application domain concerns agreements about the distribution of marital property. Family Winner (see Chapter 5) attempts to meet both parents' interests to basically the same degree. In the modified version called AssetDivider, counsellors at Relationships Australia determine what percentage of the common pool property the wife should receive (e.g. 60%). See Bellucci (2008) for full details.

In conjunction with Relationships Australia, Zeleznikow and Bellucci (2006) have developed the Family_Mediator System. Family_Mediator uses linguistic variables, rather than numerals, to indicate users' preferences. It also has techniques to bias property distribution advice using the input of mediators from Relationships Australia. However, whilst Family_ Winner and Family_Mediator promote integrative (win–win) rather than adversarial (win–lose) solutions and are conducted through processes that are fair and are perceived by the parties to be fair, Relationships Australia (and indeed Victoria Body Corporate Services) also have other needs, including:

(1) the need for decisions to comply with prevailing ethical/legal principles (such as the rights of the child and tenancy laws);
(2) the prevention of further conflict through the development of clear arrangements (such as prenuptial arrangements between partners and clear guidelines for apartment owners); and
(3) the promotion of collaborative problem-solving between parties.

A current project, 'Developing negotiation decision support systems that promote constructive relationships following disputes',[22] is meeting these needs, hence enhancing the services of Relationships Australia and Victoria Body Corporate Services. Once these and associated goals of

(1) promoting effective communication, and minimising the use of coercive strategies between parties; and
(2) allow for evaluation and feedback (i.e. are intelligent and learn from experience)

[22] LP0882329 funded by the Australian Research Council's Linkage programme, with financial and in-kind support from Relationships Australia and Victoria Body Corporate Services.

have been met, Relationships Australia and Victoria Body Corporate Services will provide innovative and excellent services that will give them a marketing advantage over their competitors.

Professor Zeleznikow and Mr Klein have had numerous discussions on how negotiation support systems can be used to help managers at Victoria Body Corporate Services cope with potentially escalating disputes. This is a critical matter for both Victoria Body Corporate Services and their clients, since members of a body corporate need to live near each other and remain involved in collaborative decision-making. Likewise, divorced parents need to communicate with each other about the welfare of their children.

Both Relationships Australia and Victoria Body Corporate Services see the use of software that supports managers and mediators to advocate solutions that allow for the continuation of constructive relationships following disputes, as giving their respective organisations a competitive advantage over their competitors.

3.6 Negotiation planning – developing decision support systems that help avoid rather than settle disputes

In this book we have focused upon how to use information technology to support dispute resolution. But in fact it would be even more desirable to provide advice and plan so that the number of disputes are minimised and those disputes that do occur are not protracted. This is an issue considered by Gray *et al.* (2007).

Gray *et al.* (2006) claim that legal practice is the business of conflict prevention and conflict resolution. Negotiation is a common requirement of legal practice. The rules of law provide the epistemological structure which is carried into the negotiation procedure.

There has been no research on building conflict-prevention negotiation support systems, using ontology of possible conflict,[23] to avoid foreseeable conflicts. Gray *et al.* (2007) consider an amalgamation of integrative bargaining and negotiation planning, and develop a prototype negotiation support system that helps avoid domestic conflicts. Considerations in the ontology of possible cohabitation conflict may assist formation of prenuptial and cohabitation agreements, and lead to an increased likelihood of a successful arrangement, with ease of re-negotiation as circumstances change, and ease of termination. With other appropriate potential conflict

---

[23] An ontology is an explicit conceptualisation of a domain (Gruber 1995).

ontologies, such as in commerce, environmental use, industrial and cultural relations, inter-governmental matters, and war, similar negotiation support systems might be constructed.

Schlobohm and Waterman (1987) developed EPS (Estate Planning System). It was a prototype expert system that performed testamentary estate planning by interacting directly with clients or paralegal professionals. The result of a consultation between a client and EPS is the client's will, printed by a form-generating program that EPS accesses. The system was written in ROSIE (an expert system shell).

Estate planning is the process by which a person plans the accumulation, management, conservation and disposition of his or her estate so as to derive the maximum benefit and satisfaction during the person's lifetime and for his or her family after death. Schlobohm and Waterman (1987) note that estate planning involves planning in many diverse areas such as:

(1) Testamentary planning – planning the disposition of a client's estate on death, including charitable bequests.
(2) Lifetime planning – gifts and other dispositions of a client's estate during life. Determining how title to property should be held.
(3) Planning for specific assets – life insurance. Planning to transfer control of closely held businesses.
(4) Estate freezing – 'freezing' the value of wealthy clients' estates to mitigate federal estate tax.
(5) Other planning – post-mortem (i.e. after death) tax planning.

To develop a prototype, Schlobohm and Waterman (1987) initially limited EPS' domain to testamentary estate planning, that is, the knowledge necessary to create a client's will or revocable trust.

3.7   Examples of negotiation decision support

In Chapter 5 we will consider specific examples of intelligent negotiation support systems. In this section we examine the negotiation domains in which such systems have been constructed.

3.7.1   Australian family law and mediation

Australian family law has been an application domain for a variety of systems that provide negotiation decision support. Hence it is worthwhile to discuss the domain.

Australian family law

Australia has a federal system of government. The Australian Constitution divides authority between the states and the Commonwealth. Section 51 of the Commonwealth of Australia Constitution Act 1900 (Cth)[24] gives the Federal Parliament the power to make laws about:

> (xx) Marriage; and
>
> (xxi) Divorce and matrimonial causes; and in relation thereto, parental rights, and the custody and guardianship of infants.

Prior to 1959 there were varying state laws about divorce. The Matrimonial Causes Act 1959 (Cth) introduced the first uniform divorce laws for Australia. The principal aim of the Family Law Act (1975) was to reform the law governing the dissolution of marriage. The new Act replaced the Matrimonial Causes Act 1959 (Cth) and superseded state and territory laws about 'guardianship, custody, access and maintenance' of children of a marriage.

The Family Law Act 1975 (Cth), as well as making significant changes to the law relating to divorce in Australia, created the Family Court of Australia to interpret and apply that law to individual cases. Appeals from a first-instance decision of a Family Court judge are ordinarily heard by a Full Court of the Family Court, which must be composed of at least three Family Court judges (Dickey 1990).

Under this Act, the sole grounds for dissolution of marriage are an irretrievable breakdown of the marriage. Matrimonial fault was not deemed relevant as the basis for the distribution of property interests by the framers of the Family Law Act (1975).[25] As Zeleznikow (2004) points out, property distribution is determined relative to (1) relative needs; (2) relative contributions; and (3) the level of wealth of the marriage, but always subject to the paramount interests of the child. The Act clearly allows the decision-maker a great deal of discretion in interpreting and weighing factors relative to a property distribution. That discretion is even greater when considering child-welfare related issues.

Zeleznikow (2000) notes that, although family law in Australia has been controversial, by and large, outcomes in property proceedings can be predicted with some degree of accuracy by practitioners experienced

---

[24] In this context the abbreviation (Cth) means the legislation is Australian federal rather than state legislation.

[25] Under the Matrimonial Causes Act 1959 (Cth), fault had been a factor in property distribution.

with the way in which the court and individual judges exercise discretion. This is however not so with that part of the Act which deals with the welfare of children. Under section 64(1) (a): 'the court must regard the welfare of the child as the paramount consideration'.

Neither parliament nor the courts have clearly defined what are the paramount interests of the child, and so this is an extremely open-textured term.[26] The Act does however attempt to pose some guidelines for determining the residency of children. These include:

(1) the court shall consider any wishes expressed by the child;
(2) the court is reluctant to have siblings living in different households;
(3) the court shall consider the future education of the children.

But nowhere is a judge told that she must take these issues into account. Nor is she informed what weight to give each of these issues. And for many issues, there is no single answer as to what is in the best interests of the child. For instance, it is easy to make rational arguments for sending children to government/private/religious schools.

In determining the primary residence of a child a Family Court judge has many choices. On one hand she could have the child spend roughly equal amounts of time with both parents, whilst on the other hand she could refuse access to either parent. Thus it appears that the judge has a wide option of choices. But the judge is in fact guided by one principle: *the paramount interests of the child*. For example, when determining the residence of the child, if the parents have violent disagreements, a judge may restrict access for one of the parents, even if during the marriage both parents have been greatly involved in the raising of the child. In this case the number of options available to the judge is limited by the parents' conflict.

Zeleznikow (2000) classifies discretionary legal domains.[27] An example of bounded discretion is the percentage split distribution of marital

---

[26] *Open-textured predicates* contain questions that cannot be structured in the form of production rules or logical propositions and which require some legal knowledge on the part of the user in order to answer.

[27] A domain is *bounded* if the problem space can be specified in advance, regardless of the final definitional interpretation of the terms in the problem space. A problem space is unbounded if one cannot specify in advance which terms lie within the problem space. There are four distinct ways in which discretion can be exercised in legal domains. We define these concepts as: no discretion; narrow discretion (there are well enunciated norms that are clear from legislation, cases and/or legal opinions); bounded discretion (there are no norms: but judges know which factors should be considered in making a judgment); and unfettered discretion (these domains have no norms and judges are not even told what factors must be taken into account in reaching a decision).

property in Australian family law. The factors to be taken into account are specified in Section 75(4) of the Act. Such factors include the contributions of each partner, the future needs of each partner and the level of wealth of the marriage. However, nowhere are judges instructed on the significance or weight of each of these factors.

An example of unfettered discretion is the determination of the custody of children in Australian family law. According to the Family Law Act (1975) the only factor to be taken into account is *the paramount interests of the child*. Following considerable litigation and uncertainty the Australian Federal Parliament made minimal attempts to define what the paramount interests of a child are. We are not aware of any decision support system that provides advice about the welfare of children. Further, we would caution against the construction of such systems. Kannai *et al.* (2007) further refine Zeleznikow (2000)'s two-dimensional model of discretionary reasoning by adding a third axis: whether the decision to be made is binary[28] or continuous.[29] According to this classification, decisions on awarding of refugee status are even more discretionary than issues about the welfare of children. The argument supporting this reasoning is that a Family Court judge has a variety of options, whereas a Refugee Tribunal Member can only accept or refuse an application for refugee status.

Australian family dispute resolution[30]

Although there was a focus on Alternative Dispute Resolution in the Family Court of Australia from its inception in 1975, conciliation and counselling were initially employed and it was not until the late 1980s that mediation began to be used.[31]

In Australia, mediation – generally facilitative mediation – has been used to handle disputes in the family arena for about twenty years. The 'family arena' generally comprises property or child-related disputes arising between parents, whether married or not, and whether they have lived together or not. Such disputes may also involve other people who are related to the children or who have cared for the children; however, the overwhelming majority of disputes mediated are couple-related.

Initially it was considered essential that the couple enter mediation voluntarily. However, this is not the situation in Australia today: at least one

---

[28] Such as is the defendant guilty?
[29] Such as the percentage of marital property awarded to the wife.
[30] Much of the work in this section is due to Deborah MacFarlane.
[31] Astor and Chinkin (2002: Chapter 17).

meeting with a family mediator is mandatory before lodging an application for a parenting order in the Family Court.

The reasons for the change are complex. Certainly a major factor in the past two decades has been the huge increase in the breakdown of family relationships, resulting in excessive workloads for courts dealing with family matters. The dominance of economic rationalism has also played a significant role both because of the failure of governments under its sway to increase the number of judges and funding to the courts generally, and because economic rationalism frowns on the cost to the public purse of court action which can be dealt with more expeditiously and cheaply by other means.

Another important factor is that many studies have shown the huge emotional cost to the family of court action, a fact often not compatible with the 'paramount interests of the child' principle which theoretically governs family court actions. Finally, the very success of voluntary mediation has led decision-makers to believe that mediation is a better alternative than adjudication for the majority of family disputes, whether undertaken voluntarily or not.

In about twenty years, Australian family mediation has gone from being considered an alternative form of dispute resolution in the 1980s, to a primary form of dispute resolution in 1995, to a compulsory first step in 2007, if parents cannot reach agreement on arrangements for their children. The transition has been a very rapid one when compared with the gradual changes that normally characterise the common law.

The importance of dealing with divorce in the best possible way when 32 per cent of marriages fail, 60 per cent involving children under the age of eighteen years,[32] is clearly crucial to the well-being of the community. The fact that mediation has proved an effective way of dealing with family relationships, and the existence of a substantial body of research demonstrating the detrimental effects of conflict between parents on their children, have made it understandable why the government has made mediation compulsory before parents are permitted to lodge an application for a parenting agreement in the courts.

A number of decision support systems that support negotiation in Australian family law have been developed: DEUS (Zeleznikow *et al.* 1995), Split-Up (Stranieri *et al.* 1999), Family_Negotiator (Bellucci and Zeleznikow 1997), AdjustWinner (Bellucci and Zeleznikow 1998),

---

[32] Australian Bureau of Statistics figures, 2006.

Family_Winner (Bellucci and Zeleznikow 2006), Family_Mediator (Zeleznikow and Bellucci 2006) and AssetDivider (Bellucci 2008). These will be discussed in more detail in Chapter 5.

3.7.2   Damages claims

The Rand Corporation built numerous expert systems in the early 1980s (Waterman and Peterson 1980, 1981 and 1984; Peterson and Waterman 1985) to advise upon risk assessment.

One of their early systems, LDS, assisted legal experts in settling product liability cases. Another Rand Corporation decision support system, SAL (Waterman *et al.* 1986), also dealt with claims settlement. SAL helped insurance claims adjusters evaluate claims related to asbestos exposure. SAL used knowledge about damages, defendant liability, plaintiff responsibility and case characteristics such as the type of litigants and skill of the opposing lawyers.

These systems built by the Rand Corporation are important, for they represent early first steps in recognising the virtue of settlement-oriented decision support systems.

3.7.3   Business–consumer disputes

The parties involved in disputes between businesses and consumers are unequal by nature. Businesses have resources, power, and are repeat players. Consumers are one-time-shooters with fewer resources and not much power. With the advent of the Internet this has changed somewhat. For quite some time consumers have been organised formally in most countries (e.g. Better Business Bureau), but the Internet allows for individual consumer feedback potentially reaching a wide audience. This is why businesses should be more cautious when dealing with consumer conflicts than they have been in the past. Obviously, a good business should take the rights of consumers seriously. Due to the fact that many businesses do not, there is much law that focuses on consumer protection. This legislation means to restore the balance between both parties. As we have seen in Chapter 2, one way the legislator realises this is by forcing businesses to inform the consumers about their rights, namely disclosure of information.

E-commerce regulation aims to create trust in business in order to stimulate business-to-consumer transactions. The adequate resolution of conflict is seen as an important element contributing to this trust. In

Online Dispute Resolution the third party should be aware of the position of both parties and the assumed inequality. A problem with such disputes is that the value of the item in conflict is minimal and thus it is normally not worth entering into a dispute resolution process. Without investment from industry or government, it is very difficult to develop a profitable business model. The use of technology can play an important role here. The costs of a resolution process primarily lie in the payment of the third parties governing this process. If only technology is used, without the need for human interference, the process can be conducted for a relatively low price. This is particularly so if the volume of conflicts is high. So the use of technology makes it possible to resolve business to commerce (B2C) disputes for a relatively low price, and allows for huge numbers of conflicts to be resolved without many additional costs.

3.7.4   Industrial relations

Walton and McKersie's work and the game theory research of John Nash[33] led to a significant use of game theory to support negotiation in industrial relations. Game theory is particularly applicable in countries where employers and employees can bargain with very few restrictions.[34]

In discussing Walton and McKersie (1965), Kochan (1992) notes that:

> The book makes ample use of theoretical constructs like game theory, subjective utilities, motivation theory and psychological concepts like equity and balance theory. This was a move toward the use of a more cognitive approach. All of these concepts were not heavily used in industrial relations and collective bargaining research, and most traditional people in our field were rather hostile to those concepts.

The Australian Workplace Relations Amendment (Work Choices) Bill 2005 encourages employers and employees to conduct direct negotiations about employment conditions. Previously, under a centralised decision-making process, the Australian Industrial Relations Commission made rulings on disputes.[35] While the legislation creates a Fair Pay Commission to ensure that all agreements meet five basic principles, the legislation

---

[33] See Nash (1953). Nash received the Nobel Prize for Economics in 1994. He is the subject of Nasar (1994), which was used as the basis for the 2001 Academy Award winning film, *A Beautiful Mind*.

[34] As is the case in the United States, unlike most Continental countries in Western Europe. In most of the latter countries, there are strict safeguards for employees, such as relating to recreation and sick leave.

[35] Generally conducted between unions and employer groups.

encourages interest-based negotiation rather than arbitrated or judicial decisions. It is thus an excellent domain in which to provide negotiation decision support. Following the victory of the Australian Labour Party in the federal elections of November 2007, legislation is before the Australian Parliament to include further safeguards for workers. Thus negotiation in the domain is moving from being primarily interest-based to being a combination of justice-based and interest-based approaches.

There have been a number of prototype negotiation support systems that advise upon industrial relations:

(1) *Negoplan* (Matwin *et al.* 1989) used rule-based reasoning to success-fully model labour–management negotiations in the Canadian paper industry. They based their example on a labour-contract negotiation between the Canadian Paperworkers' Union and CIP, Ltd. of Montreal. CIP is a major pulp and paper manufacturer. The negotiations took place in May 1987. Negoplan distinguished five major phases: prepar-ation, stalemate, initial strike, full strike, and real bargaining. These phases seem to be typical in labour–management negotiation, par-ticularly when the union's position is strong.

(2) *Persuader* (Sycara 1993) integrated case-based reasoning and deci-sion-theoretic techniques to provide decision support to industrial disputes in the United States.

3.7.5   *Bargaining about charges and pleas*[36]

How do the benefits of Alternative Dispute Resolution relate to the pro-cess of negotiating about charges and pleas? Lower cost and greater speed may be major benefits for the prosecution. But whilst cost may be a factor for defendants, speed is not. This is especially the case if the plea results in gaol time.

Plea-bargaining is the process whereby the accused and the prosecutor in a criminal case work out a mutually satisfactory disposition of the case subject to court approval.[37] It usually involves the defendant's pleading guilty to a lesser offence or to only one or some of the counts of a multi-count indictment in return for a lighter sentence. In US federal courts, the Federal Rules of Criminal Procedure govern bargaining procedures.[38]

---

[36] Much of the work in this section can be found in the soon-to-be published PhD thesis of Andrew Vincent and in Zeleznikow and Vincent (2007).
[37] See Black (1990).   [38] Fed. R. Crim. P. 11.

Without the concept of plea-bargaining, the US criminal justice system would grind to a halt. Approximately 90 per cent of guilty pleas in the United States are negotiated.[39]

The fact that in most US states there are minimum sentences for the most common crimes ensures that the prosecution is able to enter into a plea bargain if they have some control over the final sentence. The success of the plea-bargaining process *depends on the prosecutor's ability to make credible threats of severe post-trial sentences.*[40] Credible threats concerning sentence severity are enhanced in jurisdictions that have determinate sentencing regimes.[41] Some scholars treat plea-bargaining as simply another case of bargaining in the shadow of a trial.[42]

In Australia, the concept of plea negotiation is widely practised in all states but practitioners and academics alike prefer different terminologies. The practice is usually known as charge negotiation[43] or plea negotiation.[44]

A major difference between the US and Australian systems is that in Australia the prosecutor is only indirectly able to influence the minimum sentence that may be prescribed by a judge through overcharging. It seems that the greatest amount of overcharging occurs in lower courts.[45] In the higher courts, where Offices of Public Prosecution, and not the police, handle prosecution, there is a tendency not to overcharge. Mack and Roach Anleu (1996) suggest several reasons for this overcharging, but the most important one is that it gives the police a better bargaining position. The police propose high charges in order to end up with what they see as a 'correct' or reasonable set of charges for a particular set of facts.

The most significant difference between the Australian system and the US plea-bargaining system is the power of the prosecution in the United States to affect a sentence based on charges that involve some type of determinate sentencing. The same arguments for the institutionalisation of plea-bargaining that are used in the United States are used in Australia to defend the practice of plea negotiation. The strongest argument is that

---

[39] Baldwin and McConville (1977).

[40] Stuntz (2004).

[41] Cf. Keller (1996) discussing judicial discretion and determinate sentencing.

[42] Bibas (2004: 2466).

[43] See Cowdery (2005) and Austl. L. Reform Comm'n, Sentencing of Federal Offenders app. B, § 4.2 (1980), available at www.austlii.edu.au/au/other/alrc/publications/reports/15 (last accessed 16 September 2008).

[44] Seifman and Freiberg (2001).

[45] Mack and Roach Anleu (1995: 32).

the bargaining process is able to move cases through the system at a more rapid rate than would otherwise occur.

Scott and Stuntz (1992) argue that whilst most legal scholars oppose the negotiation about charges and pleas (finding it both inefficient and unjust), they acknowledge that most participants in the plea-bargaining process (including the courts) seem remarkably untroubled by the process. Hollander Blumoff (1997) examines plea-bargaining through the lens of dispute resolution, exploring how practitioners approach and carry out plea negotiations and gauging whether and to what extent plea-bargaining may be analysed as negotiation.

O'Malley (1983: 130–133) notes that plea-bargaining can be understood as one factor in a process that is seemingly geared towards the 'automatic production of guilty pleas'. It is a process that has developed in response to demands for bureaucratic efficiency felt by courts at all levels, especially those at lower levels.

While efficiency looms as the most important factor in maintaining a plea-bargaining system, it is not the most important aspect in individual cases. Generally, efficiency is the overriding reason for the prosecution to enter into a plea bargain. If a small percentage of defendants exercised their rights to trial, the criminal justice system would not be able to cope with the massive extra burden this would entail.[46] The numbers of juries and judges alone would be very large. In the United States, more than 93 per cent of cases in the federal courts were disposed of by guilty pleas in 2000.[47] The number of felony convictions for 2000 was 924,700 and approximately 95 per cent of these were disposed of by guilty pleas.[48]

There are possible negative consequences of negotiating about pleas. Bibas (2004) argues that many plea bargains diverge from the shadow of trials. He claims that, rather than basing sentences on the need for deterrence, retribution, incapacitation or rehabilitation, plea-bargaining effectively bases sentences in part on wealth, sex, age, education, intelligence

---

[46] Hodge *et al.* (2005) indicate that defendants would need to be released if an organised exercise of their Sixth Amendment right to a 'speedy' public trial before an impartial jury occurred. If only another 10 per cent claimed this right, the judicial system would be brought to a halt.

[47] The US federal courts account for only a small percentage of convicted felons incarcerated in US prisons (Bibas 2004: 2466, n. 9).

[48] See Bibas (2004), indicating that is it impossible to know the percentage of guilty pleas that resulted from plea-bargaining. See also U.S. Bureau of Just. Stat., Sourcebook of Criminal Justice Statistics 2003, tbls. 5.17, 5.46, available at www.albany.edu/source-book/index.html (last accessed 16 September 2008).

and confidence. Bibas suggest that while trials may allocate punishment imperfectly, plea-bargaining adds another layer of distortions and warps the allocation of punishment.

Adelstein and Miceli (2001) develop a general model of plea-bargaining, embed it in a larger framework that addresses the costs of adjudication, the value of punishing the guilty and the costs of false convictions, and then link the desirability of plea-bargaining and compulsory prosecution to the weights given these costs and benefits in the objective function.

Gazal-Ayal (2006) investigates the economics of plea-bargaining. He proposes having a partial ban on plea bargains, which prohibits prosecutors from offering substantial plea concessions. He argues that such a ban can act to discourage prosecutors from bringing weak cases and thus reduce the risk of wrongful convictions. Tor *et al.* (2006) conducted experiments in which they determined that defendants' willingness to accept a plea bargain is substantially reduced when defendants feel that the offer is unfair, either because they are not guilty or because other defendants received better offers.

Wright and Miller (2003) believe that pervasive harm stems from charge bargains due to their special lack of transparency. They argue that charge bargains, even more than sentencing concessions, make it difficult after the fact to sort out good bargains from bad in an accurate or systematic way.

Criticisms of plea negotiation have centred around several key issues, namely: transparency, inducements and coercion, and incorrect outcomes (Bibas 2004). Mack and Roach Anleu (1996) have identified faults in the process. The significant points include:

(1) The transparency of the process: in general, plea-bargaining occurs outside the court system.
(2) Guilty pleas may be induced by the unwarranted benefits of those burdens caused by the decision to go to trial. The quantum of sentence discount that is associated with the plea of guilty is an added pressure to engage in plea-bargaining.
(3) Incorrect outcomes in terms of both the determination of guilt and the subsequent sentence imposed.

Thus, we have seen from our analysis that there is much, both academic and community, dispute about the benefits and disadvantages of charge- and plea-bargaining. Plea-bargaining brings administrative efficiency, certainty and reduced costs. But, as Hollander Blumoff (1997) claims:

> Scholars and citizens alike argue about whether the system is inevitable, fair or just. Some hold that the plea agreement process yields results that discount crime and are too soft on criminals. Others argue, conversely, that prosecutors wield too much power over criminal defendants, especially those who are indigent. Schulhofer (1992) claims plea bargains are unduly coercive and penalize defendants who do not accept agreements for exercising their right to trial.

So how can we ensure that the benefits of plea-bargaining are maintained whilst fairly allocating punishment? The issue of fairness in negotiation is important in all domains of law, but more so in sentencing where the adversaries are not two individuals, but an individual and the state. Whilst feminist legal commentators have expressed similar concerns about family mediation, unfair family mediations do not generally lead to unjust incarceration.[49]

3.7.6   Condominium disputes[50]

Condominiums, owners' corporations, or strata titles as they used to be called, are a way of dividing and individually owning lots in a multi-lot building or property located on a single piece of land. They generally have four characteristics:

(1) separate ownership of individual lots of the property;
(2) indivisible co-ownership of the common property;
(3) restrictions on partition of the common property; and
(4) a schema of rules and covenants to govern the corporation.

While day-to-day management of the corporation is usually given to a professional management company or manager the overall management of the property and its upkeep is the responsibility of the corporation.

---

[49] Although admittedly there are major concerns about domestic violence which affect family mediation.

[50] Much of the work in this section is due to Peter Condliffe, a barrister and mediator who recently was the Executive Director of the Australian Institute of Arbitrators and Mediators. Mr Condliffe is currently undertaking a PhD on the project 'Developing Negotiation Decision Support Systems that Promote Constructive Relationships Following Disputes', conducted under the supervision of Professor John Zeleznikow.

The transient nature of much of the resident population and their relations with owners and absent investor landlords complicates the management arrangements.

The Victorian Owners Corporations Act 2006, in part 10, explicitly mentions dispute resolution processes. There are now 65,000 body corporates in Victoria. The Act sees the process of ADR as part of a wider policy of dispute management. Most Australian and US states have already developed or are developing similar guidelines (Elisha and Wiltgen 2006).

Most condominium disputes fall into either quality of life or financial disputes. The former can include pets, noise, sub-letting, parking, alterations, use of common property, exterior painting and so on. The latter can include failure to pay maintenance fees, special assessments, fines, access to accounts and related matters. However, residents in condominiums not only have to manage the day-to-day demands of living side by side in close proximity but also deal with the demands of jointly managing and maintaining the property.

Because of this closeness various 'house rules' become necessary to manage everything from paint colours and pets to barbeque use. Living within these constraints requires a considerable degree of tolerance. Compliance with these rules becomes a matter of principle to some residents, especially those who are complying with the rules but witness examples of people who are not compliant. This can be exacerbated when renters, who may not share the same concerns and interests, mix in the same building or housing arrangement with owners.

Owner/occupier and neighbour disputes can be some of the most bitter and protracted types of disputes (Mollen 1999). As a sub-set of what is generally known as 'neighbourhood disputes' they are pervasive across all sections of society. They involve the investment of enormous resources, including not only the neighbours themselves but legal, local government, police, health and welfare services.

Condliffe, Abrahams and Zeleznikow at the Laboratory of Decision Support and Dispute Management, Victoria University, Melbourne, Australia, have developed model rules for dispute resolution in condominiums (Condliffe 2009). They have developed a mediation/arbitration model out of which they are now constructing a negotiation support system. This work will be discussed in Section 5.10.

4

Technologies for supporting dispute resolution

4.1 Introduction

Information technology has become an integral part of dispute resolution processes, and is of course an essential ingredient of Online Dispute Resolution (ODR). Recently, the role of IT has become prominent in the provision of offline dispute resolution services. Within the judiciary, the introduction of IT is often used as an enabler of change within the organisation (see, for example, Fabri and Contini 2001; Oskamp *et al.* 2004). A striking example of the use of IT in courts relates to Singapore (Thian 2004). Within ten years, an old-fashioned, slow-working judicial organisation with enormous backlogs became a smooth-functioning, modern judiciary with hardly any backlog.

However, no matter how influential IT currently is in the operation of the judiciary, most judicial applications do not deal with the real content of the cases before the court. Tools that support calculations are an exception: for example, calculators which are used by judges to determine alimony in divorce proceedings. Basically, IT helps in streamlining the process. Examples include case management and workflow management systems.

As distinct from traditional offline processes, ODR by nature needs IT to resolve the conflict: in the online environment all communication is inherently electronic. So, the role of technology is pivotal, and information technology is always present.

The authors of this text have roots in the field of Artificial Intelligence and Law.[1] One of the aims of Artificial Intelligence and Law is basically to apply advanced technology to the domain of law. Conflicts lie at the heart of law. The two, technology and conflicts, are naturally brought together in Online Dispute Resolution. That is what stimulated our interest in Online Dispute Resolution almost a decade ago. In this chapter we will

---

Some parts of this chapter are based on Lodder (2006).

[1] See the *Journal of Artificial Intelligence and Law* at www.springer.com/computer/artificial/journal/10506 (last accessed 5 August 2009) and Zeleznikow and Hunter (1994).

briefly discuss the basic technology used in Online Dispute Resolution. Advanced applications are discussed in Chapters 5 and 6.

In this chapter, we first discuss characteristics of communication technology, in particular the distinction between synchronous and asynchronous communication (Section 4.2). Next, we briefly introduce the three most influential ODR processes to date, namely ICANN domain-name disputes, Cybersettle and SquareTrade (Section 4.3). We continue with elaborating upon a concept central to ODR, namely the labelling of the technology as the fourth party (Section 4.4). Subsequently, we introduce the concept of the fifth party, the provider of the technology (Section 4.5), and use the concepts to discuss the nature of technology, dedicated to ODR or not (Section 4.6), and the increasing influence of technology (Section 4.7). We conclude with a section on how technology should be matched with a particular process (Section 4.8).

4.2   Basic technology: synchronous and asynchronous

The communication technology used in Online Dispute Resolution is largely similar to regular electronic communication technology. Given our familiarity with basic forms of electronic communication, it is not useful to explain each communication modality here. Rather, we briefly address an important distinction for the understanding of ODR, namely between synchronous and asynchronous communication.

Synchronous communication is direct communication, with a minimal time interval between the moment one party makes a comment in a discussion, and the other party receives this message. The other party can, in turn, almost immediately react. This is the case in face-to-face communication, and in an online environment where chat, audio-conferencing, or video-conferencing is used.

In asynchronous communication, parties do not take part in the discussion at the same time. They do not immediately receive the communication of the other party, and also do not need to react instantly. Discussion forums, e-mail and text-messages (or SMS) are the main examples of asynchronous communication.

It is important to realise that in ODR both forms of communication can be combined. For instance, relevant documents can be exchanged via e-mail or uploaded to a shared space, followed by a Skype-communication[2]

---

[2] Skype is public domain software that enables individuals and businesses to make free video and voice calls, send instant messages and share files with other Skype users. Skype is an eBay company. See http://about.skype.com (last accessed 5 August 2009).

discussing these documents. ODR providers sometimes prefer asynchronous communication, because it is not necessary to agree on a meeting time. Asynchronous communication also allows parties to think about a response quietly. The sharp edges disappear when using asynchronous communication, and unnecessary insults can be prevented. Nonetheless, some providers consider it important that parties be able to express their emotions quickly, because once the heat gets out of the discussion, parties will be able to concentrate on the real issues. The danger in expressing such emotions is that the dispute might escalate. However, heated emotions can also reveal what would otherwise remain under the surface.

There are benefits of synchronous as well as asynchronous communication. Which communication form should be preferred depends on the nature of the dispute and the parties involved. Most providers use one of either synchronous or asynchronous communication, but some do offer both. An example of a provider supporting both is the Italian provider RisolviOnline,[3] which offers both e-mail and chat. They have noted that their current group of users are not ready yet for using the instant communication of chat. The users prefer e-mail.

4.3   The major Online Dispute Resolution providers

Currently, there are three major providers of Online Dispute Resolution Services:

(1) ICANN domain-name disputes;
(2) Cybersettle;
(3) SquareTrade.

4.3.1   The ICANN UDRP[4]

The ICANN domain-name dispute resolution process was launched in the late 1990s with a primary goal to have a quick and inexpensive online arbitration procedure to resolve disputes about domain names and hence stop the actions of unreasonable domain-name grabbers. The costs of the process are somewhere between 1,000–3,000 US dollars.

---

[3] See www.risolvionline.com/?lng_id=14 (last accessed 5 August 2009).
[4] Professor Jon Bing, law professor at the Norwegian Research Center for Computers and Law (NRCCL), has been conducting research on ICANN dispute resolution processes. A forthcoming article will appear in Proceedings of the Workshop on Legal and Negotiation Support Systems 2009, in conjunction with the 12th International Conference on Artificial Intelligence and Law (ICAIL 2009).

The process has several important features. First, the registrant of the domain name commits himself when registering the domain name to undergo an online arbitration if someone files a complaint about his domain name. The arbitration process is not binding in the sense that each party can go to court if he is not satisfied with the outcome. Over the past ten years, very few parties proceeded to court following a decision by the arbitration panel. This is understandable since if the panel decides against a potential owner, he would be very unlikely to win in court proceedings. The outcome is also easily enforceable. If the complainant loses, the holder of the domain name remains the owner. If the complainant wins, the domain name will be transferred by ICANN to the complainant.

ICANN has appointed a small number of dispute resolution providers. In the beginning (1999) the National Arbitration Forum,[5] WIPO,[6] eResolution and CPR: International Institute for Conflict Prevention and Resolution were appointed. The last two are no longer offering this service. Since February 2002 the Asian Domain Name Dispute Resolution Centre was added to the list of approved providers.[7] With the introduction of the .eu domain name, a new provider was appointed, namely the Czech Arbitration Court (CAC).[8]

The WIPO is the most successful Online Dispute Resolution provider, and has handled over 10,000 cases. eResolution stopped offering their services quite soon after they started trading. There are different explanations for this outcome. One is that at that time, they offered a fully online process (with online forms) and that the market was not ready for such a process ten years ago. The other providers offered a hybrid process, where forms could be filled in offline. A further reason for their failure is that they ruled in favour of the complainant in 60 per cent of the cases, whilst for example WIPO ruled in favour of the complainant in more than 80 per cent of the cases. Hence, most complainants chose the provider that statistically was best for them, leaving eResolution with hardly any cases.

4.3.2   Cybersettle

A very simple and appealing process is offered by Cybersettle, the primary provider of the so-called blind-bidding process.[9] The first went online in

---

[5] http://domains.adrforum.com (last accessed 5 August 2009).
[6] www.wipo.int/amc/en/domains (last accessed 5 August 2009).
[7] www.adndrc.org/adndrc/index.html (last accessed 5 August 2009).
[8] www.adr.eu (last accessed 5 August 2009).
[9] www.cybersettle.com/pub (last accessed 5 August 2009).

1998. Since then it has handled over 200,000 transactions, and has settled cases worth a total amount of US$1.6 billion.[10]

The process was developed for single issue, monetary claims, e.g. between insurance companies. The process starts when the initiator or plaintiff, called the first party, is asked by the system to enter three sums of money that he would like to obtain from the other party. The last bid should be the lowest sum this party would be satisfied with. Next, the second party is asked to enter three figures corresponding with what he is willing to pay. For him, the third offer should be the maximum he is willing to pay. The system then calculates whether the bid and offer are within a predefined range and consequently whether or not the case can be closed with a settlement.

The enforcement procedure in Cybersettle cases is straightforward: the party that has to pay is asked in advance to provide the expected sum (or more) in the form of a (bank) guarantee. If the case is settled, the required sum is transferred to the other party.

Cybersettle has patented its process, and threatened many rival providers with legal action to force them to stop offering similar services. Since 2008 it has had a Canadian associate partner.

A similar program that improves upon the Cybersettle algorithm was presented by James F. Ring, entitled 'Strategic and game theoretic issues relating to traditional and online dispute resolution systems', during the Fourth International ODR Workshop held at eBay in San Jose, California.[11] With Steven Brams (of the Brams and Taylor algorithm discussed in Chapter 5) he works at Fair Outcomes.[12]

4.3.3   SquareTrade and eBay

SquareTrade has handled millions of eBay cases. Due to a change in the procedure in early 2008, it stopped offering its ODR services in the first half of 2008. An additional reason for the termination of service is that eBay itself has provided a very popular ODR programme since 2004. During the period since SquareTrade stopped offering its services, eBay handled over thirty million cases per annum. eBay's process is quite

---

[10] www.cybersettle.com/pub/home/about/factsheet.aspx (last accessed 5 August 2009).
[11] See Proceedings of the Fourth International Workshop on Online Dispute Resolution (ODRworkshop.info) in conjunction with the Eleventh International Conference on Artificial Intelligence and Law, Press, ACM Palo Alto, CA., USA. A. Lodder, C. Rule and J. Zeleznikow (eds.) 978–90–9022015–4.
[12] www.fairoutcomes.com.

similar to what SquareTrade offered, so we briefly describe the process of the latter provider, one of the pioneers in ODR.

Parties commence the negotiation first by filling in a form. In a dedicated, structured web form the parties have to indicate, from a predefined list, what their dispute is about. They also have to indicate the details of the buyer and seller. The resolution phase starts by suggesting some possible solutions to the predefined conflict that was selected by the parties. If both parties select the same solution, the system offers the parties a contract with this solution. Parties normally will sign this contract. If the parties do not reach an agreement, a mediation phase can be started. The mediation is conducted via an e-mail platform. If the mediation is not successful, the parties can ask the mediator to suggest a solution.

4.4   The fourth party – the technology

Unlike the case in traditional offline processes, ODR by its nature needs IT to resolve the conflict: in the online environment communication is inherently electronic. So, the role of technology is pivotal, and the involvement of information technology is essential. This observation led Katsh and Rifkin (2001: 93–94) to introduce the notion of the fourth party. They identified that the following stakeholders can be identified in Online Dispute Resolution:

(1) the two parties having the dispute;
(2) the independent third party (mediator, arbitrator, conciliator); and
(3) the technology, referred to as a fourth party.

The fourth party need not have a high degree of technical sophistication. Even if the ODR process consists of the mere exchange of e-mail, its use is considered as the fourth party in the proceedings. In certain cases, the fourth party can in fact replace the third party, such as in the case of blind-bidding or indeed any fully automated negotiation decision-making. In between there are many possible manifestations of the fourth party.

Katsh and Rifkin (2001) also introduced the so-called Trust–Convenience–Expertise Triangle.

The triangle reflects the elements that should be present in any ODR system. The parties using the system should trust it, the use of the system has to be convenient, and the system should offer expertise. The triangular form indicates that the amount of each of the three concepts can vary. Right in the middle (the centroid) there are equal values of convenience,

Figure 4.1   Trust–Convenience–Expertise Triangle

trust and expertise. For example, in the convenience corner, the level of expertise and trust is less present. The triangle can be helpful in trying to understand and categorise ODR systems.

The importance of introducing the concept of the fourth party is that it places an emphasis on technology. The adequate and appropriate application of technology can lead to the difference between a resolved and unresolved dispute. For example, if there is a misunderstanding due to the inadequate representation of the exchanged information during an online mediation, the mediator can observe this problem and prevent the parties from continuing with inadequate information. If no human party is involved, e.g. in case of assisted negotiation, the technology can and should help prevent misunderstanding. Whether the technology can in fact do so depends on the type of procedure, the legal domain and the intended users. By providing adequate support, the technology can help in preventing misunderstanding. Avoiding a misunderstanding is more difficult than when a human third party observes the process. On the other hand, if no human third party is involved, the transaction price of the process decreases significantly. So, providers and disputing parties should decide for themselves as to which process is most desirable for their specific case.

With the application of information technology for dispute resolution, some commentators see the lack of *face-to-face* contact as an insurmountable hurdle. For them, only video-conferencing would be a possible solution to this problem. It is, however, doubtful whether an online environment should always mimic the offline situation. Online mediation could even take place without the involvement of a human mediator, but with the help of the technology: in a way incomparable with offline mediation. For example, parties can be supported by applications that help them to structure the information of the dispute. Systems can also be used to propose settlements based on the preferences entered by the parties. We will give several examples of such applications in Chapter 5.

In the case of online arbitration, information technology (the fourth party) can play a significant role. As we will also discuss in the next chapter, it can be used to structure the positions of the parties. In many existing online arbitration applications the exchange of statements and arguments takes place in a non-structured way. Both the arbiter and the parties can profit from a structured presentation of issues and statements, and the relation between what has been put forward by the two parties. The arbiter is then capable of observing, almost immediately, the extent of the disagreement between the parties.

4.5   The fifth party – the provider of the information technology

Bol (2005) and Lodder (2006) have introduced the concept of the fifth party. The fifth party represents the provider of the technology. This concept has also been used by several others, including Wang (2008) and Cortes Dieguez (2008). The fifth party is an entity, either a natural person or a company, involved in the ODR process. This concept has been developed to explain the various existing and possible relations between the parties involved in the ODR process.

The notion of a fifth party is useful for analysing the various relationships between those involved in the ODR process. The fifth party is not a legal party; it is a technical player in the ODR process, namely the provider of dispute resolution services. The legal consequence of being a fifth party is at least equally important as technical matters relating to the fifth party. For instance, the fifth party facilitates the analysis of a whole range of different contractual relationships between the various parties in ODR, and there are general legal duties with which the fifth party has to comply.

4.6   The nature of the technology used

In case of negotiation (as well as mediation, arbitration, conciliation) the parties can either use the services of a provider specifically dedicated to dispute resolution, or use applications they have at their disposal. The use of traditional software such as e-mail or chat should be considered for Online Dispute Resolution.

Following the most common definitions, ODR is roughly described as the dispute resolution process that takes place at least partially online, no matter what technology is used. ODR implies the presence of the fourth party, namely the technology used by those involved in the conflict as well as the eventual third party. So, the fifth party as the entity that delivers the fourth party must be present in all forms of ODR. Nonetheless, from a technical perspective one could argue that cases in which parties try to solve a conflict using traditional software should not be classified as a form of ODR (in a strict sense). Similarly, e-mail would not be called music-sharing software if an e-mail with MP3-files is sent to some friends who share the same musical preferences. Neither would e-mail be called dating software if two people set a time and date to meet for a candlelight dinner. And negotiating via e-mail to conclude a contract does not make e-mail e-contracting software. Nevertheless, from a legal perspective, the particular activities of general-purpose software such as e-mail can matter, e.g. in the case of liability. If during the dispute resolution process something goes wrong, e.g. technical problems hindering the resolution of the conflict, the provider of dedicated dispute resolution technology is more likely to be held liable than the provider of mere e-mail or chat facilities. The border between what makes software dedicated or not is gradual.

At the one end of the spectrum are the providers of general communication technology. Next comes the software that is used by providers of ODR. The type of dedication here is not technical, because the software itself is not dedicated. It is the purpose for which the providers apply the software, namely dispute resolution, that makes the software dedicated. Next in the spectrum is software originally developed for other collaborative or document management purposes, and massaged to double as ODR applications (Grover 2002), e.g. a slightly adapted discussion forum. At the other end of the spectrum is software that has been especially developed for ODR. As a rule of thumb one might say that the more dedicated the software, the quicker liability can be established and the more severe disclosure duties are. In all the above-mentioned cases, technology is used to resolve a conflict online, so the fourth party is sitting at the 'dispute resolution table'.

Given the coincidental nature of the provider of the technology in the simplest case, we would not call this provider the fifth party. The fourth and fifth parties are present in most cases. If a third is involved that uses general software or the software is by nature dedicated, the fifth party comes into play. Table 4.1 gives an overview of the different possibilities.

Table 4.1 *Third, fourth and fifth parties' use of software*

	General software, no ODR purpose	Software dedicated by use	Software dedicated by nature
Third party	No	Yes	Possible
Fourth party	Yes	Yes	Yes
Fifth party	No	Possible	Yes

The first column deals with the following situation. If an employer decides to use his Hotmail account to settle a dispute with an employee also using his Hotmail account, the technology indeed plays a role in the resolution. So, the fourth party is present. We would not however argue that Hotmail is the provider of dispute resolution services. Obviously, in the same manner, if the employee uses another provider, say Yahoo!, that does not turn both providers into dispute resolution service providers.

The second column is the situation in which the use of the software by the third party makes it dedicated. One might wonder why the fifth party is possibly involved, whilst in the case that the same software is used by only the disputing parties, then there is no fifth party. The difference is subtle. The reason the fifth party could be involved is that when the third party uses general software, he may become the provider of the technology. A mediator may run general chat software on his website that he uses to mediate between the parties. He then becomes a fifth party as well.

The third column is probably the least controversial. In that case the technology is meant to be used for ODR, either through adapted general software or specially developed software. The technology can be labelled straightforwardly as the fourth party and the provider of this technology as the fifth party. This dedicated software can be employed by a third party, but also two disputing parties may decide to use negotiation software without a third party being involved.

In summary, it is important to distinguish between the nature of the technology provided and, in particular, the aim of the provider of the technology. The fifth party is present only if either the technology was developed for supporting the resolution of disputes, or the provider aims to deliver tools that help the parties in solving the conflict.

4.7 When the third, fourth and fifth parties coincide

If the computer actually decides a case, does it make sense to speak of the technology as the third party? What about if the computer mediates a case? Has the technology then taken the place of the third party?

Blind bidding is an illuminating example of computer assisted negotiation decision making. Most authors consider this process of providers such as Cybersettle as a form of assisted or automated negotiation. It is true that parties are participating in a negotiation, but in the case of Cybersettle, it is the software that does in fact decide whether a case settles.

For this reason, Rule (2002) classifies blind-bidding as a form of online arbitration. Obviously his position is controversial, but if we examine the definition normally used for online arbitration he is correct: arbitration as a process in which the third party decides the case. In Chapter 1, we defined arbitration as an adversarial process whereby an independent third party (or parties), after hearing submissions from the disputants, makes an award binding upon the parties.

A possible objection to Rule's classification is that a piece of software cannot be considered a third party. This is an argument that is used quite often, but by itself it does not really convince. It is similar to the argument that computers cannot be intelligent, because intelligence can only be attributed to humans.

Often, the disputing parties negotiate without the intervention of a third party and use software that supports their negotiation. In the offline world people may toss a coin or throw dice to decide an issue. No one would ever call the coin or the dice a third party, although it is in fact this instrument that decides the issue for the parties.

There is, however, a significant difference between these cases. The coin or dice could be used by anyone to settle an issue: it is not necessary that the disputing parties provide input or perform some action other than agreeing to use the coin or dice. In the case of blind-bidding, the input of the parties to the dispute is crucial, and the software responds to this particular input. The role of the software is an active one.

One might still argue that the input is too simple, just some numbers. Whether or not this is true would only shift the problem to deciding under what circumstances the software performs complex enough actions to label it as a third party. Besides it being difficult to come up with criteria for this purpose, once criteria are formulated it probably remains arbitrary to decide which software should be considered a third party. The criterion already in use, a party deciding the case, seems best in this respect.

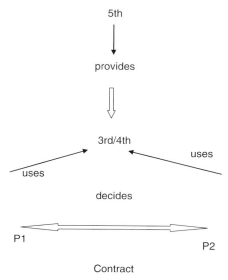

Figure 4.2   The role of the third, fourth and fifth parties in ODR

So, in our opinion, the Cybersettle software (the fourth party) acts as a third party. The company Cybersettle, as the provider of the software, is the fifth party. This leads to the following picture (see Figure 4.2).

The introduction of the fifth party, in the context of software such as Cybersettle, clarifies the role of the organisation (the human component) behind the software. This picture makes it clear that the fifth party provides the software, and does not coincide with the third party. Note that the contract between the two parties having a dispute and the fifth party is missing in the picture. The picture leaves room for the interpretation that the software is a legal actor, namely one that creates a new contract between the two parties P1 and P2 (or changing the existing contract) in which if the case settles it is decided what sum P1 needs to pay to P2. This is our interpretation, although it might be rejected by many lawyers.

An alternative interpretation is to consider the third/fourth party as an instrument.[13] The instrument is provided by the fifth party, and used by P1 and P2. The situation is somewhat comparable to auction sites. The difference is that there can be more parties bidding on an auction site, and the successful bid creates a contract between two parties who did not already have a contractual relationship. One could state that both

[13] A discussion in Dutch on software being an instrument or actor is provided by Lodder (2004). A related English paper is Wettig and Zehendner (2003).

blind-bidding sites and auction sites provide electronic contracting support tools. A more sophisticated example in this respect is Smartsettle, where the parties work on a contract in which all the issues are given certain values until both parties are satisfied, and is supported by intelligent software (Thiessen and McMahon 2000).

4.8   Matching technology with the process

In ODR, the correct use of information technology contributes significantly to the resolution of the conflict. The fifth party has to make decisions regarding what type of technology should be offered. Basically, technology in ODR can be applied for the following purposes:

(1) supporting the communication;
(2) supporting the exchange of documents and information;
(3) supporting decision-making;
(4) making decisions.

As a general rule, one might say that negotiation and mediation software should focus on communication, and arbitration on document management. A variety of factors influence what technology fits best to the conflict and the parties. Possible future research directions for online arbitration are applications that integrate document-management software and tools supporting the identification and structuring of issues. Mediation might benefit from adequate technology working in real time, and capturing the dynamics of the discussion (interaction). Negotiation software has proven successful when preformatted issues/problems are used and outcomes related to the problems are presented.

Apart from concentrating on what type of IT support fits best to

(1) given procedures;
(2) parties, and;
(3) types of conflicts.

the fifth party might make a shift in the future from delivering tools and support, depending on the specific process, to generic tools.

In such a case, different providers would deliver different functionality, and parties would not use a single provider, but choose the software that best fits their preferences. The choice of the arbiter or mediator may even depend on the choice the parties make regarding the technology. So the selection depends not only on seeing the third party as an expert on the content, but also taking into account his capacity regarding the use of specific ODR platforms and tools. In the context of mediation, Bol (2005) referred to forum-shopping, and focused on the separation between the fifth and the third party.

In the future the specialisation of the fifth party may lead to modules delivered by different providers being combined into a single ODR environment. The implementation of the three-step model discussed in Chapter 6 is an example of such an environment.

Advanced intelligent technologies for dispute resolution

In this chapter we will discuss a variety of dispute resolution decision support systems. These systems cover a wide range of disputes and many of these (particularly in the domain of family law) were constructed by the authors.

5.1 Intelligent decision support

Zeleznikow (2002) states that when considering decision-making as a knowledge-manufacturing process, the purpose of a decision support system is to help the user manage knowledge. A decision support system fulfils this purpose by enhancing the user's competence in representing and processing knowledge. It supplements human knowledge management skills with computer-based means for managing knowledge. A decision support system accepts, stores, uses, receives and presents knowledge pertinent to the decisions being made. Its capabilities are defined by the types of knowledge with which it can work, the ways in which it can represent these various types of knowledge, and its capabilities for processing these representations.

The process of decision support may generally be considered as divided into three steps:

(1) diagnosis of a problem;
(2) selection of an action; and
(3) implementation of that action.

We are particularly interested in the second step, the selection of an action as a choice among several alternatives.

Providing decision support under certainty means that the selection of an action leads to one and only one consequence. Providing decision support under conditions of risk means that several consequences are possible, each with a known probability.

It should be stressed that there is a major difference between decision support and decision-making. Decision support tools help decision-makers improve their performance. Decision-making tools automate the process, leaving a minimal role for the user.

Tools that have been used to develop intelligent negotiation support systems include:

(1) *Rule-based reasoning.* In the rule-based approach, the knowledge of a specific legal domain is represented as a collection of rules of the form IF <condition(s)> THEN action/conclusion.

For example, consider the domain of driving offences in Victoria, Australia. Drivers can lose their licence either by being drunk whilst driving, or exceeding a specified number of points in a given time. More specifically, probationary drivers (those who have held a driver's licence for less than three years) are not permitted to have even a trace of alcohol in their blood. Other drivers must have a blood alcohol level not exceeding 0.05 per cent. This knowledge can be modelled by the following rules: (a) IF drive(X) & (blood_alcohol(X) > .05) & (license(X) >= 36) THEN licence_loss(X); (b) IF drive(X) & (blood_alcohol(X) > .00) & (license(X) < 36) THEN licence_loss(X).

(2) *Case-based reasoning.* Case-based reasoning is the process of using previous experience to analyse or solve a new problem, explain why previous experiences are or are not similar to the present problem and adapting past solutions to meet the requirements. Precedents play a more central role in common law[1] than civil law and are therefore the most obvious application of adversarial case-based reasoning in the legal domain. However, partly due to the electronic availability of case law, in particular via the Internet, the role of precedents seem to become at least informally more important in civil-law countries. Using the principle of *stare decisis*, to make a decision in a new case, legal decision-makers search for the most similar case decided at the same or higher level in the hierarchy. A comprehensive discussion of the application of this approach to the legal domain is provided in Ashley (1992) and Rissland *et al.* (2005).

(3) *Machine learning.* Machine learning is that sub-section of learning in which the artificial-intelligence system attempts to learn automatically. Knowledge Discovery from Databases is the 'non-trivial extraction

---

[1] Common law is the legal tradition that evolved in England from the eleventh century onwards. Its principles appear for the most part in reported judgments, usually of the higher courts, in relation to specific fact situations arising in disputes that courts have adjudicated.

of implicit, previously unknown and potentially useful information from data'. Data mining is a problem-solving methodology that finds a logical or mathematical description, eventually of a complex nature, of patterns and regularities in a set of data (Fayyad *et al.* 1996). An in-depth discussion of Knowledge Discovery from Legal Databases can be found in Stranieri and Zeleznikow (2005).

(4) *Neural networks.* A neural network receives its name from the fact that it resembles a nervous system in the brain. It consists of many self-adjusting processing elements cooperating in a densely inter-connected network. Each processing element generates a single out-put signal which is transmitted to the other processing elements. The output signal of a processing element depends on the inputs to the processing element: each input is gated by a weighting factor that determines the amount of influence that the input will have on the output. The strength of the weighting factors is adjusted autono-mously by the processing element as data is processed. Neural net-works are particularly useful in law because they can deal with: (a) classification difficulties; (b) vague terms; (c) defeasible rules; and (d) discretionary domains. Nonetheless, the actual application of neural networks remains very limited, in particular since it is not easy, if possible at all, for neural network systems to justify their decision. Obviously, the justification of a decision is often more important than the actual decision.

We shall discuss examples of intelligent negotiation support prototypes in Section 5.4

5.2   Template-based negotiation support systems

Traditionally, negotiation support systems have been template-based, with little attention given to the role the system itself should play in negotiations and decision-making support. The primary role of these systems has been to demonstrate to users how close (or far) they are from a negotiated settlement. The systems do not specifically suggest solu-tions to users. However, by informing users of the issues in dispute and a measure of the level of the disagreement, they provide some decision support.

Eidelman (1993) discusses two template-based software systems that are available to help lawyers negotiate: Negotiator Pro and The Art of Negotiating.

Negotiator Pro has three primary features. First, it has a psychological profiling system that consists of two devices. The first is a personality profiler based upon the Myers-Briggs Type Indicator, a popular personality test that uses Jung's four typing scales (Introvert/Extrovert, Thinking/Feeling, etc.). The second device is based on a competitive/cooperative matrix of effectiveness to help judge the type of negotiators involved. After all participating parties are entered into the system, the program presents advice on how to achieve a 'win–win' solution with the given parties and their representatives.

The second feature is the Plan, which has two modes: a ten-question mode and a thirty-five-question mode. The user chooses a plan based upon the complexity of the negotiation. She answers a series of questions designed to make her think about the opportunities and obstacles involved in a particular negotiation. A window with a checklist provides an extensive list of possible answers. The result is an outline that helps her both to enter the negotiations better prepared to achieve her goals, and to recognise counter moves that the other side might attempt.

The third feature is an extensive glossary that draws more than 350 excerpts from leading books on negotiation.

The Art of Negotiating presents a menu to take the user through submenus and questions in seven areas, as follows:

(1) Subject matter of the negotiations: your side; the other side; what the negotiation is about; other important parties.
(2) Objectives: each side's objectives; conflicting and non-conflicting objectives; ranking of objectives of each side by importance.
(3) Issues and positions: issues in the negotiations; rating of the issues; positions and questions on the issues.
(4) Needs/gambits: levels of approach; needs of the other side; working for or against needs to make gambits; rating your top gambits.
(5) Climates: determining your negotiating philosophy; major climate categories; choosing climates to create; anticipating the other side's climates.
(6) Strategies: explanations of strategies; choosing your strategies; anticipating the other side's strategies; the other side's counters to your strategies; your counters to other side's strategies.
(7) Agenda: options for handling specific issues; setting up your private agenda; refining your position and questions; deciding about a general agenda; thinking about your close.

The program performs (and asks the user about) some interesting comparisons. For example, in asking the user what the negotiations are about, the program asks if the user and the other side are in agreement on the subject matter, item by item, pointing out agreements and differences. With respect to the issues, the program asks the user to type in the user's position and the opposing side's position, and questions the user has about that issue.

Eidelman (1993) claims Negotiator Pro is much more open-ended than The Art of Negotiating, with advice from hundreds of texts, hypertext interface and a free-form format. It is also more robust, more theoretical and more flexible. The ability to add templates with questions and checklists makes it particularly suitable for lawyers, who are often involved in settling large and complex matters of a specialised type.

The Art of Negotiating, on the other hand, is much more structured and focused in format, fields and advice. It is very easy to get into, to use and to get good results from. It is more specific in its suggestion of strategies, and offers an important feature that Negotiator Pro lacks – suggestions of counter-strategies to tactics either side may use.

INSPIRE (Kersten 1997) is a template-based negotiation support system that uses utility functions to graph offers, and is discussed further in Section 5.7. INSPIRE enables disputants to negotiate through the Internet, making extensive use of e-mail and web-browser facilities. The system displays previous and present offers, and uses utility functions to evaluate proposals determined to be Pareto-optimal.[2] Disputants communicate by exchanging offers and electronic mail, and can check the closeness of a package to their initial preferences through a utility graph function.

In DEUS (Zeleznikow *et al.* 1995) the goals of the parties (and their offers) in an Australian family law dispute were set on screen side by side. It is a template-based system that displays the level of disagreement, with respect to each item, between disputants. The model underpinning the program calculates the level of agreement and disagreement between the litigants' goals at any given time. The disputants reach a negotiated settlement when the difference between the goals is reduced to nil. DEUS is useful for gaining an understanding of what issues are in dispute and the extent of the dispute over these issues.

---

[2] Pareto-optimality refers to a situation where at least one party is better off, without making other parties worse off.

5.3 Negotiation support systems based upon bargaining and game theory

Perhaps the two most widely known and used negotiation support systems are Adjusted Winner[3] (Brams and Taylor 1996) and Smartsettle[4] (Thiessen and McMahon 2000). Both use game-theoretic techniques to provide advice about what they claim are *fair* solutions. Their concept of fair negotiation does not coincide with the concept of legally just negotiations that we considered in Section 1.2. Both systems require users to rank and value each issue in dispute, by allocating the sum of 100 points amongst all the issues. Given these numbers, game-theoretic optimisation algorithms are then used to optimise, to an identical extent, each person's desires.

These algorithms are fair in the sense that each disputant's desire is equally met. They do not, however, meet concerns about justice. For example, if the parents were only interested in their own desires and not the paramount interests of the children, neither system would promote the interests of the children.

Family_Winner (Bellucci and Zeleznikow 2006) also uses game theoretic techniques and artificial intelligence to provide advice about Australian family mediation. It does not, however, focus upon meeting each disputant's desires to exactly the same degree.

5.3.1   Adjusted Winner

Adjusted Winner is an algorithm developed by Steven J. Brams and Alan D. Taylor to divide *n* divisible goods between two parties as fairly as possible.[5] Adjusted Winner starts with the designation of the items in a dispute. If either party says an item is in the dispute, then it is added to the dispute list.[6]

The parties then indicate how much they value each item, by distributing 100 points across them.[7] This information, which may or may not be

---

[3] Adjusted Winner principles have now been developed by Fair Outcomes, Inc. (see www.appellex.com (last accessed 6 August 2009)) which provides parties involved in disputes or difficult negotiations with access to newly developed proprietary systems that allow fair and equitable outcomes to be achieved with remarkable efficiency. Each of these systems is grounded in mathematical theories of fair division and of games.

[4] See www.smartsettle.com (last accessed 6 August 2009), where examples of industrial relations, international conflicts and insurance disputes are given.

[5] See www.nyu.edu/projects/adjustedwinner (last accessed 17 September 2008) for examples and to use the Adjusted Winner software.

[6] The other party could of course give the item the value zero.

[7] In fact if the sum of the items was not 100, the numbers should be scaled. Essentially the disputants are being asked how they rank and value the items in dispute.

made public, becomes the basis for fairly dividing the goods and issues at a later stage. Once the points have been assigned by both parties (in secret), a mediator (or a computer) can use Adjusted Winner to allocate the items to each party, and to determine which item (there will be at most one) may need to be divided.

Suppose Bob and Carol are divorcing and wish to divide some of their assets. Suppose they distribute 100 points among the five items, as shown in Table 5.1.

Adjusted Winner works by assigning, initially, the item to the person who puts more points on it. Thus, Bob receives the home and the items in the 'other' category, whereas Carol receives the retirement account and the summer cottage. Leaving aside the tied item (investments), Carol has a total of 65 (50 + 15) of her points, and Bob a total of 40 (30 + 10) of his points. This completes the 'winner' phase of Adjusted Winner.

Because Bob trails Carol in points (40 compared to 65) in this phase, initially we award the investments on which they tie to Bob, which brings him up to 50 points (30 + 10 + 10).

The 'adjusted' phase of Adjusted Winner commences now. The goal of this phase is to achieve an equitable allocation by transferring items, or fractions thereof, from Carol to Bob until their points are equal.

What is important here is the order in which items are transferred. This order is determined by looking at certain fractions, corresponding to the items that Carol, the initial winner, has and may have to give up. In particular, for each item Carol won initially, the algorithm looks at the fraction giving the ratio of Carol's points to Bob's for that item:

(Number of points Carol assigned to the item)/(Number of points Bob assigned to the item)

Table 5.1 *Scenario using Adjusted Winner system*

Item	Carol	Bob
Retirement account	50	40
Home	20	30
Summer cottage	15	10
Investments	10	10
Other	5	10
Total	100	100

In the example, Carol won two items, the retirement account and the summer cottage. For the retirement account, the fraction is 50/40 = 1.25, and for the summer cottage the fraction is 15/10 = 1.50.

The algorithm starts by transferring items from Carol to Bob, beginning with the item with the smallest fraction. This is the retirement account, with a fraction equal to 1.25. It continues transferring goods until the point totals are equal.

Notice that if the entire retirement account was transferred from Carol to Bob, Bob would wind up with 90 (50 + 40) of his points, whereas Carol would plunge to 15 (65 – 50) of her points. Therefore, the parties will have to share or split the item. So the algorithm's task is to find exactly what fraction of this item each party will get so that their point totals come out to be equal.

Thus, let p be the fraction of the retirement account that needs to be transferred from Carol to Bob in order to equalise totals; in other words, p is the fraction of the retirement account that Bob will get, and $(1 - p)$ is the fraction that Carol will get. After the transfer, Bob's point total will be $50 + 40p$, and Carol's point total will be $15 + 50(1 - p)$. Since the point totals need to be equal, p must satisfy

$$50 + 40p = 15 + 50(1 - p)$$

Thus $90p = 15$ and so $p = 15/90 = 1/6$. Thus, Bob should get one-sixth of the retirement account and Carol should get the remaining five-sixths. Each party receives 56.67 points.

It should be noted that the greater the difference that Bob and Carol give to each item, the more points each will obtain. In their software constructed by modifying the Adjusted Winner algorithm, Bellucci and Zeleznikow (1998) noted that in the average dispute, each disputant received approximately seventy points. The reason was that the disputants were not diametrically opposed. In zero-sum games, each disputant receives fifty points because of the paradigm that whatever I win, you lose.

Brams and Taylor (1996) claim that the Adjusted Winner algorithm is envy-free,[8] equitable[9] and efficient.[10]

---

[8] Neither party would want to trade their allocation for their opponent's allocation since both would receive fewer points by accepting their opponent's allocation.

[9] Since both parties receive the same number of points.

[10] The formal proof in Brams and Taylor (1996) show that there can be *no better* allocation for both players. It should be noted that the initial allocation is efficient, since each player receives all the goods he or she most values, and the equitability adjustment step does not affect efficiency.

Fair Outcomes Inc. has developed four systems based on Adjusted Winner principles. These are:

(1) *Fair Buy–Sell.* This system is used by joint owners of property such as business partners, joint venturers, shareholders and married couples who wish to bring their joint ownership to an end on terms that are mutually acceptable and legally enforceable. This relatively simple but powerful new system provides an excellent introduction to some of the basic game-theoretic principles that underlie all of the systems offered by our company.

(2) *Fair Division.* In cases in which two parties must divide up multiple items of property or resolve multiple issues that are in dispute, this system enables the parties to do so in a fair, efficient and legally binding manner. It has been applied to conflicts ranging from divorce to international border disputes and is founded upon some of the most important research that has been done in fair division and game theory in recent decades.

(3) *Fair Proposals.* In cases in which one party is seeking money or other concessions from another party, this system allows either party to formulate and commit itself to a reasonable proposal in a manner that deprives the other side of an incentive or excuse for failing to do the same prior to a fixed deadline. Each party's proposal remains confidential unless the system determines that it is acceptable to the other side, at which point it becomes the resolution.

(4) *Fair Reputations.* In cases where a transaction has given rise to a dispute that may result in damage to a party's reputation, such as where a purchase or sale on an e-commerce site has resulted in negative 'feedback' that may adversely affect a party's 'online reputation', this system allows that party to take unilateral steps to restore, preserve and protect its reputation.

5.3.2 *Smartsettle*

In his 1950 PhD thesis, John Nash[11] developed a model showing that competitive behaviour among decision-makers leads to a non-optimal equilibrium (now known as the *Nash Equilibrium*). This radical idea challenges the classical economic theory of Adam Smith, where free competition leads to best-possible results, and is in contrast to classical Darwinian

---

[11] Nash (1950).

theory, where natural selection leads to improvement in the species. The dynamics of unregulated competition can actually be disastrous according to Milnor (1998). Many political commentators argue that the economic crises of 2008 were exacerbated by the failure of the US government to adequately regulate the governance of financial markets.

Nash (1953) showed that a unique optimal solution could be found by maximising the product of the utilities for cooperative negotiators. Nash theorised that 'we idealize the bargaining problem by assuming that the two individuals are highly rational, that each can accurately compare his desires for various things, that they are equal in bargaining skill, and that each has full knowledge of the tastes and preferences of the other'. These were also the arguments for this solution being the fairest possible outcome.

Ernie Thiessen's research commenced in 1976, working as a consulting engineer and researcher in both Canada and Nepal. During the 1980s, his work related to water resource systems, planning and development. A notable achievement was the facilitation of negotiations between His Majesty's Government of Nepal, the United Mission to Nepal and the local beneficiaries on the Andhi Khola Project regarding an unconventional plan to develop an irrigation project in such a way as to give unprecedented benefits to the poorest of the community. Thiessen received his doctorate from Cornell University in 1993 (Thiessen 1993), majoring in Water Resource Systems in the School of Civil and Environmental Engineering. While at Cornell University, Thiessen developed an efficient methodology to solve very complex negotiation problems.

In Thiessen *et al.* (1998) he described the algorithms and results obtained using an interactive computer program developed to assist those involved in negotiating agreements among parties having conflicting objectives. This Interactive Computer-Assisted Negotiation Support system (ICANS) can be used during the negotiation process by opposing parties or by a professional mediator. On the basis of information provided to the program, in confidence, by each party, it can help all parties identify feasible alternatives, if any exist, that should be preferred to each party's proposal. If such alternatives do not exist, the program can help parties develop counter-proposals.

Through a series of iterations in which each party's input data, assumptions and preferences may change, ICANS can aid each party in their search for a mutually acceptable and preferred agreement. This paper describes the algorithms used for analysing preferences and for generating alternative feasible agreements. Also presented are the results of some limited experiments involving water resource system development and use conflicts that illustrate the potential of programs such as ICANS.

Of course, at that time, none of these negotiation support systems were online. They all ran on single computers, albeit possibly large ones.

Thiessen and McMahon (2000) cite seven current challenges of conventional negotiation that often prevent participants from achieving better outcomes:

(1) adversarial tactics;
(2) piecemeal thinking;
(3) tedium;
(4) high costs;
(5) irrational decisions;
(6) complexity; and
(7) win–lose outcomes.

They claim (in 2000) that new negotiation support systems with powerful optimisation algorithms and enhanced by a maturing cyberspace are now providing a real alternative to conventional negotiation in business arrangements as well as the settlement of litigation. These new systems reduce negotiating time and cost for decision-makers by putting them in control of a process that quickly clarifies trade-offs, recognises party satisfaction on all types of negotiation issues, and generates optimal solutions.

They claim that the basic theory underlying the optimisation algorithms of negotiation support systems can be illustrated effectively using the efficiency frontier concept. The efficiency frontier concept represents the best possible outcomes for all parties in a negotiation case.

They argue that every potential resolution in a negotiation problem is associated with an expected satisfaction level for each negotiation party. The efficiency frontier is a line defining the greatest level of joint satisfaction that parties can get in a particular negotiation.

They continue to describe One Accord, a negotiation support system that networks multiple parties located anywhere in the world and manages their confidential information with a neutral Internet site. With the aid of a facilitator, the parties proceed through the various phases in the following sequence:

(1) qualify interests;
(2) quantify satisfaction;
(3) establish equity;

(4) maximise benefits;
(5) secure commitment.

Thiessen and McMahon claim that preliminary research shows significant potential for negotiating parties to gain from using such systems. Thiessen *et al.* (1998) report that in a Cornell University study the average gains were 16 per cent for each party. This methodology has been patented and is now being used by Smartsettle.

In his work on the Smartsettle system, Ernie Thiessen noted that real-world negotiators do not cooperate in that way. He specified a secure neutral site to fulfil the knowledge requirement. In his PhD thesis,[12] he wanted to develop a rule for fairly distributing benefits when generating an optimal solution relative to an existing tentative agreement among any number of negotiators. The mathematical framework was also inspired by Raiffa (1982). Since Thiessen's goal was to develop a computer program to demonstrate the results of his research, an important criterion was that the methods would perform well in practical implementation. Thiessen came up with a rule called 'Maximize the Minimum Gain'.[13]

5.3.3   Family_Winner

Bellucci and Zeleznikow (2006) observed that an important way in which family mediators encourage disputants to resolve their conflicts is through the use of compromise and trade-offs. Once the trade-offs have been identified, other decision-making mechanisms must be employed to resolve the dispute. They noted that:

(1) the more issues and sub-issues in dispute, the easier it is to form trade-offs and hence reach a negotiated agreement; and
(2) they choose as the first issue to resolve the one on which the disputants are furthest apart – one party wants it greatly, the other considerably less so.

In assisting the resolution of a dispute, Family_Winner (Bellucci and Zeleznikow 2006) asked the disputants to list the items in dispute and to attach importance values to indicate how significant it is that the disputants be awarded each of the items. The system uses this information to

---

[12] Thiessen (1993).
[13] See www.smartsettle.com/resources/articles/21-smartsettle-and-a-beautiful-mind (last accessed 18 September 2008).

form trade-off rules. The trade-off rules are then used to allocate issues according to a 'logrolling' strategy.[14]

Family_Winner accepts as input a list of issues and importance ratings that represent a concise evaluation of a disputant's preferences. In forming these ratings, the system assumes that the disputants have conducted a comparison of the issues. As noted by Sycara (1993), bargainers are constantly asked if they prefer one set of outcomes to another. Thus Sycara suggests considering two issues at a time, assuming all others are fixed. Family_Winner uses a similar strategy in which pair-wise comparisons are used to form trade-off strategies between two issues.

The trade-offs pertaining to a disputant are graphically displayed through a series of trade-off maps (Zeleznikow and Bellucci 2003). Their incorporation into the system enables disputants to visually understand trade-off opportunities relevant to their side of the dispute. A trade-off is formed after the system conducts a comparison between the ratings of two issues. The value of a trade-off relationship is determined by analysing the differences between the parties, as suggested by (Mnookin *et al.* 2000).

Consider as an example a family law dispute in which the wife is awarded the marital home and the husband awarded the holiday house. Depending on how the husband and wife rated various issues, one might be compensated following the allocation of property to the other. Compensation is considered as an external reward, one that is not related to the issues on the table. Family_Winner awards compensation to parties that have either lost an issue they regard as valuable, or have been allocated an issue of little importance.

The system implements compensation by either increasing or decreasing a party's rating. It is then expected that changes made to a rating will influence the decision of a future allocation. The amount of any compensation resulting from the triggering of a trade-off has been empirically determined from an analysis of data. This means that even though we have tried explicitly to define utility functions, they are indeed developed implicitly and are only approximations.

The input consists of:

(1) Issues in dispute. Both disputants are requested to enter the issues in dispute. The issues may consist of a series of sub-issues.

---

[14] Logrolling is a process in which participants look collectively at multiple issues to find issues that one party considers more important than does the opposing party. Logrolling is successful if the parties concede issues to which they give low importance values. See Pruitt (1981).

(2) Ratings. Once the issues and sub-issues have been established, the user enters numbers that reflect the importance of an issue or sub-issue (this is called a rating).

(3) Mutual exclusiveness. An issue is mutually exclusive of another issue, if as a result of allocating one issue, both issues are allocated simultaneously. For example, the issues of primary residency and visitation rights to children are mutually exclusive, since if one parent has residency, then the other, save for exceptional circumstances, is allocated visitation rights.

Unlike the case of input, the method by which output is presented by the system is not characterised by a sequential standard process. These outputs include:

(1) Trade-off maps. Once new information has been entered into the system, or changes occur in the negotiation (for example to ratings following an allocation), the system displays two trade-off maps. Each map represents the preferences and trade-offs pertaining to a party. These diagrams provide disputants with an opportunity to diagrammatically assess their position in relation to all other issues.

(2) Summary report. Once an issue has been allocated to a party, a summary report describing the current state of issue allocation with respect to the preferences of both parties is displayed. The summary report lists the issue recently allocated and the party to which it is allocated, all prior allocations, the value of issues before allocation and their current value, and a hierarchical map of all issues yet to be resolved.

Family_Winner uses the Issue Decomposition Hierarchy (as described in Bellucci 2004) to store all issues (and sub-issues) and makes use of trade-off maps to deliver a compensation strategy. The output consists of a list of allocations, which forms the basis of the advice provided by the system.

An explicit description of utility functions developed for the Family_Winner System can be found in Bellucci and Zeleznikow (2006). We now illustrate how Family_Winner operates through an example developed by Emilia Bellucci and first shown on the CNNMoney programme.[15]

---

[15] See Desktop Divorce by Ben Tinker, CNNMoney programme, 12 October 2007, http://money.cnn.com/video/#/video/news/2007/10/12/tinker.desktop.divorce.cnnmoney (last accessed 18 September 2008).

The case description of this real-life divorce scenario and the relative point allocations have been extracted from Brams and Taylor (1996: 105). The trial *Jolis* v. *Jolis* commenced on 5 December 1980, and concluded on 30 October 1981. The case was heard in New York City, at a time when a new law subjecting all martial property to a 50–50 split was being introduced. The couple had been married for forty-one years, of which they spent thirty-three years together. The wife had given up her early and successful career to care for the couple's four sons. The couple had lived together in substantial wealth, primarily due to the expansion of the husband's diamond business.

There were both real estate and liquid assets to be divided. The husband's diamond business was not treated as marital property, as its growth was primarily due to market forces, especially the diamond boom of the 1970s. The children's welfare was not included as an issue as they were no longer considered minors at the time of separation.

The above case, using the ratings mentioned in Table 5.2, was presented to the system. The screenshot shown in Figure 5.1 indicates how the system accepts the case input, specifically the names of issues in dispute.

The system next accepts the ratings of issues from party A and party B separately. Figures 5.2 and 5.3 show the input into the system of the husband's ratings (party A) and the wife's ratings (party B).

Now that the system has all the information it needs, it starts to allocate issues. The first issue to be allocated is the *Paris Apartment*. The *Paris Apartment* is allocated first to the wife, as her rating of the *Paris Apartment*

Table 5.2 *Point allocations taken directly from Brams and Taylor (1996)*

Issues	Husband's ratings	Wife's ratings
Paris Apartment	35	55
Paris Studio	6	1
New York Coop	8	1
Farm	8	1
Cash and Receivables	5	6
Securities	18	17
Profit-sharing Plan	15	15
Life Insurance Policy	5	4
Total	100	100

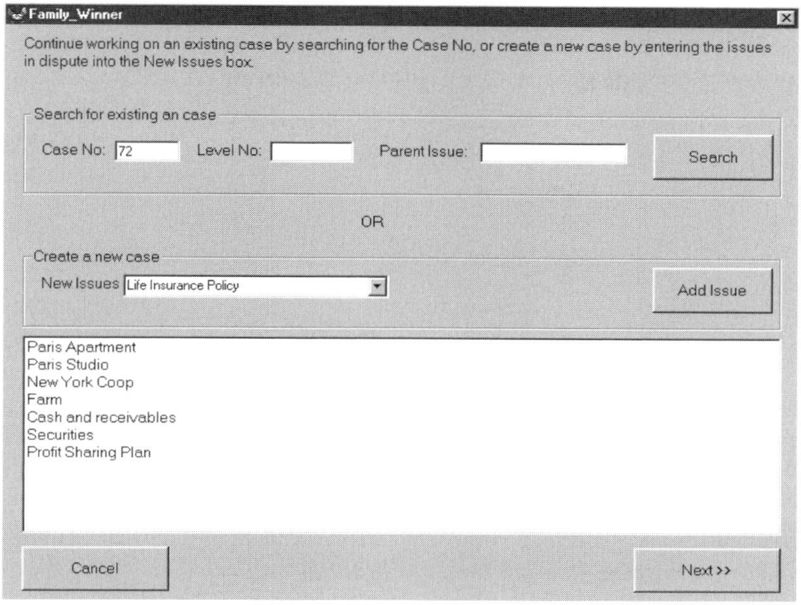

Figure 5.1   Input into Family_Winner of the names of issues in dispute

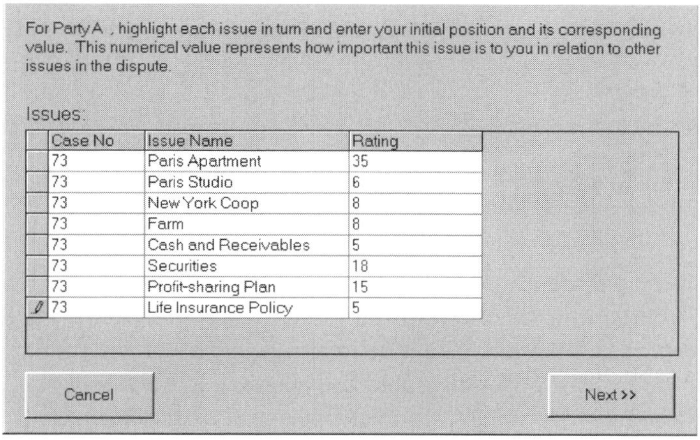

Figure 5.2   Input of the husband's ratings per issue (party A)

at 55 exceeds the husband's corresponding rating of 35. Changes made to issues as a result of relative trade-offs are detailed in Table 5.3.

As the husband lost a relatively important issue, the changes made to his ratings are significant – a 50 per cent change. Therefore the husband

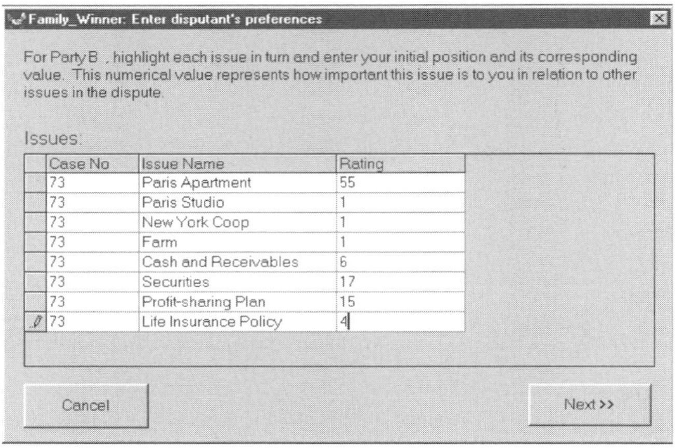

Figure 5.3   Input of the wife's ratings per issue (party B)

Table 5.3 *Changes made to issues after the allocation of* Paris Apartment *to the wife (Figure 5.4 details this information)*

Issues	Husband's ratings	Wife's ratings
Paris Studio	9 (50% change)	1.325 (32.5% change)
New York Coop	12 (50% change)	1.325 (32.5% change)
Farm	12 (50% change)	1.325 (32.5% change)
Cash and Receivables	7.5 (50% change)	8.325 (38.75% change)
Securities	27 (50% change)	25.5 (50% change)
Profit-sharing Plan	22.5 (50% change)	22.5 (50% change)
Life Insurance Policy	7.5 (50% change)	5.45 (36.25% change)

is compensated for losing the *Paris Apartment* to the wife, by ensuring he has a better chance of obtaining the remaining issues in the following rounds of allocation. The wife's ratings experienced comparatively smaller gains, as she was allocated the primary issue. Issues she valued less significantly did however increase, so as not to disadvantage the wife. Her issues gained points relative to the amount they were valued. For example, issues valued not important are increased by 32.5 per cent so as to enable the wife a greater chance of their allocation in the following rounds. Issues of greater importance were increased to 50 per cent of their value, so to enable the wife a greater chance of obtaining issues she wanted.

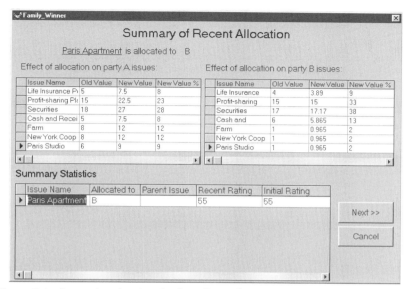

Figure 5.4   Screenshot showing the first allocated item, *Paris Apartment*

The next issue to be allocated was *New York Coop*. It was allocated to the husband. Table 5.4 lists the changes in remaining ratings as a consequence of *New York Coop*'s allocation to the husband. Figure 5.5 shows the allocation of *New York Coop*.

Changes to the wife's ratings reflect the loss of an issue of little importance to the party, and consequently there existed little need to compensate them for this loss. Nevertheless, two issues gained points from this allocation, *Cash and Receivables* and *Profit-sharing Plan*. Both these issues were valued highly by the wife. These issues increased their rating, thus enabling the wife a greater chance of being allocated those issues considered important to her. The values of the issues for the husband were increased according to the importance value each displayed. Although most issues gain some points, these gains are minimal, as the party won the *New York Coop* issue.

Farm is the next issue to be allocated. It was awarded to the husband. The resulting changes as a result of the allocation of *Farm* are described in Table 5.5. Figure 5.6 shows the allocation of *Farm*.

Farm is allocated in a similar manner to that of *New York Coop*. The wife was not greatly compensated as she did not value *Farm* greatly (only 1.325 out of a possible 100), and the remaining issues were not of great

Table 5.4 *Changes made to issues after the allocation of* New York Coop *to the husband*

Issues	Husband's ratings	Wife's ratings
Paris Studio	10.575 (17.5% change)	1.325 (0% change)
Farm	15 (25% change)	1.325 (0% change)
Cash and Receivables	8.625 (15% change)	8.325 (0% change)
Securities	33.75 (25% change)	35.06 (37.5% change)
Profit-sharing Plan	22.5 (0% change)	28.68 (27.5% change)
Life Insurance Policy	8.625 (15% change)	5.45 (0% change)

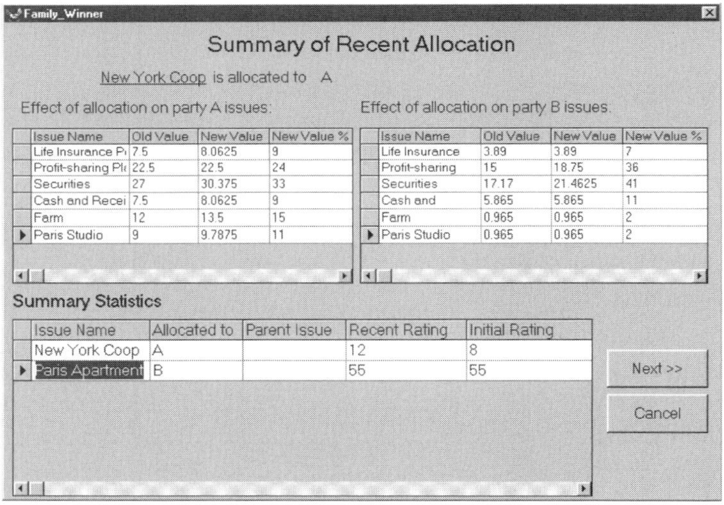

Figure 5.5   Screenshot of the allocation of *New York Coop*

importance to her. Similarly, the husband's ratings increased as a result of the allocation, to enable him a greater chance of being allocated issues deemed important.

The next issue to be allocated was the *Profit-sharing Plan*. It was given to the wife. Changes made to the issues as a result of *Profit-sharing*'s allocation are shown in Table 5.6.

The wife won the profit-sharing issue. As a result, her ratings increased to reflect her preference to be allocated other issues considered important to her. The husband's ratings increased, even though

Table 5.5 *Changes made to issues after the allocation of the* Farm *to the husband*

Issues	Husband's ratings	Wife's ratings
Paris Studio	12.16 (15% change)	1.325 (0% change)
Cash and Receivables	9.48 (10% change)	8.325 (0% change)
Securities	42.18 (25% change)	35.06 (0% change)
Profit-sharing Plan	24.18 (7.5% change)	41.59 (45% change)
Life Insurance Policy	9.48 (10% change)	5.45 (0% change)

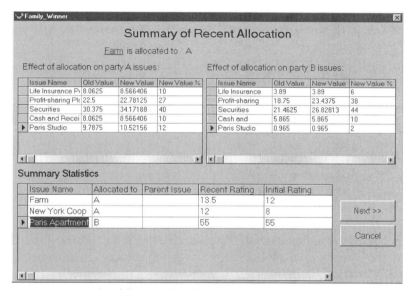

Figure 5.6   Screenshot following the allocation of *Farm*

not to the same extent, as his issues were not considered as important to him. At this point, the husband received *New York Coop* and *Farm*. Both these issues were considered important to him. The wife obtained the *Paris Apartment* and *Profit-sharing Plan*, issues considered important to her.

The next issue under consideration was the *Paris Studio*. It was awarded to the husband. Table 5.7 displays the changes evidenced after allocation of the issue.

Table 5.6 *Changes made to issues after the allocation of* Profit-sharing *to the wife*

Issues	Husband's ratings	Wife's ratings
Paris Studio	15.2 (25% change)	1.97 (48.75% change)
Cash and Receivables	11.86 (25% change)	12.48 (50% change)
Securities	52.73 (25% change)	43.82 (25% change)
Life Insurance Policy	11.86 (25% change)	8.17 (50% change)

Table 5.7 *Changes made to issues after the allocation of* Paris Studio *to the husband*

Issues	Husband's ratings	Wife's ratings
Cash and Receivables	13.93 (17.5% change)	12.48 (0% change)
Securities	83.3 (77% change)	43.82 (5% change)
Life Insurance Policy	13.93 (17.5% change)	8.17 (0% change)

The *Paris Studio* was not valued highly by the wife, and therefore remaining issues experienced minimal change. The husband's ratings increased more significantly due to their greater importance to the wife than to the husband.

Securities was the next issue to be allocated. It was given to the husband, as the wife's evaluation of the issue at 83.3 was greater than the husband's rating of 43.82. Table 5.8 lists changes made to the remaining issues in dispute.

The wife was compensated for the loss of *Securities* by a substantial amount (50 per cent increase), while the husband suffered a loss of 21 per cent as a result of its allocation. The husband valued the issue quite highly, and therefore lost a substantial amount of points across the remaining issues of *Cash and Receivables* and *Life Insurance Policy*.

The second last issue to be allocated was *Cash and Receivables*. It was given to the wife. *Life Insurance Policy* was the remaining issue in dispute. As a result of *Cash and Receivables* being allocated to the wife, the husband's valuation of *Life Insurance Policy* increased by 25 per cent to compensate the party for the previous loss. The husband's remaining rating was increased by 7.5 per cent as the issue was valued as Moderately

Important. Table 5.9 describes the changes to the remaining issue of *Life Insurance Policy.*

As the husband's rating of *Life Insurance Policy* was greater than that of the wife, the husband was allocated the issue. As the final issue to be allocated, the negotiation has now concluded. Table 5.10 give a summary of issue allocations made to the parties. Figure 5.7 shows Family_Winner's summary screen of allocations.

Although the husband gained 50 per cent more issues than the wife, the solution is considered a fair outcome once analysis is performed

Table 5.8 *Changes made to issues after the allocation of* Securities *to the husband*

Issues	Husband's ratings	Wife's ratings
Cash and Receivables	11.0 (–21% change)	18.73 (50% change)
Life Insurance Policy	11.0 (–21% change)	12.26 (50% change)

Table 5.9 *Changes made to the remaining issue, after the allocation of* Cash and Receivables *to the wife*

Issues	Husband's ratings	Wife's ratings
Life Insurance Policy	13.76 (25% change)	13.18 (7.5% change)

Table 5.10 *Summary of allocations for the family law dispute negotiations*

Husband	Wife
New York Coop	Paris Apartment
Farm	Profit-sharing Plan
Paris Studio	Cash and Receivables
Securities	
Life Insurance	

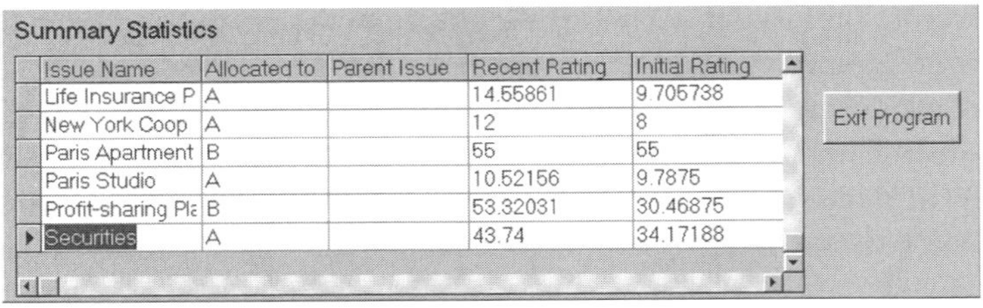

Summary Statistics				
Issue Name	Allocated to	Parent Issue	Recent Rating	Initial Rating
Life Insurance P	A		14.55861	9.705738
New York Coop	A		12	8
Paris Apartment	B		55	55
Paris Studio	A		10.52156	9.7875
Profit-sharing Pla	B		53.32031	30.46875
Securities	A		43.74	34.17188

Exit Program

Figure 5.7   Summary screen displaying the list of all allocations

on the initial ratings provided by disputants. It was expected that *Paris Apartment* would be allocated to the wife, as the difference between the two ratings was extensive. Similarly, it was expected the issues of *Paris Studio*, *New York Coop* and *Farm* were to be allocated to the husband, as he valued them substantially higher than the wife's corresponding ratings. The remaining issues of *Cash and Receivables*, *Securities*, *Profit-sharing Plan* and *Life Insurance Policy* were not issues clearly identifiable with allocation to a party, as their ratings were closely weighted. Taking two issues at a time, *Cash and Receivables* and *Life Insurance Policy* were issues whose initial weighted values, assigned by both parties, were separated by just one point. It is reasonable to expect one party to be allocated either *Cash and Receivables* or *Life Insurance Policy*, with the remaining issue being given to the opposing party. *Cash and Receivables* was allocated to the wife, while *Life Insurance Policy* was allocated to the husband. The remaining issues were *Securities* and *Profit-sharing Plan*. Again, these issues were initially valued similarly by the disputants, and were allocated in a fashion similar to that of *Cash and Receivables* and *Life Insurance Policy*. *Securities* was allocated to the husband, while *Profit-sharing Plan* was allocated to the wife.

In this section we have focused upon how game theory can be used to provide negotiation decision support. We now investigate how the use of artificial intelligence techniques can provide negotiation decision support.

5.4   Artificial intelligence and negotiation support systems

Over the past decade research systems have been developed which use artificial intelligence techniques to provide decision support to human negotiators.

(1) As mentioned in Section 3.7.2, the earliest negotiation support systems that used artificial intelligence were developed by the Rand Corporation in the early 1980s to advise upon risk assessment in damages claims. LDS (Waterman and Peterson 1981) assisted legal experts in settling product liability cases. LDS's knowledge consisted of legislation, case law and, importantly, informal principles and strategies used by lawyers and claims adjustors in settling cases. SAL (Waterman *et al.* 1986) helped insurance claims adjusters evaluate claims related to asbestos exposure. SAL used knowledge about damages, defendant liability, plaintiff responsibility and case characteristics such as the types of litigant and skill of the opposing lawyers. These two systems represented the first steps in recognising the virtue of settlement-oriented decision support systems.

(2) As discussed in Section 3.7.4, NEGOPLAN (Matwin *et al.* 1989) is a rule-based system written in PROLOG. It addresses a complex, two-party negotiation problem containing the following characteristics:

  (a) many negotiation issues that are elements of a negotiating party's position;
  (b) negotiation goals that can be reduced to unequivocal statements about the problem domain, and that represent negotiation issues;
  (c) a fluid negotiating environment characterised by changing issues and relations between them; and
  (d) parties negotiating to achieve goals that may change.

The NEGOPLAN method does not simulate the entire negotiation process. It gives one party a competitive advantage. The opposing party's goals and subgoals are hidden from the side supported by NEGOPLAN. The opposing party reveals only those issues that are the subject of the bargaining.

NEGOPLAN has been used to advise upon industrial disputes in the Canadian paper industry.

(3) PERSUADER (Sycara 1993) integrated case-based reasoning[16] and game theory to provide decision support with regard to US labour disputes.[17] One of the crucial characteristics of negotiation support is systems that are capable of improving their performance, both in terms of efficiency and solution quality, by employing machine

---

[16] Case-based reasoning is the process of using previous experience to analyse or solve a new problem, explain why previous experiences are or are not similar to the present problem and adapting past solutions to meet the requirements of the present problem.

[17] See Section 3.7.4 for further details.

learning techniques. The model integrates case-based reasoning and decision theoretic techniques (multi-attribute utilities) to provide enhanced conflict resolution and negotiation support in group problem-solving. PERSUADER uses case-based reasoning to learn from its experience. In contrast to quantitative models or expert systems that solve each problem from scratch and discard the solution at the end of problem solving, case-based reasoning retains the process and results of its computational decisions so that they can be re-used to solve future related problems. Case-based reasoning is a powerful learning method since it enables a system not only to exploit previous successful decisions, thus short-cutting possibly long reasoning chains, but also to profit from previous failures by using them to recognise similar failures in advance so they can be avoided in the future.

(4) MEDIATOR (Kolodner and Simpson 1989) used case retrieval and adaptation[18] to propose solutions to international disputes. The MEDIATOR's task domain is common-sense advice-giving for the resolution of resource disputes. The MEDIATOR is loosely modelled after the style of negotiations suggested by the Harvard Project on Negotiation (Fisher and Ury 1981; Raiffa 1982). An analysis of the mediation task that influenced the implementation and decision model used in the MEDIATOR system can be found in Simpson (1985). The MEDIATOR program is responsible for understanding a problem, generating a plan for its solution, evaluating feedback from the disputants, and recovering from reasoning failures.

(5) GENIE integrates rule-based reasoning and multi-attribute analysis[19] to advise upon international disputes (Wilkenfeld *et al.* 1995). It can aid crisis negotiators in identifying utility-maximising goals and in developing strategies to achieve these goals. GENIE provides the user with a strong set of tools which aid in the search for utility-maximising goals and strategies. However, in a complex negotiating situation, this identification alone does not guarantee that the individual will be able

---

[18] Case adaptation takes a retrieved case that meets most of the needs of the current case and turns it into one that meets all of the case's needs.

[19] Multi-criteria decision analysis or multi-criteria decision-making (MCDM) is a discipline aimed at supporting decision-makers who are faced with making numerous and conflicting evaluations. It aims at highlighting these conflicts and deriving a way to come to a compromise in a transparent process. Measurements are derived or interpreted subjectively as indicators of the strength of various preferences. Preferences differ from decision-maker to decision-maker, so the outcome depends on who is making the decision and what their goals and preferences are (Saaty 2005).

to be successful in achieving utility maximisation. The actions of the other negotiators affect the ability of the decision support system-supported negotiator to achieve his/her goals. Despite this fact, the experimental results show that the decision support system users generally achieved higher utility scores, and groups in which decision support system users participated achieved higher overall group scores. There has been much recent work on using an agent approach for providing negotiation support. Abrahams and Zeleznikow (2008a, 2008b and 2009) and Zeleznikow and Abrahams (2009) use agent theory to support negotiations in Australian family law. Kraus et al. (1998), Jennings et al. (2000), Kraus (2001) and Kraus et al. (2008) use agent theory to provide decision support for multilateral negotiations.

5.4.1   The Split-Up system

Split-Up provides advice on property distribution following divorce (Stranieri *et al.* 1999). The aim of the approach used in developing Split-Up was to identify, with domain experts, relevant factors in the distribution of property under Australian family law. They then wanted to assemble a dataset of values on these factors from past cases that can be fed to machine learning programs such as neural networks. In this way, the manner that judges weighed factors in past cases could be learnt without the need to advance rules. The legal realist jurisprudence movement inspired this approach (Llewellyn 1962).

Ninety-four variables were identified as relevant for a determination in consultation with experts. The way the factors combine was not elicited from experts as rules or complex formulas. Rather, values on the ninety-four variables were to be extracted from cases previously decided, so that a neural network could learn to mimic the way in which judges had combined variables.

However, according to neural network rules of thumb, the number of cases needed to identify useful patterns given ninety-four relevant variables is in the many tens of thousands. Data from this number of cases is rarely available in any legal domain. Furthermore, few cases involve all ninety-four variables. For example, childless marriages have no values for all variables associated with children so a training set would be replete with missing values. In addition to this, it became obvious that the ninety-four variables were in no way independent.

In the Split-Up system, the relevant variables were structured as separate arguments following the argument structure advanced by Toulmin (1958). Toulmin concluded that all arguments, regardless of the domain, have a structure that consists of six basic invariants: claim, data, modality, rebuttal, warrant and backing. Every argument makes an assertion based on some data. The assertion of an argument stands as the claim of the argument. Knowing the data and the claim does not necessarily convince us that the claim follows from the data. A mechanism is required to act as a justification for the claim. This justification is known as the warrant. The backing supports the warrant and in a legal argument is typically a reference to a statute or a precedent case. The rebuttal component specifies an exception or condition that obviates the claim.

A survey of applications of the Toulmin Structure has revealed that the majority of researchers do not apply the original structure but vary it in one way or another. Figure 5.8 illustrates the structure used in Split-Up (Stranieri *et al.* 2001).

Figure 5.8 illustrates one argument from the Split-Up system. We see from that figure that there are three data items. Each of these is the claim item of other arguments leading to a tree of arguments where the ultimate claim of the system is the root of the tree.

Figure 5.9 shows the full argument structure for Split-Up.

In the argument in Figure 5.8, the inference mechanism is a neural network. The network, once trained with appropriate past cases, will output a claim value (percentage split of assets) given values of the three data items.

In twenty of the thirty-five arguments in Split-Up, claim values were inferred from data items with the use of neural networks whereas

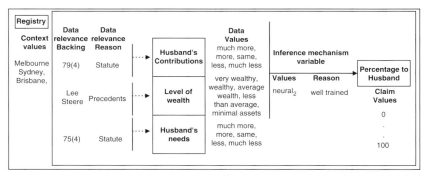

Figure 5.8   The generic Toulmin argument for the percentage split of assets awarded to the husband

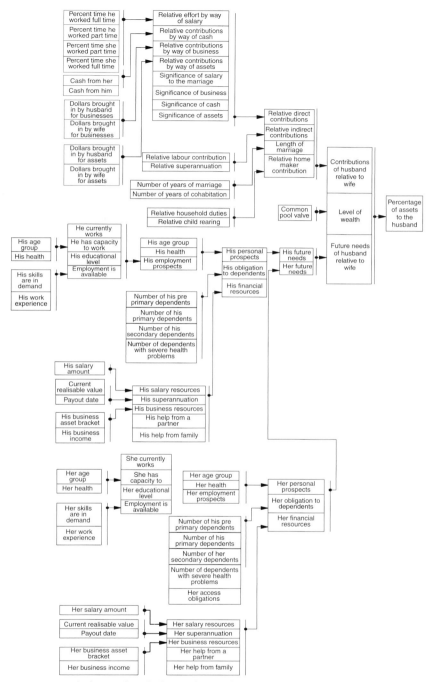

Figure 5.9 The hierarchy of relevant factors for a percentage of split determination used in the Split-Up system

heuristics were used to infer claim values in the remaining arguments. The neural networks were trained from data from only 103 commonplace cases. This was possible because each argument involved a small number of data items due to the argument-based decomposition.

The Split-Up system produces an inference by the invocation of inference mechanisms stored in each argument. However, an explanation for an inference is generated after the event, in legal realist traditions by first invoking the data items that led to the claim. Additional explanatory text is supplied by reasons for relevance and backings. If the user questions either data item value, she is taken to the argument that generated that value as its claim.

The Split-Up system performed favourably on evaluation, despite the small number of samples. Because the law is constantly changing, it is important to update legal decision support systems. Currently, the tree of arguments is being modified in conjunction with domain experts from Victoria Legal Aid to accommodate recent changes in legislation. In particular:

(1) The recent tendency by Family Court judges to view domestic violence as a negative financial contribution to a marriage.
(2) The re-introduction of spousal maintenance as a benefit to one of the partners. Under the *clean-break philosophy*, Family Court judges were reluctant to award spousal maintenance, since it would mean one partner would continue to be financially dependant on his/her ex-partner. However the increasing number of short, asset-poor, income-rich marriages has led to a reconsideration of the issue of spousal maintenance.
(3) The need to consider superannuation and pensions separately from other marital property.

The argument-based representation facilitates the localisation of changes and makes maintenance feasible. The use of the argument-based representation of knowledge enables machine learning techniques to be applied to model a field of law widely regarded as discretionary.

5.4.2　*Split-Up as a negotiation support system*

Whilst the Split-Up system was not originally designed to support legal negotiation, it is capable of doing so. Split-Up can be directly used to proffer advice in determining your BATNA. The following example, taken from Bellucci and Zeleznikow (2001), illustrates this point.

Suppose the disputants' goals are entered into the Split-Up system to determine the asset distributions for both W and H. Split-Up first shows

Table 5.11 *Outputs of the Split-Up system for several variations of a family law case*

Resolution	H's %	W's %
Given one accepts W's beliefs	35	65
Given one accepts H's beliefs	58	42
Given one accepts H's beliefs but gives W custody of children	40	60

both W and H what they would be expected to be awarded by a court if their relative claims were accepted. The litigants are able to have dialogues with the Split-Up system about hypothetical situations. Given the requirements of W and H in a hypothetical example, the Split-Up system provided the following answers as to the percentages of the distributable assets received by each partner (see Table 5.11).

Clearly, custody of the children is very significant in determining the husband's property distribution. If he were unlikely to win custody of the children, the husband would be well advised to accept 40 per cent of the common pool (otherwise he would also risk paying large legal fees and having ongoing conflict).

While Split-Up is a *decision* support system rather than a *negotiation* support system, it does provide disputants with their respective BATNAs and hence provides an important starting point for negotiations. However, more than a BATNA calculation is required of negotiation support systems. Namely, a negotiation support system should model the structure of an argument, provide advice on how to sequence the negotiation, and propose solutions.

In Chapter 6 we will explain our three-step model for Online Dispute Resolution. This model includes providing advice about BATNAs and trade-offs and providing support for disputants to argue and explain their desires.

5.5   Extending interest-based bargaining

5.5.1   *The Family_Mediator system*

The Family_Winner system was designed to help mediators encourage disputants to settle their disputes through the use of trade-offs. The system focuses upon trying to determine each of the disputant's interests and then uses game theory to suggest good solutions (not necessarily optimal). But Australian family law focuses upon the paramount interests of the children, not upon the interests of the parents.

In late 2005, the Family_Winner system achieved much media attention, including over a dozen radio interviews in all Australian states and on BBC Radio 5 and, separately, the BBC World Service, articles in the *Sydney Morning Herald*,[20] *The Times* of London, the *Australian Financial Review* and *The Economist*.[21] The inventors were asked to compete on ABC's (Australian Broadcasting Commission) *New Inventors* television show on 16 November 2005. They won their heat.[22]

As a result of this publicity, Professor Zeleznikow and Dr Bellucci received much interest in commercialising Family_Winner. One expression of interest came from the Queensland branch of Relationships Australia. One of its tasks is to provide advice to couples that are contemplating divorce. The Queensland branch of Relationships Australia wants to use a modified version of Family_Winner to provide decision support for their clients. The application domain is agreements about the distribution of marital property.

Instead of Family_Winner attempting to meet both parents' interests to basically the same degree, mediators at Relationships Australia determine what percentage of the common pool property the wife should receive (e.g. 60 per cent). This advice could indeed be tendered by the Split-Up system. However, Relationships Australia preferred that their mediators make individual decisions, rather than use a decision support system.

A major issue of concern to Relationships Australia is how to equate the percentage of property with the interests of the couple. It is not necessary that there be a direct connection between the financial value of an item and the point value that each party in the dispute attaches to the item. Indeed, a major issue in dispute may involve determining the value of the item. For example, following a divorce, the husband may agree that the wife should be awarded the marital home. In this case it would be in his interests to overvalue the house (say he suggests it is worth $1,200,000) whilst it is in the wife's interests to undervalue the house (say she suggests it is worth $800,000).

---

[20] See http://smh.com.au/articles/2005/09/20/1126982062322.html and www.smh.com.au/news/next/game-theory-for-negotiators/2005/11/14/1131816858584.html (last accessed 22 September 2008).

[21] See http://economist.com/displaystory.cfm?story_id=E1_VVSTQRG (last accessed 22 September 2008).

[22] See www.abc.net.au/tv/newinventors/txt/s1504763.htm (last accessed 22 September 2008).

So how can the new system that Zeleznikow and Bellucci (2006) invented, Family_Mediator, help resolve the issue?

(1) The mediator involved in helping resolve the dispute makes decisions about how many points the husband and wife should each receive. The Mediator could use the Split-Up system if this is seen as beneficial. Say the wife receives X% and husband Y% where $X + Y = 100$.

(2) The Mediator decides on the value of each item in dispute.

(3) Both the husband and wife give points to each of the items in dispute.[23]

(4) The Family_Mediator system then suggests trade-offs and compensations so that the wife receives $T^*(100 + (X - Y)/2)$ points and the husband receives $T^*(100 + (Y - X)/2)$ points where T is the number of points each party would receive under the original Family_Winner system.[24]

The development of Family_Mediator allows the concept of interest-based negotiation as developed in Family_Winner to be integrated with notions of justice. The advice about principles of justice can be provided by decision support systems that advise about BATNAs (e.g. Split-Up) or human mediators.

Unlike the Family_Winner system, the Family_Mediator system allows users to input negative values.[25] This development is necessary because family mediation clients often have debts (such as credit-card debts and mortgages) which are as much items in the negotiation as assets.

Further, to ensure that Family_Mediator proposes an acceptable solution, it might be necessary to include, as a universal issue in all disputes, a cash variable payment item. For example, where the wife has identified that her highest preference is to retain the family home, an outcome might provide for her to keep the matrimonial home and the mortgage.[26] In order to reach an acceptable settlement, the wife might need to make a cash payment to the husband. Hence we have stipulated the requirement that a variable appear in the output.

---

[23] As in the entering of the points into the Family_Winner system, the points should total 100. If this is not the case, then the numbers are scaled so that they add to 100.

[24] The decision to give the wife $T^*(100 + (X - Y)/2)$ points and the husband $T^*(100 + (Y - X)/2)$ points came from an empirical comparison of algebraically developed formulae.

[25] Thanks are due to Natasha Rae of Relationships Australia (Queensland) for this suggestion.

[26] Which is clearly a negative item.

Table 5.12 *Likert scale for linguistic variables used in the Family_Mediator system*

Description	Points
Irrelevant	0
Little Significance	10
Marginal	20
Moderate	30
Important	40
Very Important	50
Essential	60

A further limitation of the Family_Winner system (arising from its adaptation of the Adjusted Winner algorithm) is the need for users to enter numerical values. Whilst disputants can probably linearly order[27] the significance to them of all items in dispute, it is unrealistic to expect them to give a numerical value to each item. But it is not unreasonable for the users to assign a linguistic variable[28] to each item. We suggest a seven-point scale which can then be converted into points (see Table 5.12).

Suppose the parties enter the following terms for the issues in dispute in the example given in Bellucci and Zeleznikow (2006) (see Table 5.13).

The husband's total score is 200. Thus to scale his scores each number is multiplied by $100/200 = 0.5$. The wife's total score is 190. Thus to scale his scores each number is multiplied by $100/190 = 0.53$. This hence leads to a points table (Table 5.14).

These points are then utilised by the Family_Mediator algorithm.

5.5.2   The AssetDivider system

AssetDivider (Bellucci 2008) is a system developed to meet the needs of family dispute resolution practitioners at Relationships Australia (Queensland). It generalises Family_Winner by including financial values of property and allowing mediators to bias the negotiation (so as to meet the *paramount interests of the children*) in favour of one party to the negotiation.

---

[27] A set Y is linearly ordered if we can place it in the form $y1 <= y2 <= ... <= yn$.

[28] Describing in words how they value each item.

Table 5.13 *Husband and wife's linguistic variable allocation for the given family law dispute*

Item	H description and thus unscaled points	W description and thus unscaled points
Residency	Little Significance *10*	Essential *60*
Visitation Rights	Very Important *50*	Irrelevant *0*
Shares	Important *40*	Little Significance *10*
Superannuation	Little Significance *10*	Moderate *30*
Child Support	Moderate *30*	Irrelevant *0*
Matrimonial Home	Irrelevant *0*	Important *40*
Investment Unit	Marginal *20*	Irrelevant *0*
Holiday House	Irrelevant *0*	Marginal *20*
Mitsubishi Car	Marginal *20*	Irrelevant *0*
Holden Car	Irrelevant *0*	Moderate *30*
Boat	Marginal *20*	Irrelevant *0*

Table 5.14 *Scaled points for the husband and wife*

Item	H scaled points	W scaled points
Residency	5	32
Visitation Rights	25	0
Shares	20	5
Superannuation	5	16
Child Support	15	0
Matrimonial Home	0	21
Investment Unit	10	0
Holiday House	0	11
Mitsubishi Car	10	0
Holden Car	0	16
Boat	10	0

Family_Winner takes a list of issues (usually items for distribution between two parties) and allocates them based on a rating given by the parties in dispute. Two sets of ratings are provide, one for each party in dispute. This rating (a numerical value between 0 and 100) does not represent the monetary value of the item; instead it symbolises how important the item is to the party. We assume that a party wants to keep an item they feel is important to them.

Similarly, AssetDivider accepts a list of items together with ratings (two per item) to indicate the item's importance to a party. In addition it also accepts the current monetary value of each item in dispute. Bellucci assumes that this dollar value has been negotiated (if necessary) before AssetDivider is used.[29] Hence, only one dollar value is entered per item.[30] The proposed percentage split is also entered; this reflects what percentage of the common pool items in dispute each party is likely to receive in the settlement. The system is not capable of determining the percentage split; this figure has to be derived from the mediator's knowledge in past cases or from computer systems such as Split-Up (see Stranieri *et al.* 1999), which can provide a percentage split given certain characteristics and features of divorce cases.

The order by which issues are allocated is of paramount importance in a negotiation. Bellucci (2008) claims that professional mediators have indicated that issues attracting little disputation should be presented foremost for allocation, so as to help foster a positive environment in which to negotiate. Family_Winner allocates items to parties according to whoever values them the most. Once an item has been allocated to a party, the remaining ratings (of items still in dispute) are changed by trade-off equations. These modifications try to mimic the effect that losing or gaining an item will have on the rest of the items still in dispute. The equations directly modify ratings by comparing each one against that of the item recently lost or won (each party's set of ratings are modified as a result of an allocation). The equations update ratings based on a number of variables – whether the item allocated was lost or gained, the value of the allocated item in relation to items still in dispute and the value of the item whose rating will change as a result. In Family_Winner, the extent to which ratings were modified was determined through an analysis of data collected from mediation cases provided by the Australian Institute of Family Studies.

AssetDivider accepts items, a rating per issue and the monetary value of an item (unlike Family_Winner, which does not consider the monetary

---

[29] Future research will consider what happens if the party cannot agree on the value of the item. Such conflict often occurs: for example, if the husband wishes to transfer the matrimonial house to the wife, it is in his interest to have the value of the house as high as possible, whereas it is in the wife's interest to keep it as low as possible.

[30] The decision to only enter one dollar value per item can in fact be the basis of protracted dispute. One option is to use blind-bidding to decide upon the dollar value of each item.

value of items at all). The allocation strategy, as described above, is similar to that in Family_Winner, except that the equations have been modified to reflect, according to Relationships Australia (Queensland), increased fairness.[31] Items are not only allocated on interests (that is, whoever values them most) but also by considering their monetary value.

AssetDivider's allocation strategy works by provisionally allocating an item to the party whose rating is the highest. It then checks the dollar value of items it has been allocated previously (that is, their current list of items), the dollar value of the item presently allocated and the dollar amount permitted under the percentage split given by mediators. If by allocating the item in question the party exceeds its permitted amount, the item is removed from its allocation list and placed back into negotiation. In this case, the item has not been allocated to a party. If the dollar value of the item was within the limits of the amount permitted under the percentage split rule, then the allocation proceeds. Once an allocation has occurred the 'losing party' is compensated by the trade-off equations modifying ratings (whereas in Family_Winner both winning and losing parties were affected).

In Chapter 6 we will investigate how to incorporate argumentation and bargaining about trade-offs to develop negotiation support systems. This will occur as part of the consideration of Lodder and Zeleznikow's (2005) three-step model for Online Dispute Resolution.

5.5.3   The Australian Telephone Dispute Resolution Service

Online Dispute Resolution makes it possible to provide family law mediation services to parties who are geographically remote. In the past the process of separation and divorce would be done extensively by correspondence and expensive litigation, involving the costs of time, travel and accommodation. Given that Australia is both a country and a continent, there is an important section of the population who live in remote regions. The provision of government services to such communities is both difficult and expensive.

To meet such needs the Australian government initiated the Family Relationship Advice Line (FRAL).[32] The Advice Line is a national

---

[31] How to value fairness in negotiation was considered in Section 1.2.
[32] See www.ag.gov.au/www/agd/agd.nsf/Page/Families_FamilyRelationshipServices OverviewofPrograms_ForFamilyRelationshipServicesPractitioners_ FamilyRelationshipAdviceLineResources (last accessed 16 August 2009).

telephone service established to assist people affected by relationship or separation issues. The Advice Line provides information on family relationship issues and advice on parenting arrangements after separation. It can also refer callers to local services that can provide assistance.

It is important to note that the Advice Line complements the services offered by the Family Relationship Centres. It ensures that people who are not able to attend a Centre can receive help. None of FRAL, the Australian Telephone Dispute Resolution Service or the Australian Online Family Dispute Resolution Service has been developed to replace the services offered by the Family Relationship Centres (FRCs).[33] Rather, each complements these services and offers support to those who find it difficult to use traditional family dispute resolution services.

The Family Relationship Advice Line is available from 8am to 8pm, Mondays to Fridays, and 10am to 4pm on Saturdays (local time), across Australia. Because of the two-hour time difference between the Australian east and west coasts (three hours during daylight summer time), this means telephone dispute resolution is available 8am to 11pm, Mondays to Fridays, and 10am to 7pm on Saturdays (Eastern Standard Time), or eighty-four hours per week – far longer than the standard forty hours provided by traditional Family Relationship Centres.

In a major addition to traditional family dispute resolution services, FRAL provides the organisation of telephone dispute resolution for people unable to attend a family dispute resolution service. The Telephone Dispute Resolution Service (TDRS) was established from Australian government funding in 2007. Potential clients cannot automatically contact TDRS. They need to be referred either through the Family Relationship Advice Line (the vast majority of TDRS clients) or a Family Relationships Centre. Because FRAL is publicly advertised, whilst TDRS is not, potential clients see the provider of mediation services as the Australian government, rather than trusted mediation and counselling services.

Upon referral from FRAL or an FRC, TDRS asks potential clients if they wish to register their dispute. Once they agree to register the dispute, the telephonist asks some demographic questions, advises upon the TDRS process and then schedules an intake appointment (which is often immediate). This can be compared to time taken to mediate a dispute at

---

[33] As part of the reform of the family law system in 2005, the Australian government launched community resource centres for families called Family Relationship Centres. Currently, sixty-five Family Relationship Centres (FRCs) have opened across Australia. A major task of the FRCs is the provision of family dispute resolution services.

an FRC. For example, Fletcher (2008) says it takes an average ninety-four days for men and 109 days for women from the time of initial interview to dispute resolution.[34]

Many of the TDRS disputes involve domestic violence. This is because victims often want to move as far as possible from the perpetrator. The intake is performed by mediators from the same pool as those conducting the eventual mediation – and if possible the same person does both intake interviews and the mediation.

The intake officer decides if it is appropriate to proceed with the dispute and if her conclusion is positive she discusses with the first party (Party A) how to approach the second party (Party B). She then phones Party B, indicating to him that a letter is coming regarding the dispute. If Party B indicates he is willing to participate, then he to goes through the registration and intake process.

Prior to the scheduling of the mediation session, an assessment of the case is performed by a senior practitioner. Questions asked include whether the case is ready for mediation, and if there a need for shuttle mediation, co-mediation, a translator or child or legal representatives.

Currently, 80% of the cases presented to TDRS result in agreements: 57% in full agreements and 23% in partial agreements. This is similar to traditional family mediation. In a report prepared for the Australian Family Court,[35] the percentage of cases resolved through mediated agreements was 61% in 2004–2005 and 60% in 2005–2006.

The Family Court of Australia provided detailed statistics on the percentage of its Final Orders Cases resolved through mediated agreement. The committee was disappointed to read that the percentage of cases resolved by mediated agreements has decreased steadily from 69% in 2003–2004 to 57% in 2006–2007.[36]

Thus, TDRS has a similar success rate to traditional FRCs, whilst being able to handle its caseload more cheaply, efficiently and quickly. For example TDRS has handled 3,500 new cases in the past few years.

Following the success of the Telephone Dispute Resolution Service and the roll-out of the Australian government's National Broadband

---

[34] The time is longer for women as they are more likely to initiate the process and hence be the first party to be interviewed.

[35] Report on Court performance, Part 3, www.familycourt.gov.au/wps/wcm/resources/file/eb52a30eee48a26/Part_3_Court_Performance_AR06.pdf, figure 5, performance (last accessed 16 August 2009).

[36] Annual Report of Family Court of Australia, 2008, www.aph.gov.au/senate/committee/legcon_ctte/annual/2008/report2/c02.pdf (last accessed 17 August 2009).

Network,[37] the Australian Attorney General has supported the development of an Online Family Dispute Resolution Service.

Currently, a prototype Online Family Dispute Resolution Service (OFDRS) is being developed. The technologies to be used for communication (such as Skype and Elluminate) are being examined. Issues of access to appropriate technology have been examined. As OFDRS is an alternative to existing services and most people having disputes about the care of children are under forty-five, it is believed that 95 per cent of the disputants will have familiarity with and access to the appropriate technology. Access to the technology is readily available at both local libraries and FRCs. A further measure that is being considered is buying or hiring laptops for disputants. Compared to the costs of litigation or even prolonged Alternative Dispute Resolution, the purchase or hire cost of a laptop is minimal.

5.5.4   The Australian Online Family Dispute Resolution Service

The Australian Online Family Dispute Resolution Service (OFDRS) provides disputants with benefits that are not as readily available in face-to-face and telephone dispute resolution. This is especially so at the intake stage.

One of the major impediments to a successful mediation is the lack of knowledge disputants bring to mediation. Fisher and Ury (1981) highlight the need for those entering a negotiation to be prepared. One way to prepare disputants for a negotiation is to provide them with videos that advise upon the process, expectations and reasonable behaviour in a dispute. Most Family Relationship Centres invite disputants (separately) to training sessions, and TDRS sends disputants relevant materials, including pre-education videos.

The Harvard Program on Negotiation has recognised the importance of simulated videos in training disputants.[38] The family mediation videos will be immediately available at the OFDRS website. As well as advising upon process, they will illustrate to disputants as to what are reasonable behaviours. Ross (1995) introduced the notions of (1) *reactive devaluation,* which refers to the fact that the very offer of a particular proposal or concession – especially if the offer comes from an adversary – may

---

[37] See www.news.com.au/technology/story/0,28348,25301686–5014239,00.html (last accessed 17 August 2009).

[38] See www.pon.org/catalog/index.php?manufacturers_id=12&osCsid=6004a22081997c5 44c3751781707e8e8 (last accessed 19 August 2009).

diminish its apparent value or attractiveness in the eyes of the recipient and (2) *optimistic overconfidence* – people have a tendency to develop an overly optimistic view on their chances in disputes.

These behaviours hinder negotiation. By providing relevant training and education through viewing role-playing, disputants might identify unreasonable behaviour in others, which they would accept in themselves. For example, an ex-husband, seeking shared parenting, believed it would be reasonable to share the marital property equally. But when it was pointed out that his annual salary was $200,000 whilst that of his wife is $40,000, and that this would result in his son spending 50 per cent of his time sleeping on a mattress in the living room, his attitude changed.

The OFDRS also provides commentary on recent changes in the law (e.g. a presumption of shared parenting and mandatory mediation) and links to the law and cases (to the few who might want to read these).[39]

The OFDRS provides the opportunity for disputants to read blogs and participate in discussion and support groups. The process of divorce and developing new parenting patterns is traumatic. Nevertheless, 40 per cent of Australian parents go through this process, with no preparation to support them. Self-help groups can provide invaluable support and help parents to share their experiences.

A further support tool in the intake stage can provide advice about BATNAs. The communications stage during an OFDRS mediation is similar to that occurring in Family Relationship Centres and telephone dispute resolution. AssetDivider is being used to help disputants identify their desires and provide advice upon trade-offs.

5.6   The BEST-project: BATNA establishment using semantic web technology[40]

The BEST-project commenced in 2005. Van Harmelen and Lodder initiated this project, because they were interested in automatically providing information on BATNAs by using semantic web technologies. The aim of the project was to investigate if and to what extent semantic web technologies could help in retrieving relevant case law.

In Computer Science terms, the problem of finding relevant case law in order to determine a BATNA can be reduced to the problem of finding

[39] See www.austlii.edu.au/cgi-bin/sinosrch.cgi?method=auto&meta=%2Fau&mask_path=&mask_world=&query=family+law+legislation&results=50&rank=on&callback=off&legisopt=&view=relevance&max= (last accessed 19 August 2009).

[40] See www.best-project.nl (last accessed 12 August 2009).

closely related documents in a large, semi-structured collection. Computer Science has developed a number of techniques for this problem, ranging from 'knowledge free' techniques based on shallow text-parsing and statistical analysis to 'knowledge intensive' methods, such as ontology-based search and navigation.

The paradigm of *ontology-based search and navigation* is particularly well-suited in cases where the application domain is sufficiently well structured, and where user-queries need substantial amounts of refinement, typically in an interactive dialogue with a system. The ontology serves multiple purposes for search and navigation in the document set:

(1) to disambiguate search terms;
(2) to semantically narrow or broaden searches when too many or too few results are returned;
(3) to suggest semantically related queries that involve syntactically different terms.

Each of these points contribute to an interactive exploration interface where the classical distinction between searching (starting from a precise query) and browsing (undirected navigation through the document set) disappears.

Substantial experience in building such interfaces was derived through a number of projects:

(1) The Skillfinder application for Swiss Life (Reimer *et al.* 2003) used a middle-sized light-weight ontology of around 1,000 concepts to support the search process for personal with required skills for a given project among the Swiss Life workforce (11,000 employees).
(2) The Enersearch knowledge portal (Iosif *et al.* 2003) facilitated the access of stakeholders to the portal website of the Enersearch think-tank in the energy sector.
(3) DOPE browser, built for Elsevier Science publisher (Stuckenschmidt *et al.* 2004), uses a large commercial ontology on medical drugs[41] and a very large document set[42] to provide disambiguation and refinement of keyword-based queries.

The results of the project are described in Van Laarschot *et al.* (2005), Klein *et al.* (2006) and Wildeboer *et al.* (2007). Currently, a system has been

---

[41] EMTREE, which has 60,000 concepts and was developed by Elsevier; see www.ovid.com/site/products/fieldguide/embx/EMTREE_Thesaurus.jsp (last accessed 12 August 2009).
[42] Over fifteen million medical abstracts from MedLine.

developed that supports users by retrieving relevant case law on liability. In this way parties are given the opportunity to form a judgment about whether they could hold another party liable for certain caused damages or if they could be held liable themselves. Also, parties can determine the zone of possible agreements for negotiation.

In the BEST system for the intelligent disclosure of case law the retrieval is based on search terms provided by laypeople. The main challenge is to match the different terminology used in case law and by laypeople. Laypeople describe cases in their own words, which differ from the vocabulary used by legal experts and in legal texts. The BEST project decoupled the task of giving a meaningful description of the legal case at hand from the task of retrieving similar case law from the public available case law database: www.rechtspraak.nl.[43]

5.7   InterNeg/INSPIRE

Kersten and Noronha (1999) discuss the InterNeg project that involves:

(1) the construction of InterNeg, a website 'for and about negotiation' at http://interneg.org/interneg/tools/inspire/;[44]
(2) the development of decision and negotiation support methods and systems;
(3) the use of existing and the development of new 'auxiliary' systems for data processing, the storage and analysis of negotiation records, and the exchange of multimedia type transactions;
(4) the preparation of teaching and training tools and materials;
(5) research on the use of the computer and communication technologies in negotiation;
(6) research on the difference in negotiation styles that result from the differences in culture, education, age, gender, and related issues; and
(7) a study of the negotiations between humans, and between humans and computer systems.

The INSPIRE system has been specifically developed to study negotiation processes and negotiators' behaviour. This system allows for a large-scale systematic study of cultural differences in negotiation, which were previously nonexistent.

There are key differences between INSPIRE and other studies:

[43] Last accessed 12 August 2009.
[44] Last accessed 22 September 2008.

(1) the use of computer and communication technologies to observe the process of negotiation in a controlled setting;
(2) negotiations can be conducted anonymously, thus the cultural bias may be reduced;
(3) negotiators have access to decision and negotiation support tools;
(4) the negotiation case allows for specification of subjective preferences among issues and options; and
(5) negotiations may be conducted over several weeks with or without imposed deadlines.

Kersten and Noronha (1997) claim that the two trends that may potentially lead to widespread use of Negotiation Support Systems in real negotiations are:

(1) the maturity of formal methods for decision and negotiation analysis, and
(2) the expansion of the use of web-based systems in business and other transactions.

Zartman (1993) argues that decision analytic methods based on multi-attribute theory, simulation modelling, statistical analysis and cognitive mapping have shown their usefulness. The INSPIRE system uses decision theory and supports construction of utility functions. There are four main support functions in INSPIRE. One function allows the user to construct a utility function that is used to evaluate her own and her opponent's offers. The second is to present negotiation dynamics in a graph on which all offers and counter-offers are plotted. The third function is to record all messages and offers, and to create a negotiation history. The fourth function allows the system to verify the Pareto-optimality of the compromise (if achieved) and if a Pareto non-optimal compromise is achieved it is used to provide negotiators with Pareto improvements that they may consider in the post-settlement stage.

The InterNeg site is organised into five departments in addition to general information about the site, its history, users and developers. Each department has a different focus:

(1) Reference desk: an archive of reference material on negotiation and negotiation support, including answers to frequently asked questions, bibliographies, software catalogues, glossaries and computing dictionaries.
(2) Research and studies: research output from the InterNeg group, its worldwide collaborators and other researchers.

(3) Support tools and aids: software that is usable on the web. This includes software produced as part of the InterNeg project, e.g. INSPIRE and INSS, and tools contributed by other researchers.
(4) Learning and training: negotiation learning and teaching resources, e.g. tutorials, essays on and guidelines for negotiation strategies, course information, university programmes and other training aids.
(5) External links: links to negotiation-related sites other than InterNeg, and to resources in other negotiation-related disciplines such as software agents, e-commerce, computer-supported cooperative work, etc.

Kersten and Noronha (1997) claim INSPIRE is the first system designed to conduct negotiations on the web. Developed in the context of a cross-cultural study of decision-making and negotiation, the system has been primarily used to conduct and study negotiation via the World Wide Web as well as in the teaching of information systems, management science, international business, and English as a second language.

INSPIRE views a negotiation as a process occurring in a particular context. It comprises a series of activities beginning with pre-negotiation which involves preparation for negotiation, proceeding through the actual conduct of the negotiation during which messages, arguments, offers and concessions are exchanged and evaluated by the parties until an agreement is reached and, finally, implementation of the agreement. It is usually inappropriate to assume that reaching an agreement is the goal of the negotiation, as is often assumed in low-context societies such as in the United States (Hofstede 1989). Indeed, in many high-context cultures such as the Japanese, an agreement is viewed as merely the beginning. Revision of the contract and re-negotiation are integral aspects of the negotiation process.

INSPIRE currently addresses the preparation, conduct and post-agreement re-negotiation aspects of the whole process. For example:

(1) preparation involves understanding the negotiation problem, issues and options, and preference elicitation via hybrid conjoint analysis leading to the construction of a utility function;
(2) the conduct of negotiation involves support for offer construction and counter-offer evaluation by means of ratings based on the utility function, and graphical representation of the negotiation's dynamics; and
(3) post-settlement involves computation of packages that dominate the most recent compromise.

In addition to the above three major functions there is a range of smaller support features. Also, during the offer exchange the user may re-evaluate issues and options and modify his or her utility function. During the preparation phase each user individually performs activities that enable him or her to comprehend the problem, the main negotiable issues and options, the possible offers (packages) and criteria. This phase also involves specification of preferences leading to the construction of the user's utility function.

The conduct of negotiations is divided into four standard stages, namely climate-setting, presenting, mid-point bargaining, and closing. These four stages are not clearly distinguished in INSPIRE. However the system's two modes of communication, that is, structured offers and free text messages, allow the users to perform activities corresponding to all the stages.

Offers have a predefined format: that is, they contain names of the issues and options (issue values). While constructing or analysing an offer, users automatically obtain its utility value. An offer may be accompanied with a message, which allows for argumentation and backing. Users may also send separate messages in order to, for example, set the climate, request explanations, or press their counterpart for a reply.

To support users in reviewing the negotiation and its dynamics, the system groups together all the past messages and offers, including utility values. In addition, a graph displaying negotiation dynamics is also available. It depicts all the offers made by both parties over time and the users' rating scales.

During negotiation users may review and revise their ratings, effectively updating their utilities. It has been observed that the graphical facility and offer scores become a focal point with some users and they tend to revise their preferences frequently, apparently with the objective of getting a satisfactory graph with high final scores.

Once a compromise has been achieved during the conduct phase, INSPIRE checks it for efficiency (Pareto-optimality). This is the stage when the system acts as a mediator and takes into consideration the utilities of the two parties. Negotiation ends if the compromise is efficient. Otherwise the system computes efficient packages and displays several of them to both users. The displayed packages include those which increase one party's utility alone, as well as the mid-point solutions.

Three major factors affect the INSPIRE design:

(1) They wish to enable users with nothing more than a web browser and an Internet connection to avail of INSPIRE's services. This implies a

tremendous degree of portability and gives the researchers access to users in remote countries with minimal computing resources.

(2) Current trends in net-centric computing are towards pay-per-use software: programs that reside at their developers' home sites and are automatically downloaded and executed whenever the user needs a particular piece of functionality. This induces a tendency towards an architecture in which the server (INSPIRE's home site) plays a central role, regardless of the structure of communication needs.

(3) Since one of INSPIRE's primary goals is to observe and log user activities as completely as possible for the cross-cultural study, and since it is difficult to monitor actions on the user's host machine, it is desirable that all non-trivial activities be conducted through the INSPIRE site.

One other factor that significantly influenced the design is the fact that the negotiations supported are asynchronous: since the two parties negotiating with each other typically reside in faraway countries with different time zones, it is rare for both sides to be simultaneously logged on. Therefore, INSPIRE is designed to interact independently with each user, saving the state resulting from each user's actions in a form that can be retrieved when the counterpart logs on some time later.

The primary uses of the system are training and research. Between July 1996 and April 1997, 281 bilateral negotiations were conducted through the system by managers, engineers and students from over fifty countries. INSPIRE has been used at eight universities and training centres. Ability or willingness to understand others in the case of anonymity also appears to be rooted in culture. An important finding of this work is a general and high acceptance of INSPIRE and its features. The system was designed for training and research purposes; nevertheless the users see its practical usefulness which, in fact, surprised us. Out of the 192 users who evaluated the system, 89% stated that they would use it for training and practice of negotiation skills, 83% to prepare for actual negotiations, and 61% stated that they would use the system in actual negotiations. This very high acceptance of the system led Kersten and Noronha to work on the INSS system that already has many more capabilities in handling negotiators' requests.

The Indian and US participants were in their mid-thirties on average. Their negotiation experience is similar, but Indians have the lowest rates (of the population who participated in the project) of usage of the Internet. The Indians also have little experience with Decision Support Systems and/or Negotiation Support Systems. Their ability to achieve expected compromises or surpass them and attain a high level of satisfaction with the process and their own performance suggest that the system and web-based negotiations do not introduce a significant burden or additional complexity into the already complex negotiation process.

The results of this study indicate that negotiators are often reluctant to improve an already achieved compromise despite the fact that they are provided with several packages superior to the one they agreed upon. The underlying reasons for accepting inefficient compromises are being studied further. As Kersten and Noronha (1999) state:

> A significant amount of work has to be done with the existing numerical and categorical data. Even more work is required to analyze messages. Text analysis is a potentially fascinating area of study in INSPIRE negotiations. We know from the interactions with some of the users and from the messages we receive that many of them consider INSPIRE negotiation extremely important. There are cases when users feel cheated by their opponents, get angry and emotional. This shows that the system has a value as an effective negotiation tool and that virtual negotiations may not take away all the frustration and anxiety which is associated often with face-to-face negotiations.

Rubin and Sander suggest that while cultural differences exist, it often happens that much of the reported differences are the results of expectations and perceptions (1991). The InterNeg project allows for an unbiased as possible communication among negotiators who do not know the identity or even the nationality of their opponents.

5.8   GearBi[45]

Vreeswijk and Lodder (2005) worked on a prototype application for online arbitration. After examining existing services available from providers of online arbitration they noted the following:

(1) A different form should be used for each party: *if an intake form is similar for both the complainant and the respondent this can be confusing.*

(2) Information should be structured in obvious fields with not too much information accompanying each field: *only if the fields into which the parties should enter their information are straightforward, can the*

---

[45] Much of the research in this section is based on Vreeswijk and Lodder (2005).

parties do so easily. Otherwise, people may stop using an application because it takes them too much time to understand how it operates.

(3) The instructions should be short. More elaborate instructions should be provided via linking: *people do not want to spend time on reading 'manuals'. And they lose the overview if too much information is provided.*

(4) Parties should be kept informed as much as possible about the stages and status of the arbitration, and about the time constraints that hold at any particular moment: *parties should know what the next steps are, and if they are waiting what the reason for the delay is. Otherwise they may become suspicious about the delay, e.g. thinking that the third is discussing matters with the other party.*

(5) Information that is already known by the provider should be included; information should not be asked twice; information should not be represented twice (cf. WIPO).[46] *This contributes to the convenience of the application, and is one reason why information technology is superior to paper.*

(6) It is of benefit to the arbitration process if a distinction is made between different sorts of replies. For example, submitting a new claim is entirely different from submitting a simple comment on a previous claim. *The communication should be labelled and processed in line with its purpose.*

Elaborating upon the lessons, the design of GearBi is based on four design principles, namely:

(1) simplicity,
(2) awareness,
(3) orientation, and
(4) timeliness.

The principles of simplicity, awareness, orientation and timeliness originate mainly from interaction design and usability engineering, even though they are often discussed in different contexts and in isolation. We will now explain these four principles and how they apply to GearBi.

Firstly, simplicity seems to be the most obvious factor. The development of GearBi has shown that simplicity is hard to manage. Usability engineering research points out time and again that complex systems,

---

[46] In software engineering, it is an important principle to keep the design orthogonal. In speech, this is called the DRY principle (Hunt and Thomas 2000).

and in particular systems with a high cognitive workload, simply will not be used. In this context, it is difficult to present arguments that go against simplicity, and find arguments for a more complete and complex arbitration environment. One argument against simplicity could be that arbitration environments are typically used by specialised employees with a knowledge of the domain and with knowledge of the relevant rules of conduct in arbitration. For this reason, arbitration environments could allow for more complexity than environments where laypeople are involved, for example in business-to-consumer oriented environments. Still, the best policy is to keep the environment as simple as possible in order to keep the arbitration process central. Therefore, throughout the project simplicity was considered to be a key factor.

Awareness is an important second requirement of arbitration systems. Users should know of each other's whereabouts in order to enhance their online visibility. For example, it would be highly convenient for users to know from each other when they last visited the arbitration site. Other means to make users more aware of each other's whereabouts are the registration of each user's last action, and tying personal notifications to important events within the process. Carroll *et al.* (2003), for example, argue that people working collaboratively must establish and maintain awareness of one another's intentions, actions and results. Notification systems are typical instruments to increase such awareness factors, but other tools may be used to support awareness of more complex activities. Carroll *et al.* (2003) have stressed the importance of activity context factors like planning and coordination and their work suggests design strategies for notification systems to better support collaborative activity. Awareness is an important issue, not in the least because research has pointed out that systems with a high awareness factor make users feel more involved in the whole process (see, for example, Blanchard 1993; Endsley 1995; Gutwin and Greenberg 1998).

A third important requirement of an arbitration environment can be summarised under the header 'orientation'. By this we mean that, at each point in the environment, users must know where they came from, where they are, and what their possible next step might be. Factors that contribute to orientation are, for example, the automatic generation and maintenance of to-do lists, time-stamped user input, and personalised 'what next?' pages. The use of a uniform graphical user interface also highly contributes to orientation.

By timeliness we mean that parties should know that arbitration is a process that takes place at a certain time and that user input is to be expected within certain time intervals. This is not to say that these time intervals must be taken literally, but the general principle of timeliness still applies.

Dufner *et al.* (1999) and Nakano (2001) argue that websites must reflect that their content is an up-to-the-minute reflection of the current topical interests. If this is not the case, then outdated content and the absence of time-indicators decrease the trust of users in the overall accuracy of the site. Factors that enhance timeliness are time-stamped user input, visible milestones, visible deadlines, and tying personal notifications to important events within the process.

GearBi maintains its own database of cases and presents each case to its end users as a collection of tabsheets, of which the most important ones are entitled 'claimant', 'respondent', 'arbiter', 'parties', 'status', 'done', 'timeline' and 'documents'. The tabsheets 'claimant', 'respondent' and 'arbiter' contain the data that belong to the claimant, the respondent and the arbiter, respectively. The tabsheet of the claimant, for example, contains sections corresponding to the first row of Table 1 of Vreeswijk and Lodder (2005), and the same is true for the tabsheets of the respondent and the arbiter.

GearBi works with so-called *views* on tabsheets, which means that the presentation of a tabsheet depends on the party viewing that sheet. Fields of the tabsheet 'claimant', for example, can be edited only by the claimant, while other parties can only view this sheet. These kind of permissions are also briefly indicated at the top of every tabsheet (for example, 'This page is owned by the claimant and is read-only').

As with other tabsheets, the 'documents' sheet contains sections for each party under which header the documents contributed by that party are collected. Only after an explicit action of the owner (called 'publish' in the online environment) are tabsheets made permanent and readable to other parties.

To make all parties more aware of each other's presence, the tabsheet at which the parties are registered contains, besides names and other personal data, a time-stamp of the time and date the party has last visited or browsed the case in question. This is possible because parties can only browse their case if they log in and identify themselves. After that, every retrieval of a case page is registered (but not necessarily communicated to the other parties). Furthermore, the tabsheet entitled 'parties' contains, for every party, a description of the last action executed by that party. For example, if the respondent issued a comment on 22 February 2009, and browsed the site afterwards, the last action registered for the respondent is 'Comment on 22 February 2009 (X days ago)', where X depends on the time interval between giving the comment and the retrieval of a particular page. In addition, all fields of all forms are supplied with a time-stamp once edited. This increases the awareness of the parties involved.

In order to enhance the orientation aspect of GearBi, the developers decided to include tabsheets named 'done', and 'status'. The tabsheet entitled 'done' summarises the contributions made so far in an aspect-oriented format. The latter means that contributions are presented not chronologically as happens in a logbook, but rather in a topic-oriented structure in the spirit of Table 1 of Vreeswijk and Lodder (2005). The tabsheet 'status' indicates the current status of the case and the next step that the viewer or another party is supposed to take. If the next step is to be taken by the party viewing the case, this is indicated and followed by a link to the relevant page.

To enhance timeliness, all input fields are time-stamped, and may be made permanent ('frozen') by their owners. To enhance time-awareness, GearBi offers each party the opportunity to specify deadlines. Deadlines are points in time at which certain aspects, or stages, of the arbitration process should have been completed. Thus, the claimant, the respondent and the arbiter may attach deadlines to different phases of an arbitration process. It follows from the roles of the parties involved that deadlines announced by the arbiter bear a different status than deadlines that are indicated by the other two parties. Typically, a deadline announced by the claimant or the respondent may be interpreted as a desideratum, while a deadline announced by the arbiter may be interpreted as binding. In this respect, the term 'deadline' may be a bit misleading. Still, GearBi uses the term 'deadline', because this term is frequently used for time limits as for completion of an assignment.

GearBi allows the arbiter to explicitly indicate, or mark, deadlines as binding. It does not matter for GearBi, however, whether a deadline is binding or not. At all times, it is up to the arbiter to decide how to proceed if certain milestones, or deadlines, pass without notice. In particular, GearBi does not take any special measures if a deadline has expired. An example of such a measure might be to block parties from editing certain pages. However, we can imagine that arbiter(s) prefer, for example, the automatic blocking in case a deadline has passed. We therefore included this as an option.

Deadlines may be modified by their owners at all times. As with all input fields in GearBi, deadlines are time-stamped, and may publicly be made permanent ('frozen') by their owners.

Once the claimant is satisfied with his request, there is the possibility to publish it. After a request is published, GearBi sends a YAML-update to the eventual involved administrative body (e.g. the International Court of Arbitration), and an e-mail to the respondent in which the respondent is invited to peruse the claimant's request. Naturally, from that moment on the claimant's page is visible to the respondent. The e-mail contains a URL in which the number of the case, the respondent's identity, and an entry point to the portal of the provider (tabsheet) are incorporated in an encrypted form.[47]

When the respondent views the page of the claimant, he sees exactly what the claimant sees, except that the respondent can comment upon every entry that is inputted by the claimant. He can do so by highlighting a relevant piece of text and pressing on a button entitled 'comment'.

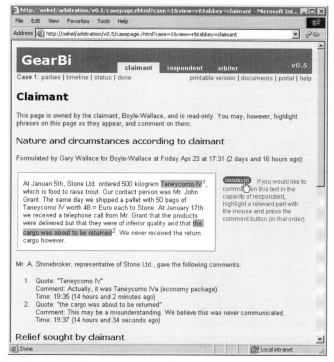

Figure 5.10   Example of where the respondent has just entered two comments on the claimant's page

---

[47]   The prototype works with unencrypted URLs.

This can be done multiple times. As soon as the respondent starts to enter data, we may assume that the respondent agrees to participate in the process via the provider (in this case GearBi), thus circumventing the need to check this explicitly with the respondent.

The respondent 'owns' a similar page as the one of the claimant, where it is possible to formulate his view on the matter. The input of the respondent can be commented upon by the claimant, in the claimant's view on the page of the respondent.

The page of the arbiter contains a summary of the data of the two contestants. This page also contains information about interim or partial awards, preferences of the participants, or, if the process is running to its end, a final award. Depending on the role that this information plays in the process, a number of items of the arbiter's page are invisible to the contestants. The ordering of the information entered by both the claimant and the respondent allows the arbiter to quickly assess the commonalities and differences between both parties.

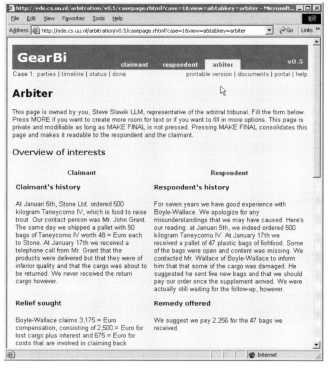

Figure 5.11   The arbiter's page

5.9 Plea-bargaining

Building systems to support the various parties involved in the sentencing process is fraught with difficulties. Tata (2000) has detailed the effort in the construction of the Scottish Sentencing Information System and discusses some of the reasons why judicial decision support systems are not well received by the judiciary. One of the primary reasons for judicial ambivalence is the fact that most systems do not accurately reflect either the manner in which judges reach their decision or are so complicated that they are virtually useless. Until now, there has been little discussion about the link between how a sentencing decision is reached and how the reasons for the sentence are articulated. In Australia written decisions are not always made available for sentencing decisions at first instance. The opaqueness of the process is further exacerbated by the lack of articulation of reasons.

We now describe a decision support system that Zeleznikow and Vincent (2007), Mackenzie *et al.* (2007 and 2008), Vincent and Zeleznikow (2007) and Vincent *et al.* (2007) have developed to assist criminal defence lawyers at Victoria Legal Aid to provide advice about sentencing. The sentencing decision support system is being extended into a plea-bargaining support system, using the three-step Online Dispute Resolution environment of Lodder and Zeleznikow (2005).[48]

As with the Split-Up system, the approach to modelling the discretionary and intuitive domain of sentencing is based on the model of argument proposed by Toulmin (1958) and discussed in Vincent and Zeleznikow (2005). The Toulmin model is concerned with showing that logic can be seen as a kind of jurisprudence rather than science.

The claim of one argument can be used as the data item for the next. The Toulmin argument structure offers those interested in knowledge engineering a method of structuring domain knowledge. It also enables the reasoning behind certain claims to be made explicit. In any system that will be of use to decision-makers, reasons for decisions are important, especially for transparency.

In a sentencing verdict the judges do not enter into a dialogue in an effort to explain the reasons. A sentence verdict stands like a tombstone unless challenged by an appeal. Stranieri *et al.* (2000) have suggested that discretion is intimately associated with the way knowledge is represented. They suggest that the way in which discretion is operationalised,

---

[48] This will be discussed in detail in Chapter 6.

in particular knowledge representations, is important for the design of computer-based systems that support decision-makers. While this may be particularly obvious to policy-makers who construct complex legislation, it has not been recognised or articulated very often in information systems research. A rule-based system offers no discretionary action to a user; similarly, a mandatory sentencing scheme offers little discretion to a sentencing judge. It would be inappropriate to attempt to capture the complicated discretionary area of sentencing by a rule-based system, since there would be too many rules and so the system would be virtually useless to all but the most patient users. The approach is very beneficial in attempting to model the sentencing domain due to the ability of the system to provide information to a sentencing judge or defence lawyer. Information can be stored around clusters of arguments. The use of Toulmin argumentation has been discussed above under the Split-Up System (pp. 111–114).

The modelling phase of the sentencing system was undertaken by knowledge engineers in conjunction with domain experts to establish the practical nature of the sentencing environment in Victoria. After reading the relevant parliamentary acts governing the Victorian sentencing system, both knowledge engineers and domain experts developed the decision and argument trees. The modelling procedures and steps are more fully discussed in Hall *et al.* (2005).

A group of Australian professionals and university professors built a sentencing decision support system to help new defence lawyers at Victoria Legal Aid make arguments to support their clients to receive the least onerous sentences. The modelling framework they adopted used Toulmin argument structures as defined below. Discretion is operationalised as the selection of alternate ways to combine existing factors and the option to include or ignore new factors. Therefore, it is appropriate for modelling reasoning in 'bounded discretion'[49] fields such as sentencing.

The top-level flow of reasoning in sentencing is depicted using a decision tree,[50] part of which is illustrated in Figure 5.12 and continued in Figure 5.13. The remaining models are argumentation trees and depict the discretionary elements of the sentencing decision. Figure 5.14 shows a top view of the factors involved in the discretionary decision.

[49] In that all relevant factors are known beforehand, even if it is not known how they interact.

[50] A decision tree is an explicit representation of all scenarios that can result from a given decision. The root of the tree represents the initial situation, whilst each path from the root corresponds to one possible scenario.

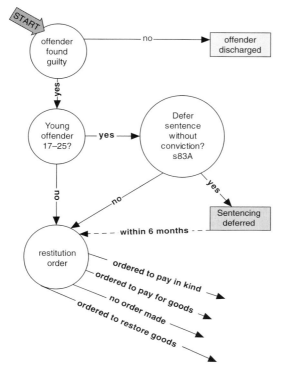

Figure 5.12   Part of the sentencing procedural decision tree

Figure 5.13 shows part of the procedural decision tree. 'Impose sentence' is a discretionary decision, and the factors that influence this decision are shown in more detail in Figure 5.14.

Figure 5.14 depicts two argumentation models and should be read from right to left. Argumentation models are one means of demonstrating the contributing factors to a discretionary decision. The right-hand model shows the top-level argumentation model for the main node 'impose sentence' (refer to Figure 5.13 where this decision forms part of the procedural decision tree). The right-hand model of Figure 5.14 shows the sentencing outcomes of the 'impose sentence' decision and the seven main factors contributing to this discretionary decision. Each of the seven factors can vary in significance. The possible data values for the first factor, 'serving the purposes of sentencing', are shown fully expanded. The left-hand model of Figure 5.14 shows the node 'serving the purposes of sentencing' further expanded, including data values for its first node. The potential

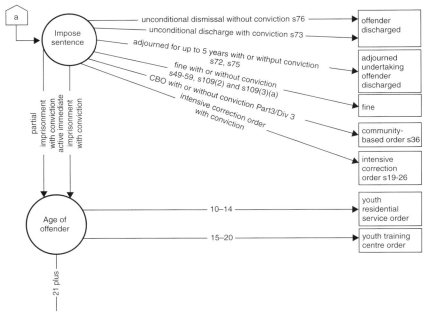

Figure 5.13   Second part of the sentencing procedural decision tree

outcomes of the left-hand model in turn become the input data values to the right-hand model.

With the support of a grant from the Victorian Partnership for Advanced Computing, TAMS software is being used to convert free-text sentencing decisions into a fixed format. Following from the successful use of neural networks in the family law domain (Zeleznikow *et al.* 1996; Stranieri *et al.* 1999) the project is using neural networks and association rules to glean how sentencing decisions are made.

Criticisms of plea negotiation have centred on several keys issues, namely: transparency, inducements and coercion, and incorrect outcomes (Bibas 2004). Mack and Roach Anleu (1996) have identified faults in the process. The significant points include:

(1) The transparency of the process: in general, plea-bargaining occurs outside the court system.
(2) Guilty pleas may be induced by the unwarranted benefits of those burdens caused by the decision to go to trial. The quantum of sentence discount that is associated with the plea of guilty is an added pressure to engage in plea-bargaining.

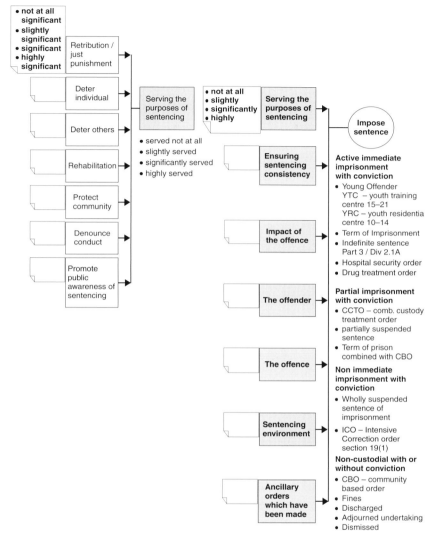

Figure 5.14   Top-level sentencing argumentation model with expansion of first node

(3) Incorrect outcomes in terms of both the determination of guilt and the subsequent sentence imposed.

These three main areas of concern are all present in the Victorian Contest Mention system. If the accused decides to plead guilty to the charges filed, the charges are dealt with at the time of the Contest Mention hearing. The facts of the case are presented orally to the magistrate by the prosecutor by way of a written summary of the offence, which has been agreed to by the defence lawyer. There is no transparency in this process, as the magistrates are presented with only an altered copy of the summary and it is this summary alone that is preserved on the record.

The Victorian Magistrates' Court deals with over 95 per cent of all criminal offences that are resolved in Victorian courts.[51] Of the 130,890 matters finalised in 2003–2004, 9,082 were finalised via the Contest Mention.[52]

Zeleznikow and Vincent (2007) are constructing a plea negotiation support environment for Contest Mentions in the Victorian Magistrates' Court and more broadly plea negotiations in other jurisdictions. The current system is intended to be used by Victorian Legal Aid lawyers to support plea negotiations and possibly to train inexperienced advocates. The system consists of two major parts.

The first part is a sentencing decision support system which provides information as to possible range of sentences and also the probability of attaining the recommended sentence. The second part is an environment for plea negotiation. The first and integral part of the overall system advises on possible sentence so as to properly apprise defendants of all the possible negotiation outcomes. The effects of suggested charge changes can be assessed using the sentencing information system part of the overall system. The system is being constructed using the Lodder–Zeleznikow framework, namely the provision of BATNA, and support for communication and negotiation.

The sentencing decision support system described above provides a BATNA. It system provides advice concerning possible sentences, as well as giving information about how these sentences might be combined, either cumulatively or consecutively in the case of multiple charges. It must be remembered, however, that the sentence is not being negotiated; it is a plea of guilty to a particular charge or set of charges that needs to be decided.

---

[51] The figure of 95 per cent is derived from the Victorian Magistrates' Courts Sentencing Statistics: 1996/1997–2001/2002, p. 1. A brief examination of both the Victorian Magistrates' Courts Sentencing Statistics: 1996/1997–2001/2002 and the Victorian Higher Courts Sentencing Statistics: 1997/1998–2001/2002 leads to a figure of around 97 per cent of all defendants who had charges decided without resort to either bench or jury trial.

[52] Magistrates' Court of Victoria 2003–04 Annual Report, 15.

BATNA advice in plea negotiation, at present, is not provided by specific electronic tools. Once an offer is made it must be measured against the BATNA. The step of reality testing is very important in the process of ADR. De Vries *et al.* (2005) indicate that in the final stage of the negotiation process, reality testing provides an excellent method of ensuring that parties are fully aware of the agreement they are about to reach.

The plea negotiation process is a form of shuttle bargaining, an offer followed by a counter-offer. The defence lawyer evaluates the quality/benefit of the offer and either accepts or rejects the offer and makes a new offer. This is the case in the Contest Mention system as it operates in Victorian Magistrates' Courts. Unless the defence lawyer is experienced, the types of negotiations that occur before the beginning of the Contest Mention can be very problematic and difficult. A less experienced lawyer might accept a plea that might not be the best achievable outcome in the situation even though it may have been perfectly adequate for another defendant in a different case.

6

A three-step model for Online Dispute Resolution

Bellucci *et al.* (2004) and Lodder and Zeleznikow (2005) have developed a three-step model for Online Dispute Resolution. The Online Dispute Resolution environment should be envisioned as a virtual space in which disputants have a variety of dispute resolution tools at their disposal. Participants can select any tool they consider appropriate for the resolution of their conflict and use the tools in any order or manner they desire, or they can be guided through the process. The proposed three-step model is based on a fixed order. In this chapter, we discuss the model in detail. At the end of this chapter we add to the model some considerations on how fairness in negotiation can be obtained.

6.1   The three-step model

In considering the principles and theory underlying their integrated Online Dispute Resolution environment, Lodder and Zeleznikow first evaluated the order in which online disputes are best resolved. The system that they propose conforms to the following sequencing, which in our opinion produces the most effective Online Dispute Resolution environment:

(1) First, the negotiation support tool should provide feedback on the likely outcome(s) of the dispute if the negotiation were to fail – i.e. the 'best alternative to a negotiated agreement' (BATNA).

(2) Second, the tool should attempt to resolve any existing conflicts using argumentation or dialogue techniques.

(3) Third, for those issues not resolved in step two, the tool should employ decision analysis techniques and compensation/trade-off strategies in order to facilitate resolution of the dispute.

Finally, if the result from step three is not acceptable to the parties, the tool should allow the parties to return to step two and repeat the process recursively until either the dispute is resolved or a stalemate occurs. A stalemate occurs when no progress is made when moving from step two to step three or vice versa. Even if a stalemate occurs, suitable forms of ADR (such as blind-bidding or arbitration) can be used on a smaller set of issues.

6.2   BATNA establishment

In Chapter 5 we discussed a number of decision support systems that provide advice about BATNAs. In Section 5.4.2 we discussed how the Split-Up system provides BATNAs for commencing fair negotiations.

Such BATNA advice is now being provided on the Internet. One such example, discussed in Section 5.6, is the BEST-project (*BATNA Establishment using Semantic web Technology*), which is based at the Free University of Amsterdam. The BEST-project aims to explore the intelligent disclosure of Dutch case law (namely damages disputes) using semantic web technology.[1] It uses ontology-based research.[2]

In Section 5.9 we discussed how Zeleznikow and Vincent (2007) have developed a decision support system to assist criminal defence lawyers at Victoria Legal Aid to provide advice about sentencing. The system provides advice about BATNAs for lawyers engaging in plea-bargaining.

Calculating one's BATNA is an important step in the decision as to whether to go to court or to mediate – in family law, commercial disputes and even criminal law. The concept is just as valid in international disputes, e.g. do you try to conciliate or go to war if another nation enters what you consider to be your territory?

Ideally, a decision on whether or not to negotiate[3] is based on a well-informed choice although, unfortunately, the information necessary to make such a decision is often lacking. One of our aims is to employ intelligent systems research to provide litigants with information about the expected outcome of court proceedings.

As Zeleznikow (2006) states, we cannot build a generic decision support system that advises upon BATNAs in all negotiation domains because, for example, family law disputes are very different from disputes about international treaties or decisions to accept plea bargains. Knowing about the context of the dispute is essential. It is possible, however, to build systems that allow disputants to communicate with each other and to build

---

[1] See www.best-project.nl/description.sthml (last accessed 4 August 2008).
[2] An ontology is an explicit conceptualisation of a domain (Gruber 1995).
[3] See, for example, Mnookin (2003).

systems that advise upon trade-offs. Split-Up, BEST and the plea-bargaining system are attempts to provide specialised BATNA advice.

6.3   Rational communication

In Chapter 4 we investigated standard (as distinct from intelligent systems) technologies that support dispute resolution. In Section 4.2, we looked at systems for supporting communication. Techniques considered included e-mail, SMS, chat, video conferencing, discussion groups, telephone and fax.

We should emphasise that most current Online Dispute Resolution systems provide opportunities for some or all of the above communication facilities, but little else. For example, The Claim Room[4] provides most of these facilities. Its Online Dispute Resolution software enables licensee organisations to have platforms developed to their own configuration, and supports:

(1) the creation of case files with multiple collaborative forums and subject to user access/read/write privileges;
(2) anonymous brainstorming;
(3) audio-visual teleconferencing and desktop sharing;
(4) blind-bidding facilities

The Claim Room's bespoke mediation tools are used by the UK's Ministry of Justice, two US federal government agencies, European Consumer Centres and the Law Council of Australia.

There has been much work in the domain of Artificial Intelligence and Law on the topics of communication and argumentation. Certainly, the most common argumentation technique used in Artificial Intelligence and Law is Toulmin argumentation.

According to Freeman (1991), argumentation involves a family of concepts that can be broadly grouped into three categories:

(1) concepts related to the process of engaging in an argument;
(2) procedures or rules adopted to regulate the argument process; and
(3) argument as a product or artefact of an argument process.

The first two categories, process and procedures, are intimately linked to a dialectical situation within a community of social agents.

---

[4] Also known as The Mediation Room, www.themediationroom.com (last accessed 24 September 2008).

Freeman (1991: 20) defines a dialectical situation as 'one that involves some opposition among participants to a discourse over some claim, that it involves interactive questioning for critically testing this claim and this process proceeds in a regimented, rule governed manner'. A dialectical situation need not occur between two independent human agents in that monologues can be represented dialectically.

The Toulmin structure (see Section 5.4.1) has been used to structure knowledge in many studies. The representation facilitated the organisation of complex legal knowledge for information retrieval by Dick (1987), Marshall (1989) and Ball (1994). Clark (1991) represented the opinions of individual geologists as Toulmin structures so that his group decision support system could identify points of disagreement between experts. Johnson *et al.* (1993) identified different types of expertise using this structure, Bench-Capon *et al.* (1991) used Toulmin Argument Structures to explain logic programming conclusions, and Matthijssen (1999) represented user-defined tasks with Toulmin Argument Structures. Branting (1994) expands Toulmin Argument Structure warrants as a model of the legal concept *ratio decidendi*.[5]

Toulmin proposed his views on argumentation informally and never claimed to have advanced a theory of argumentation. He does not rigorously define key terms such as warrant and backing. He only loosely specifies how arguments relate to other arguments and provides no guidance as to how to evaluate the best argument or identify implausible ones.

6.3.1   Lodder's approach to argumentation and negotiation

The argument tool used in Lodder and Zeleznikow's proposed ODR environment is based on Artificial Intelligence and Law research about dialogical models of legal reasoning, in particular on DiaLaw,[6] a dialogical model of justification.[7] In the Artificial Intelligence and Law field, scholars have created a number of models that concentrate on various characteristics of legal reasoning. For example, the Pleadings Game was

---

[5] *Ratio decidendi* is Latin for the 'reasons for decision', that is the legal reasons why the judge came to the conclusion that he or she did. It is the fundamental basis for the rule of law in common-law systems. *Stare decisis* says that the *ratio decidendi* will apply to subsequent cases decided by courts lower in the hierarchy.

[6] See Lodder and Herczog (1995), Lodder (1999), Brin (2000) and Stulberg (2000).

[7] Legal justification is a specific type of legal reasoning. Some legal statements are self-evident and do not need to be justified. For most legal statements, however, justification is essential. In general, the acceptability of a legal statement depends on the quality of its justification. A classic but simple justification, at least in civil-law countries, is to support

developed to identify what issues – both legal and factual – exist between disputing parties.[8] The HELIC-II system attempts to represent a unified model of legal reasoning; its creators also provide a portable software tool based on such a model.[9]

Loui, in Loui *et al.* (1993 and 1997), stresses unremittingly that argumentation is a process. He is primarily interested in the development of 'dialectical protocols', rules that guide this process and that can guarantee that the procedure is fair and the outcome legitimate.[10] Another important element of his work is the study of rationales of rules and cases (Loui and Norman 1995).

Most of the Artificial Intelligence and Law research on dialogical reasoning has roots in legal philosophy. For example, Chaim Perelman's rhetorical theory (Perelman and Olbrechts-Tyteca 1969)[11] and Jurgen Habermas' consensus theory of truth (Habermas 1973)[12] are influential.

DiaLaw (Lodder 1999) is a two-player dialogue game designed to establish justified statements. It is a procedural model in which logic and rhetoric are combined. Logic is used to force, under certain circumstances,

---

a statement by the facts of the case and a rule of which the conditions are subsumed by the facts. Dialogical models focus on the *process* of justification: the exchange of information that is introduced step by step in order to justify a statement. A statement is justified if, after a sequence of one or more claims, the other party is convinced of the tenability of the statement being justified.

[8] Gordon (1995).

[9] Nitta and Shibasaki (1997).

[10] In his lecture 'One Hundred Observations about Fair Games' at the international Views on Legal Argumentation workshop held in Maastricht on 4 June 1998 (on file with Arno Lodder), Ronald Loui said: 'Almost all games are social processes, and most social processes are games' and 'Ideal fairness for ideal players reduces to a probabilistic substantive fairness. Consider the extensive form of any two-player finite game. By backward induction from game outcomes, with incomplete information, we can construct a probability distribution for each outcome. With complete information, of course, the game is solvable. The appropriateness of such a game depends on the willingness to bias the coin, and the game is no better a proxy than a biased coin.'

[11] An argument is logically valid if based on a reasoning scheme (e.g. *modus ponens*: if A then B; A, therefore B, whereby the truth of the premises guarantees the truth of the conclusion). Rather than focusing on the structure of arguments, Perelman and Olbrechts-Tyteca concentrate on the effects of argumentation on an audience (see pp. 13–62). The procedural, dialogical models developed in Artificial Intelligence and Law represent the process in which the opponents aim to convince each other.

[12] Habermas' work has influenced how we consider whether a statement is true or not. In Habermas' theory, truth can be established on the basis of consensus. Thus, something is true if we agree it is. The procedural, dialogical models in Artificial Intelligence and Law build on this idea by declaring the outcome of the process true or justified where the parties agree.

an opponent to accept a statement.[13] The rhetoric element is represented in that the model defines as justified any statement on which the parties agree.

A dialogue in DiaLaw starts when a player introduces a statement she wants to justify. The dialogue ends if the opponent accepts the statement (justified) or if the statement is withdrawn (not justified). The rules of the game are rigid and the language used in the game is formal. This rigidity and formality help in presenting a clear picture of the relevant arguments. Due to its formal language and the fact that it was not designed to be used in practice in its prototypical form, DiaLaw is not an easy game to play.[14] That said, the ideas underlying DiaLaw make it well-suited for supporting a natural language exchange.

Lodder and Huygen (2001) have created an ODR tool they call eADR,[15] based on the principles behind the construction of DiaLaw. Through a careful structuring of the information entered, the tool aims, in particular, to support parties engaged in an arbitration procedure. Nonetheless, Lodder and Huygen claim that the tool could also be used for other types of Online Dispute Resolution such as negotiation and mediation.[16]

The argument tool used in the ODR environment proposed by Lodder and Zeleznikow (2005) operates as follows:

'*Statements*' are natural language sentences. A party using the argument tool can enter one of the following three types of statements:

(1) *Issue*: a statement that initiates a discussion. At the moment of introduction, this statement is not connected to any other statement.
(2) *Supporting statement*: each statement entered by a party that supports statements of the same party.

---

[13] To give a simple example, if someone accepts a reason for a conclusion, he is then forced to accept the conclusion as well unless he can put forward reasons against the conclusion. Note that it is necessary that the reason is accepted. Even if only one reason for a conclusion is adduced and no reasons against, if the reason is not accepted, the opponent cannot be forced to accept the conclusion.

[14] The following natural language dialogue illustrates this inherent difficulty: '(1) It was not permissible to search Tyrell', '(2) Why do you think so?', '(3) Only if someone is a suspect may he be searched, and Tyrell was not a suspect' would be formally represented (where '~' means 'not') as (1) (claim, ~search_allowed(Tyrell)), (2) (question, ~search_allowed(Tyrell)), (3) (claim, reason(~suspect(Tyrell), ~search_allowed(Tyrell)).

[15] The parties using this tool can enter natural language statements. The tool asks the user to enter an issue in normal text. Once a party has introduced an issue, which is a statement initiating the discussion, the tool then asks the party to enter a statement supporting the issue, if such a statement exists (which will normally be the case).

[16] See also Lodder (2002b), in which Lodder further outlines the applicability of the tool for other types of Online Dispute Resolution.

(3) *Responding statement*: each statement entered by a party that responds to statements of the other party.

Any statement that is entered by the parties is represented as follows: P(E, Q(C)),[17] where P is the party who adds the statement, E is the entered statement, C is the statement connected to E, and Q is the player who claimed C.[18] If a statement is an issue, then it is represented as P(E, P(E)). From the definition of the other statements above, it follows that:

P(E,Q(C)) is a supporting statement if and only if P = Q;
P(E,Q(C)) is a responding statement if and only if P ≠ Q.

After a party enters a statement (E), the statement is added as an 'element' P(E, Q(C)) to a set of elements collectively called the 'game board' (G). Because an issue is the only statement not connected to other statements at the moment of introduction, the first statement added to the game board is always an issue.

The tool presented here differs from the tool constructed by Lodder and Huygen (2001) in that it is no longer a game in which parties take turns.[19] Rather, parties can add statements at any given moment, and even simultaneously. We believe that for negotiation/mediation, this is a more natural way of exchanging information, especially in an online environment.

6.3.2   Using the argument tool: an example involving family law

When viewed on a computer screen, the implemented argument tool presents issues at the left of the screen, indents supporting statements under the statement they support, and places responding statements to the right side of the statement to which they react. For example, the game board G, with H(usband) and W(ife) as the parties could be described in a linear fashion as follows:

> H ('I want custody', H('I want custody')).
> H ('I would take good care of the children', H('I want custody')).

---

[17] This is the internal representation, not how the users see it. They are using a graphical interface of which a simple example is depicted later in this section.

[18] One might wonder why P(E) is not simply added to the game board if a party P adds a statement E. The answer is that the additional information is needed in order to structure the information exchange, since it reveals how the statements are connected.

[19] To use this tool during an arbitration, the first party claims issues and provides support; when that party is finished, he or she then hands over the game board to the other party. The second party can, during its turn, add any of the three statement types defined later in this section.

W ('I want custody', H('I want custody')).
W ('I am a better parent than H', W('I want custody')).
H ('In the past I have been good for the children', H('I want custody')).
W ('You were working all the time', H('In the past I have been good for the children')).

As implemented in the environment, the same set would be presented roughly as follows:[20] the statement 'I want custody' is claimed simultaneously by both H and W. The introduction of identical statements is not unique in negotiation. In existing formal systems, such as DiaLaw, this would be modelled in two different steps: W would first claim that she does not want H to have custody, and then consecutively claim in support that she wants to have custody herself. This sequence might be necessary from a formal point of view, but if natural language is used, one cannot expect that the parties would enter their statements in such an unnatural sequence.

Existing formal systems do not allow the parties to state identical issues as follows:

H: custody(husband)
W: custody(wife)

The argument tool, however, can handle this sequence of moves, owing to the system's acceptance of natural language (anything can be entered in reaction to a statement by the other party) as opposed to formal language elements. The use of natural language does not detract from the tool's ability to help represent the structure of the dialogue. Thus, the statement of W is clearly a response to the statement of H; both players can provide support for the statements they introduced.

Another statement players can claim is similar to that of the notion of a question in dialogue games.[21] The question in a dialogue is used to ask for an explanation or a justification.[22] For example, in response to a statement

---

[20] When fully implemented, the use of graphics will make the representation more convincing and appealing.

[21] In dialogue games, the most common speech acts (called '*moves*') are '*claim*', '*accept*', '*withdraw*' and '*question*'. A '*claim*' introduces a statement. There is an '*accept*' when one party accepts the statement of the other. A '*withdraw*' refers to the revocation of a statement. The argument tool proposed by the authors allows only the input of claims in principle. The speech act '*withdraw*' does not seem necessary to the function of the model, although we might add it if users at the testing stage demand the possibility of withdrawal.

[22] In philosophy and argumentation theory, the distinction between explanation and justification is an important one. See Walton (2004). For example, you cannot attack someone who is merely explaining that he is arguing in a wrong or fallacious way. The reason this is

by the husband that he desires custody of the children, the wife might ask
the question 'why?'. Technically, the rules of application for the argument
tool require that all inputs be in the form of statements, not questions.
Nonetheless, because questions can be structured as statements, players can still functionally ask questions using the tool. For instance, after
the husband states that he wants custody, the wife could add the statement 'I do not understand why you should have custody.' Technically this
statement is not a question; it is just a sentence expressing uncertainty.
Functionally, however, the wife is asking the question: 'Why should you
have custody?'[23]

   Another possible response the parties can make is 'OK' or 'I agree'. Such
responses are problematic for the tool because the system does not interpret them as statements. Consequently, while the parties will notice that
agreement has been reached (they recognise 'OK' or 'I agree'), the tool,
by itself, cannot recognise such an agreement. This concern is especially
problematic given that the argument tool is merged with a negotiation
support system which can only function effectively where it can identify
any agreement regarding the issues. As Lodder and Zeleznikow do not
want to restrict the parties by requiring specific formats for the statements they enter, which would be necessary for the tool to automatically
recognise agreement, the system provides that each introduced issue will
be accompanied by an OK-button. If one party clicks the OK-button in
response to the other party's statement, the system recognises that agreement has been reached. The added element is then:

$P(OK, Q(C))$, given that $Q(C, Q(C))$[24] is an element of G.

6.4   Game theoretic decision support

We often know what criteria are important in making a decision but
are unsure how these criteria interact. This is particularly true when

---

        so is that fallacies are faults in argumentation, and accusing someone of these faults who
        is not arguing (hence, he is explaining) is not fair.
[23] Note that because the proposed system does not check the format of what the parties
        enter, in principle they could enter a genuine question even though that would technic-
        ally violate the rule requiring statements. A possible solution is to make a question icon
        available to the parties (similar to the OK-button proposed to represent agreement, as
        discussed in the text). Parties could attach the icon to statements that are not yet sup-
        ported by the opponent, or that, even if supported, are not fully understood.
[24] The reason this element is not simply $Q(C)$ is that it is formally more elegant for all elem-
        ents in the set to have the same form.

important criteria appear to be in conflict. As an example, for a husband involved in divorce proceedings, the knowledge that the chance of his retaining custody of the children is low might compel him to give the criterion of obtaining primary residency (also known as custody) of the children a low weight. However, if the husband wants to maintain the family home, he might give this criterion a higher weight. In such situations, using a multi-criteria decision support tool could help highlight possible *best* alternatives.

Zeleznikow *et al.* (2002) have previously used the multi-criteria decision-making approach.[25] The most typical approach requires the user to directly assign values to each alternative for a given criterion. Under an alternative approach known as the Analytical Hierarchy Process (Saaty 1994), the user responds to a series of pair-wise comparisons: given two alternatives, the user is asked to express her preference for one over the other.

An application of the Analytical Hierarchy Process is demonstrated in the Family_Winner application,[26] which uses the concept of hierarchical decomposition to determine the order by which allocation is to occur, and to enable the formation of sub-issues or items. After setting forth the issues, the disputants must decompose such issues into sub-issues until their positions are reflected in the sub-issues. Each issue is broken down so that allocation issues are binary in form: each issue is allocated to either the husband or the wife. Family_Winner uses a theory of pair-wise comparisons to determine whether the husband or wife is allocated an item or an issue. Upon reaching the lowest level in the hierarchy (as specified by the disputants), the system mathematically calculates the value of each sub-issue or item with respect to the relative super-issues or items. It does so for each party. Once completed, the system calculates which party is allocated particular sub-issues or items through pair-wise comparisons over the derived values from both parties (Bellucci and Zeleznikow 2001).

---

[25] Multi-criteria decision analysis, or multi-criteria decision-making (MCDM), is a discipline aimed at supporting decision-makers who are faced with making numerous and conflicting evaluations. It aims at highlighting these conflicts and deriving a way to come to a compromise in a transparent process. Measurements are derived or interpreted subjectively as indicators of the strength of various preferences. Preferences differ from decision-maker to decision-maker, so the outcome depends on who is making the decision and what their goals and preferences are (Saaty 2005).

[26] See Section 5.3.3.

Although there is an argument that one should assume bounded ration-ality and the presence of incomplete information in developing real-world negotiation support systems (Sycara 1998), Lodder and Zeleznikow's model of legal negotiation assumes that all actors behave rationally. The model is predicated on economic bases, that is, it assumes that the protagonists act in their own economic best interests. While much human negotiation is not necessarily based upon rational economic behaviour, the goal of nego-tiation support systems is to provide rational advice. The environment that they are developing therefore assumes the existence of rational actors.

6.5   The integrated system

In their three-step model Lodder and Zeleznikow (2005) suggest that the parties commence with the argument tool. If the parties do not reach agreement on all issues through use of the argument tool, they can then use the negotiation support system. If the proposal suggested by the nego-tiation support system is not acceptable, then the argument tool can be used again to provide additional support or a response. In fact, the parties can at any point go back to the argument tool in order to discuss further issues introduced during use of the negotiation support system.

Lodder and Zeleznikow could have recommended that the parties begin with the negotiation support system phase, moving to the argu-ment tool to discuss one or more (sub-)issues if the negotiation support system failed to suggest an acceptable proposal. If agreement was not reached on one or more (sub-)issues, the parties could further consult the negotiation support system.

They recommend commencing with the use of the argument tool because the use of a negotiation support tool first might discourage the parties from conducting a dialogue. It is important that the parties discuss the issues in dispute and become aware of the opposing side's arguments prior to trade-offs being suggested. An important task of a mediator is to have the parties communicate with each other. This task is hindered if a decision support system automatically suggests trade-offs before any attempt at communication or conciliation occurs.

Another problem with beginning with the negotiation support system as opposed to the argument tool is that the parties would then need to assign values to the issues before discussing them. Following a dialogue, the disputants might realise they wish to reallocate points – perhaps because their opponent was awarded an issue which, on reflection, they realise they greatly desired.

Notwithstanding the concerns Lodder and Zeleznikow have raised, should parties choose to begin with the negotiation support system, they believe that the above examples of potential problems are exceptional cases. Generally, the combination of the negotiation support system and the dialogue tool will lead to satisfactory results. Parties simply will not cede issues that are very important to them. Also, the party who wins issues in the dialogue worth sixty points to her would be wise to accept the proposal of the negotiation support system. Otherwise, her eventual return may be less than sixty points, or include issues less important to her.

Consensus remains the leading principle of Lodder and Zeleznikow's ODR environment. No party will be confronted with an undesired outcome. For example, assume that the wife is awarded several issues in the dialogue, and that, while using the negotiation support system, the husband gets only half of the remaining issues. If the husband accepts this proposal, so be it. The conflict is solved with mutual satisfaction. If not, the dialogue tool would be used again, and it would be wise for the wife to accept that the husband receives at least some of the issues desired by him. Nonetheless, if a party does not like a (partial) outcome, he or she has the right not to accept it.

The goal of the model is to satisfy the disputing parties, not to ensure that the disputing parties receive an equal number of the artificially created points. Lodder and Zeleznikow imagine that ultimately both the negotiation support system and the argument tool will be offered in the online environment, and the parties will be left to decide in which order to use them.

Some proponents of mediation consider ADR superior to litigation.[27] On the other hand, some opponents of mediation believe parties should litigate because only then can fundamental rights such as a fair trial be truly guaranteed.[28] We do not consider mediation superior to litigation. Rather, we believe that litigation is the best procedure for some disputes while mediation is desirable for most conflicts. The challenge is to develop systems that can advise people on what is the most effective procedure

---

[27] For example, in the Netherlands a book series on mediation is called 'Effectieve geschillenoplossing', which means to express that generally mediation is more effective than litigation. In a similar way, the Centre for Effective Dispute Resolution (CEDR) propagates ADR/mediation as being more effective. What is important to realise, though, is that which procedure is most effective is not an a priori given fact, but depends on the particularities of the case.

[28] Attorneys are often quite sceptical about mediation.

given their dispute type, their intentions and their background, among other issues.

6.5.1   *Resolving disputes through dialogues*

Ideally, after determining one's BATNA, the starting point for the mediation in our proposed system is to form the set of issues in dispute. Based on research by Bellucci and Zeleznikow (2001), here is an example of a dialogue in which agreement is reached.

Tom and Mary have decided to divorce. They have two children. The relevant issues in dispute can be divided into child-related issues and financial issues. The child-related issues are split into the following sub-issues:

(1) private school,
(2) residency of the children,
(3) religion, and
(4) visitation rights.

Tom starts the discussion by introducing the private-school issue. Mary does not understand why the children should go to a private school and therefore asks Tom why this issue is so important to him. Tom explains that he wants the children to be well educated, and that he is afraid that public schools provide an inferior education to private schools. After hearing Tom's explanation, Mary says that it is OK if the children attend a private school. The current state of the negotiation is as follows, with the sequence of the information exchange being indicated in parentheses.

Note that Tom introduced support for his position only after Mary asked him to do so because Tom expected Mary would automatically accept his position. The dialogue also illustrates that Tom did not wait for

Table 6.1 *Example of dialogue where agreement is reached*

Tom: Children should go to a private school (1)	Mary: I do not understand why they should (2)
	Mary: OK (5)
Tom: Children should be well educated (3)	
Tom: Public schools provide an inferior education (4)	

Mary's reaction after introducing the first supporting statement. Instead, he introduced the two supporting statements consecutively.

The issue concerning private schools can now be placed in the resolution set A. Any other issues that Tom and Mary resolve using the dialogue tool are also added to set A. Unresolved issues, in set N, are then addressed in the third step, use of the negotiation support system.

6.5.2   Negotiation support through the use of compensation strategies and trade-offs

If use of the argument tool is not entirely successful, H and W are then asked to give a significance value to each of the issues in dispute, in a similar manner that users of the Family_Winner system (see Section 5.3.3) are asked to allocate points.

The Lodder and Zeleznikow environment differs slightly from the Adjusted Winner model in that it does not require the points to be equally distributed. An equal distribution of points is not the major goal of their system. Rather, their aim is to have both parties reasonably satisfied, or at least 'equally dissatisfied' with the proposed resolution of the dispute. Thus, if both parties agree after the dialogue step, then points need not be allocated. Similarly, if the negotiation support stage is used, then the points may not be equal. One may speculate that there is a potential problem in that someone who wins an issue using the argument tool will be more likely to give such issue a lower point value in the negotiation support process. However, once an issue is resolved under the argument tool, the issue is recorded as resolved and taken off the dispute board. Hence it is not considered at the negotiation support step.

6.5.3   The outcome of the dispute resolution process

The parties in dispute may reach agreement after using only the dialogue tool, or after using both the dialogue tool and the negotiation tool. If after using both procedures in sequence not all issues have been resolved, the parties may return to the dialogue tool in order to re-address the remaining issues in dispute.

This process continues until either all issues are resolved or a stalemate is reached. A stalemate occurs when no further issues are resolved on moving from the argumentation tool to the negotiation support system, or vice versa.

In brief, use of our Online Dispute Resolution environment will result in one of the following scenarios:

(1) No issues are resolved after use of either the argumentation tool or the negotiation support system and total failure is reported.
(2) Some issues are resolved, but a stalemate occurs. One of two scenarios can then occur:
   (a) either the parties do not agree to accept the partial resolution of the issues resolved during the process and no progress is reported, or
   (b) the parties agree to some or all of the issues resolved during the process and partial success is reported.
(3) The dispute is resolved and success is reported.

If (2b) occurs, a further form of dispute resolution could be used (such as arbitration) or the case could be litigated on a reduced set of factors. This should lead to reduced costs and a speedier resolution of the conflict.

What happens if parties disagree about what issues are in dispute? In our description of the negotiation, the set of issues in dispute is the union of the set of issues provided by each party. Thus, if either side says an issue is in dispute, then it is in dispute. However, this approach is not optimal under all circumstances. For instance, in an e-commerce dispute, a seller might say that a book was in good condition. The buyer disagrees and wants either some of his money back or to be able to return the book. Possible issues include the following:

(1) the condition of the book;
(2) whether the buyer will be refunded the money he spent on the book;
(3) who will pay for the eventual return of the book.

In this example, the parties will need first to establish what the actual condition of the book was. Only after this has occurred will the other issues become relevant. Neither the negotiation support system nor the argument tool is particularly helpful in the case of such factual differences of opinion. To build computer software to help resolve this problem, we need to investigate how to build computer systems to analyse evidence. This is a major strand of current research in Artificial Intelligence and Law.

6.6   Principles of fair negotiation

In Section 1.2 we examined current research on fairness and justice in Alternative Dispute Resolution. We now wish to develop a framework for developing just negotiation support systems.

6.6.1   Transparency

As we have seen from a discussion of negotiating about pleas and charges, it is essential to be able to understand and, if necessary, replicate the process in which decisions are made. In this way unfair negotiated decisions can be examined and, if necessary, be altered. The same statement holds in family mediation.

Van Boven *et al.* (2003) state that:

> Thompson (1991) has shown that when negotiators have different priorities, negotiators who provide information about their priorities to their partners fare better than those who do not. The **illusion of transparency** may lead negotiators to hold back information about their priorities in the mistaken belief that one has conveyed too much information already. By leading negotiators to believe that their own preferences are more important than they really are, the illusion of transparency may give rise to the belief that the other side is being less cooperative than they are themselves – which may lead each negotiator to hold back even more. The process can thus spiral in the wrong direction toward greater secrecy.

The November 2001 declaration of the Fourth Ministerial Conference of the World Trade Organization, held in Doha, Qatar, developed guidelines for the organisation and management of their free-trade negotiations. One of their principles (number 49)[29] says:

> The negotiations shall be conducted in a transparent manner among participants, in order to facilitate the effective participation of all. They shall be conducted with a view to ensuring benefits to all participants and to achieving an overall balance in the outcome of the negotiations.

Bjurulf and Elgstrom (2004) discuss the importance of transparency in negotiations regarding the European Union directives on public access to European documents. They argue that the development of norms helps facilitate fair negotiations.

---

[29] See www.wto.org/english/thewto_E/minist_E/min01_E/mindecl_E.htm#organization(last accessed 29 July 2008).

Alternate opinions are held by Finel and Lord (1999). They claim that transparency often exacerbates crises in international disputes. They claim that:

a). The media – a major factor in transmitting information made by available by transparency – may have an incentive to pay more attention to belligerent statements than more subtle, conciliatory signals.

b). Transparency may actually undermine behind-the-scenes efforts at negotiated settlements … in the prelude to the war of 1812,[30] leaders on both sides felt constrained to limit concessions that might be perceived as giving in to the extremists on the other side.

c). A lack of transparency may actually help states to avoid conflict, as in the case of the Chinese–Russian border disputes of 1969. Had the two states, which engaged in belligerent rhetoric, also been transparent, the crisis might have spiraled out of control. In contrast, the onset of World War One was made possible by the fact that neither Russia nor Germany was able to perceive correctly the relatively limited goals of the other side.

d). Transparency may make it difficult for observers to determine which groups will contain a given policy decision. In the Suez War of 1956, Nasser may have drawn false conclusions about Israel's willingness to go to war due to the division of opinion in the Israeli government.

Finel and Lord (1999) suggest the possibility of a curvilinear relationship between transparency and the ability to resolve crises peacefully. They postulate that both a very high transparency – because it accurately signals intentions – and very low transparency – because it prevents the noise of domestic policies from overwhelming diplomatic signals – allows states to defuse crises.

We can in fact also consider two distinct forms of transparency: transparency about the process and transparency of the data in a particular negotiation.

Transparency in negotiation processes

There is widespread support for the development of transparent processes in dispute resolution. For example, at the commencement of all mediation conferences, Relationships Australia (Queensland) clearly indicates to the disputants how the process will be managed. It follows the model discussed in Sourdin (2005):

- Opening parties' statements
- Reflection and summary

---

[30] Between the United Kingdom and the United States.

- Agenda-setting
- Exploration of topics
- Private sessions
- Joint negotiation sessions[31]
- Agreement/closure

Whilst this model of mediation is regularly used in primary family dispute resolution and most commercial mediation,[32] it is not used in negotiations about charges and pleas.

The above model involves a formal turn-taking exercise, which is inappropriate in less formal settings of negotiation such as plea-bargaining. Some of the criticism of plea-bargaining is that it does not, in general, follow a formal transparent model. However, even in plea-bargaining, changes are occurring.

For example, the Northern Territory office of the Director of Public Prosecutions argues that:[33]

> Negotiations between the parties are encouraged and may occur at any stage of the process of a matter through the courts, Charge negotiations must be based on principle and reason, not on expedience or convenience alone.

But nowhere in the guidelines is there any discussion on how the charge negotiation should be conducted, nor what fair principles to follow are. However, section 6.8 does state that:

> Records must be made as events occur for transparency and probity.

To emphasise the importance of transparency in charge negotiations, Wright and Miller (2003) believe that pervasive harm stems from charge bargains due to their special lack of transparency. Charge bargains, even more than sentencing concessions, make it difficult after the fact to sort out good bargains from bad in an accurate or systematic way. They further argue that:

> Transparency is one of the greatest challenges to the administrative criminal justice process. Because the disputed facts[34] are not presented in open

---

[31] The process can shuttle between private sessions and joint negotiation sessions, as is necessary for the individual dispute.

[32] See for example the policies of LEADR (Australasian Association of Dispute Resolvers) at www.leadr.com.au (last accessed 1 August 2008).

[33] www.nt.gov.au/justice/dpp/html/guidelines/charge_negotiation.shtml (last accessed 1 August 2008).

[34] We discuss this later in the failure to disclose or discover data in a negotiation.

court (or in any public forum), the quality of a criminal conviction in an administrative system is difficult to judge. Only by improving transparency can we address the underlying concerns, such as convicting innocent defendants or providing prosecutors with such complete control over outcomes that defendants retain no realistic access to judges, trials or trial rights.

To improve the dilemma of plea-bargaining, Wright and Miller (2002) introduce the notion of *prosecutorial screening*. The prosecutorial system they envisage has four interrelated features: early assessment, reasoned selection,[35] barriers to bargains[36] and enforcement.[37]

Bibas (2006) argues that a great gulf divides insiders and outsiders in the criminal justice system, whether in litigation or negotiating about charges and pleas. He claims that by making decision-making more transparent, the criminal justice system can help minimise injustices.

Transparency and discovery

Even when the negotiation process is transparent, it can still be flawed if there is a failure to disclose vital information. Such knowledge might greatly alter the outcome of a negotiation.

Take for example the case of a husband who declares his assets to his ex-wife and offers her 80 per cent of what he claims is the common pool. But suppose that he has hidden 90 per cent of his assets from his ex-wife.[38] Thus, in reality, he has only offered her 8 per cent of the common pool.[39]

Discovery, the coming to light of what was previously hidden (Black 1990), is a common pre-trial occurrence. As Cooter and Rubinfeld (1994) and Shavell (2003) point out, in litigation, the courts may require that a litigant disclose certain information to the other side; that is, one litigant may enjoy the legal right of *discovery* of information held by the other side. Interestingly enough, Shavell claims that the right of discovery significantly increases the likelihood of settlement, because it reduces differences in parties' information. This benefit is often lost in a negotiation.

The failure to conduct adequate discovery can be a major flaw in negotiation. But how can we conduct sufficient discovery without losing many of the benefits that derive from negotiation?

---

[35] Prosecutors must file only appropriate charges.
[36] The office must severely restrict all plea-bargaining and most especially charge bargains.
[37] There must be sufficient training, oversight and other internal enforcement mechanisms to ensure uniformity in charging and relatively few changes to charges after they have been filed.
[38] In trusts and other property.
[39] 0.8 x 0.1 = 0.08 or 8 per cent of the pool.

Cooter and Rubinfeld (1994) claim:

> Trials occur when the parties are relatively optimistic about their out-
> come, so that each side prefers a trial rather than settlement on terms
> acceptable to the other side. When the parties are both optimistic (rela-
> tive to the expected outcome with complete information), at least one of
> them is uninformed. Revealing information to correct the other side's
> false optimism creates an advantage in settlement bargaining for the dis-
> closing party. This fact provides a strong incentive to voluntarily disclose
> facts correcting the other side's false optimism before trial. Consequently,
> discovery increases settlements and decreases trials by organizing the
> voluntary exchange of information.

This benefit is often lost in a negotiation, especially if important information is not disclosed or, even worse, hidden. Relationships Australia
claims to be child focused, but in providing evaluative mediation advice,
does little discovery on determining what is in the best interests of the
child. In many family disputes, information about marital property or
child abuse might not be disclosed. Given the failure to disclose, how can
we ensure negotiations are fair?

Requiring specified aspects of disclosure in a negotiation might help
enhance the fairness of the negotiation process.

6.6.2 Using bargaining in the shadow of the law in negotiation

As discussed in Section 1.2, most negotiations in law are conducted in
the shadow of the law, i.e. bargaining in legal domains mimics the probable outcome of litigation. These probable outcomes of litigation provide
beacons or norms for the commencement of any negotiations (in effect
BATNAs). Bargaining in the shadow of the law thus provides us with
standards for adhering to *legally just* and *fair* norms.

By providing disputants with advice about BATNAs and bargaining in
the shadow of the law, and incorporating such advice in negotiation support systems, we can help support fairness in such systems.

For example, in the AssetBuilder system, interest-based negotiation is
constrained by incorporating the paramount interests of the child.[40] By
using bargaining in the shadow of the law, we can use evaluative mediation (as in Family_Mediator) to ensure that the mediation is fair.

---

[40] In this case, Relationships Australia (Queensland) inputs into the system what percentage of the Common Pool both the husband and the wife will receive.

The Split-Up system models how Australian Family Court judges make decisions about the distribution of Australian marital property following divorce. By providing BATNAs it provides suitable advice for commencing fair negotiations.

The BEST-project (*BATNA Establishment using Semantic web Technology*), based at the Free University of Amsterdam aims to explore the intelligent disclosure of Dutch case law using semantic web technology.[41] They use ontology-based search and navigation. The goal is to support negotiation by developing each party's BATNA.

6.6.3   *The negatives in using transparency and bargaining in the shadow of the law for negotiation support*

In Sections 6.6.1 and 6.6.2, we outlined the benefits of promoting transparency and bargaining in the shadow of the law to support fair negotiation. There is, however, a certain danger in promoting transparency and bargaining in the shadow of the law for negotiation support.

(1) *Disputants might be reluctant to be frank* – one of the benefits of negotiation (as opposed to litigation) is that outcomes are often kept secret. Thus the resulting negotiation does not act as a precedent for future litigation. If this benefit is lost, then parties[42] might be more reluctant to negotiate. This desire to keep negotiated decisions secret has led to Edwards (1985) claiming that such negotiated decisions are not just.

(2) *Mediators might be seen to be biased* (such as in evaluative mediation) – Honeyman (1985) indicates that there can be three groups of biases in mediation – personal, situational and structural. If mediators need to offer advice about transparency and bargaining in the shadow of the law, then both the disputants and other interested parties might be reluctant to engage in the negotiation.[43]

---

[41] See www.best-project.nl/description.sthml (last accessed 4 August 2008).

[42] Such as defendants in tobacco litigation disputes who will only settle if the outcome is kept secret. If outcomes are published the tobacco companies are less likely to settle the cases.

[43] The issue of whether mediator bias is undesirable is considered by Kydd (2003). He claims: 'mediators are often thought to be more effective if they are unbiased or have no preferences over the issue in dispute. This article presents a game theoretic model of mediation … which highlights a contrary logic. Conflict arises in bargaining games because of uncertainty about the resolve of the parties. A mediator can reduce the likelihood of conflict by providing information on this score. For a mediator to be effective, however, the parties must believe that the mediator is telling the truth, especially if

(3) *The difficulty and dangers of incorporating discovery into negotiation support systems* – discovering appropriate information is complex, costly and time consuming. As previously noted, Katsh and Rifkin (2001) state that, compared to litigation, Alternative Dispute Resolution includes advantages of lower cost, greater speed and a less adversarial process. By insisting upon certain basic levels of discovery, we might lose these benefits.

(4) *The inability to realise the repercussions of a negotiation* – often disputants focus upon resolving the dispute at hand. They fail to realise that the resolution they advocate may have larger scale repercussions.

In 2005, the Australian Competition and Consumer Commission (ACCC) convened a number of examinations of VISY executives (whose chairman was Richard Pratt) over allegations that VISY entered illegal price-fixing and market-sharing arrangements with arch-rival Amcor. Initially VISY denied any wrongdoing.[44] In October 2007, Pratt secured an early negotiated settlement with the Australian Competition and Consumer Commission, avoiding months of potentially damaging publicity for Mr Pratt and Amcor. But his changed evidence led, in June 2008, to the Australian Competition and Consumer Commission beginning criminal proceedings in the Federal Court against Mr Pratt for allegedly providing false or misleading evidence in the course of an investigation.[45] Despite receiving expensive legal advice, Mr Pratt did not realise that his negotiated civil plea negotiation with the Australian Competition and Consumer Commission could lead to later criminal proceedings against him.[46]

Thus, our proposed principles for developing fair negotiation support systems also have some drawbacks.

the mediator counsels one side to make a concession because their opponent has a high resolve and will fight. An unbiased mediator, who is simply interested in minimizing the probability of conflict will have a strong incentive to make such statements even if they are not true, hence the parties will not find the mediator credible. Only mediators who are effectively **on your side** will be believed if they counsel restraint.'

[44] See Cameron Stewart, 'Richard Pratt to Admit Breaking Law', *The Australian*, 6 October 2007, www.theaustralian.news.com.au/story/0,25197,22539478–601,00.html (last accessed 6 August 2008).

[45] See www.accc.gov.au/content/index.phtml/itemid/832393 (last accessed 6 August 2008).

[46] This issue is now moot since, in April 2009, Mr Pratt was diagnosed with prostate cancer. Given this information, the criminal charges against him for giving misleading and false information to the Australian Competition and Consumer Commission were dropped. Mr Pratt passed away on 28 April 2009. See www.theaustralian.news.com.au/story/0,25197,25402486–601,00.html (last accessed 6 August 2009).

7

Future prospects

We have entered a new era. Technology has become an integral part of society, and the Internet is no longer just an infrastructure used to book a flight, buy a book or send e-mails. We watch videos on YouTube, keep in touch with our friends via social networking sites such as MySpace and Facebook or follow our professional contacts via LinkedIn. We download music and movies via Torrent-sites such as The Pirate Bay and other P2P (peer-to-peer) networks, and get the latest news via Twitter. All the above services are delivered via the Internet. In at least two ways, developments such as these contribute to the importance of technology-enhanced dispute resolution, in particular Online Dispute Resolution.

Firstly, they illustrate that many daily activities shift from the physical to the online world. Indeed, virtual communities and virtual worlds have become popular places on the Internet, with some visited even more than Google.[1] The most extreme exponent of this development is the notion of virtual worlds: such as World of Warcraft, Lineage and Second Life. Each of these is visited by millions of participants from all over the world. They spend many hours daily in this online environment which they sometimes consider as 'the real world'.

In three-dimensional virtual worlds of which World of Warcraft and Second Life are the best-known examples, humans use virtual identities called avatars to socially interact. Virtual worlds that partly mimic the real world are growing exponentially, becoming platforms in which we shop, play, socialise, work and learn, and ... have conflicts.

Secondly, online activities generate new conflicts. As Ethan Katsh often indicates, the more people go online, the more conflicts the online environment generates. This is in particular true for the Web 2.0 movement, under which most of the above mentioned virtual worlds and online communities fall. The underlying idea of this second wave of the World Wide Web (hence the name Web 2.0) is that the users create and share content,

[1] For instance, in early 2007 MySpace was visited more than Google.

opinions, news, etc. Since professional bodies are no longer central in delivering these services, the number of parties providing information has increased tremendously. Many of those people are not familiar with laws on privacy and intellectual property. The resulting conflicts can best be addressed with technology-enhanced dispute resolution.

Using a wide range of social science research, Larson (2006) indicates that current youth are becoming always available and always connected. They will demand that service professionals be able to help them resolve disputes online.

Further, the caseload of the traditional court systems in many countries is facing an almost total breakdown (Quirchmayr 2006). To deal with such problems, technology-enhanced dispute resolution, in particular ODR, is likely to become one of the central methods of dispute resolution in the future.

In this book we have provided an overview of the theory behind dispute resolution from three perspectives that can be considered the pillars of technology-enhanced dispute resolution, namely law, technology, and Alternative Dispute Resolution and provided insight into many research projects in this field. By choosing relevant theory and research projects as the starting point for our book, and whenever necessary addressing practical developments, we believe we have delivered a robust text that can be used for years to come.

In Chapters 1 and 3 we addressed the central concepts and leading theories on how to resolve disputes. In Chapter 2 we elaborated upon the necessary legal safeguards that should be taken into account when developing technology-enhanced dispute resolution.

The core of the book deals with technology. However, we have not discussed technology for its own sake, but rather always had in mind the aim for which the technology is applied: resolving disputes in the shadow of the law. At the end of the Chapter 3 we presented some general examples of domains where negotiation support can be useful. The forth chapter laid the technological foundations for all dispute resolution: basic techniques and concepts were presented. Chapter 5 provided a very rich overview of a wide range of applications of technology in dispute resolution. Anyone wishing to develop technology-enhanced dispute resolution should carefully read what technology has been used, in what way, and why. Finally, our well-known three-step model of dispute resolution was presented in Chapter 6.

Even after reading this book at least one question has not yet been fully answered: *can technology-enhanced dispute resolution indeed be a good alternative to litigation*? The easy answer to this question is that it does not have to be an alternative, since litigation is also enhanced by technology. Therefore, most of what is in this book is relevant for litigation as well.

We believe that in most processes, both litigation and Alternative Dispute Resolution, technology can play a central role. We do not claim, however, that all dispute resolution should be enhanced by technology. In the end, it will always depend on the interests at stake, the parties involved and the technology available. Nonetheless, the indications are there that in due time more and more dispute resolution processes will make use of technology. An important illustration of this point concerns a pilot project carried out by JURIPAX in the first half of 2009. In this project 200 divorcing couples used the JURIPAX[2] software during their process of divorce. It appeared that a majority considered the use of technology beneficial to reaching an outcome to their dispute in a satisfactory way.

For the coming five or ten years we do not doubt that the influence of technology in dispute resolution will increase. This process can evolve either gradually or rapidly. If the developments continue in the way they currently do, the use of alternative methods supported by technology, as well as technology-enhanced litigation, slowly but surely will become the default. We expect that in 2020 more than half of all dispute resolution processes will be supported by technology.

The other possible scenario is more spectacular. We must admit that although progress in the field of technology-enhanced dispute resolution is obvious, no momentous application has been developed yet. The moment someone develops a platform with the convenience and attractiveness of Google or YouTube, the offline and traditional dispute resolution processes will simply fade away. Even if this never happens, the future for technology-enhanced dispute resolution is a bright one. With this book, we expect to have contributed a small but noteworthy addition to these developments.

---

[2] JURIPAX provides online dispute resolution services including online-intake and pre-mediation solutions, online discussion-room and conference facilities and digital-document and case-management solutions. See www.juripax.com/index.php?section=20&LNG=en (last accessed 26 August 2009).

Adjusted Winner   Adjusted Winner is a two-party point allocation procedure that distributes items or issues to people on the premise of whoever values the item or issue more. The two disputants are required to indicate explicitly how much they value each of the different issues by distributing 100 points across the range of issues in dispute. In this paradigm, it is assumed there are k discrete issues in dispute, each of which is assumed divisible. The Adjusted Winner paradigm is a fair and equitable procedure because at the end of allocation each party will have accrued the same number of points.

analogical reasoning   Analogical reasoning is the process of determining the outcome of a current problem (the case at bar) by comparing it to similar past experiences (precedents).

analogy   Drawing an analogy is taking an existing case and seeking to match it with the current case so that one can conclude that the outcomes should be identical.

Analytical Hierarchy Process   AHP decomposes the overall decision objective into a hierarchic structure of criteria, subcriteria and alternatives. Using the AHP, a decision-maker then compares each pair of criteria by answering the question, with respect to meeting the overall decision objective, of which of the two criteria is most important. The result is a matrix of pair-wise decisions.

and/or graphs   And/or graphs (or actually trees) are useful for representing the ways in which goals can be expanded into subgoals. The root node represents the main goal, whilst the leaf nodes represent atomic facts. The intermediate nodes represent subgoals.

	The nodes at any level are all 'ands' or all 'ors' and may alternate from level to level.
arbitration	Arbitration is an adversarial process whereby an independent third party (or parties), after hearing submissions from the disputants, makes an award binding upon the parties.
argumentation	Argumentation involves a family of concepts that can be broadly grouped into three categories: 1) concepts related to the process of engaging in an argument, 2) procedures or rules adopted to regulate the argument process, and 3) argument as a product or artefact of an argument process.
AssetDivider	AssetDivider is a system developed to meet the needs of family dispute resolution practitioners at Relationships Australia (Queensland). It generalises Family_Winner by including financial values of property and allowing mediators to bias the negotiation (so as to meet the *paramount interests of the children)* in favour of one party to the negotiation.
asynchronous communication	In asynchronous communication, parties do not take part in the discussion at the same time.
BATNA – know your best alternative to a negotiated agreement	The reason you negotiate with some one is to produce better results than would otherwise occur. If you are unaware of what results you could obtain if the negotiations are unsuccessful, you run the risk of entering into an agreement that you would be better off rejecting, or rejecting an agreement you would be better off entering into.
Bayesian belief networks	Bayesian belief networks are graphical models which allow the representation of dependencies among subsets of attributes. They can also be used for classification. They are defined by two components: 1) a directed acyclic graph where each node represents a random variable and each arc represents a probabilistic dependence. Each variable is conditionally dependent of

	its nondescendents in the graph, given its parents. The variables may be discrete or continuous; 2) a conditional probability table for each variable, $P(X|\text{parents}(X))$.
Bayesian classifiers	Bayesian classifiers are statistical classifiers that can predict class membership probabilities – such as the probability that a given sample belongs to a particular class.
Bayesian inference	Bayesian methods provide a formalism for reasoning about partial beliefs under conditions of uncertainty. In this formalism, propositions are given numerical values, signifying the degree of belief accorded to them. Bayes' theorem is an important result in probability theory, which deals with conditional probability. It is useful in dealing with uncertainty, as well as the use of Bayesian inference networks for information retrieval. An application of Bayesian inference networks is the recent WIN (Westlaw Is Natural) legal database.
Bayes theorem	Bayes theorem states that $Pr(Ai|J) = Pr(J|Ai) * Pr(Ai) / [\ \Sigma k=1\ k = n\ Pr\ \{(J|Ak) * Pr(Ak)\}\ ]$ and thus allows one to evaluate certain conditional probabilities given other conditional probabilities.
belief functions	Belief functions are an alternative to probability theory for representing uncertainty in expert systems. Belief functions allow the user to bound the assignment of probabilities to certain events, rather than give events specific probabilities.
BEST project	The BEST project provides advice about BATNAs using semantic web technology.
bounded domain	A domain may be said to be bounded if the problem space can be specified in advance, regardless of the final definitional interpretation of the terms in the problem space.
bounded rationality	Bounded rationality involves choosing strategies from less-than-complete considerations and striving for satisfactory rather than optimal levels of utility.
brainstorming	In brainstorming, the parties, with or without the mediator's participation, generate many possible solutions before deciding which of those best fulfil the parties' joint interests.

burden of proof	In the law of evidence, the burden of proof is the necessity or duty of affirmatively proving a fact or facts in dispute on an issue raised between the parties in a cause.Except as otherwise provided by the law, the burden of proof requires proof by a preponderance of the evidence. In a criminal case, the government, beyond a reasonable doubt, must prove all the elements of the crime. Except in cases of tax fraud, the burden of proof in a tax case is generally on the taxpayer.
case adaptation	Case adaptation takes a retrieved case that meets most of the needs of the current case and turns it into one that meets all of the case's needs.
case-based reasoning	Case-based reasoning is the process of using previous experience to analyse or solve a new problem, explain why previous experiences are or are not similar to the present problem and adapting past solutions to meet the requirements of the present problem.
case knowledge base	In case-based reasoning, the case knowledge base is that part of the system that stores the cases.
civil law	Civil law may be defined as that legal tradition which has its origin in Roman law, as codified in the *Corpus Juris Civilis* of Justinian and as subsequently developed in Continental Europe and around the world. Civil law eventually divided into two streams: the codified Roman and uncodified Roman law. Civil law is highly systematised and structured, and relies on declarations of broad, general principles, often ignoring the details. Civil-law systems are closed, in the sense that every possible situation is governed by a limited number of general principles.
The Claim Room	The Claim Room is a UK ODR environment that provides support conferencing, brainstorming and blind-bidding.
common law	Common law is the legal tradition that evolved in England from the eleventh century onwards. Its principles appear for the most part in reported judgments, usually of the higher courts, in relation to specific fact situations arising in disputes that courts have adjudicated. Common-law systems are

	open, in the sense that new rules may be created or imported for new facts.
compensation	Compensation in negotiation involves one side receiving what it desires and the other side being compensated by being awarded another issue as compensation.
confirming evidence trap	The notion that disputants strongly adhere to positions taken and are more likely to actively collect information that confirms the validity of their position, and downplay or ignore information that refutes their choice.
critical legal studies	Critical legal studies theorists contend that rules and principles are not used to determine an outcome but are invoked after a conclusion has been reached in order to support and justify an outcome.
data mining	Data mining is a problem-solving methodology that finds a logical or mathematical description, eventually of a complex nature, of patterns and regularities in a set of data.
data-mining pattern	A data-mining pattern is interesting if: 1) the pattern is easily understood by humans; 2) the pattern is valid (with some degree of certainty) on new or test data; 3) the pattern is potentially useful; 4) the pattern is novel.
decision analysis	Decision analysis, generated from statistical decision theory, is a methodology typically used to support decision-makers actively in assessing alternative courses of action.
decision tree	A decision tree is an explicit representation of all scenarios that can result from a given decision. The root of the tree represents the initial situation, whilst each path from the root corresponds to one possible scenario.
DEUS	DEUS is a template-based system that displays the level of disagreement, with respect to each item, between disputants. The model underpinning the program calculates the level of agreement and disagreement between the litigants' goals at any given time. The disputants reach a negotiated settlement when the difference between the goals is reduced to nil. DEUS is useful for gaining an

	understanding of what issues are in dispute and the extent of the dispute over these issues.
discretion	Discretion is a power or right conferred upon decision-makers to act according to the dictates of their own judgment and conscience, uncontrolled by the judgment or conscience of others.
easy cases	Easy cases are those cases which can be disposed of on the basis of well-established law and where the facts are sufficiently indisputable that no real issue arises.
expanding the pie	Expanding or enlarging the pie involves the parties in a dispute creating additional resources so that both sides can maintain their major goals.
expert system	Expert systems are computer programs capable of providing advice and functioning at the standard of (and sometimes even at a higher standard than) human experts in given fields.
Family_Winner	Family_Winner asks disputants to list the items in dispute and to attach importance values to indicate how significant it is that the disputants be awarded each of the items. The system uses this information to form trade-off rules. The trade-off rules are then used to allocate issues according to a 'logrolling' strategy.
feature reduction	Feature reduction involves the removal of features that are not relevant or make no sizeable contribution to the data mining exercise.
feature selection	Feature selection or relevance analysis attempts to identify features that do not contribute to the data-mining task.
feed-forward neural network	In a feed-forward neural network, the neurons on the first layer send their output to the neurons of the second layer, but they do not receive any input back from the neurons on the second layer.
fifth party	In an ODR environment, the fifth party represents the provider of the technology.
fourth party	In an ODR environment, the fourth party is the information technology that supports the dispute resolution.
fuzzy logic	Fuzzy logic is a many valued propositional logic where each proposition P, rather than taking the value T or F, has a probability attached (thus between 0 and 1) of being true. It would take the

	value 0 if it were false and 1 if it were true. Logical operators and probability theory are then combined to model reasoning with uncertainty. Fuzzy rules capture something of the uncertainty inherent in the way in which language is used to construct rules. Fuzzy logic and statistical techniques can be used in dealing with uncertain reasoning.
fuzzy set theory	Fuzzy set theory uses the standard logical operators & (and), v (or), ~ (not). Thus given truth values (or membership values) μ (p) for p and μ (q) for q, we can develop truth values (or membership values) for p & q, p v q and ~p. These values are determined by (a) μ (~p) = 1 – μ (p), b) μ (p & q) = min{ μ (p), μ (q)}, c) μ (p v q) = max{ μ (p), μ (q)}.
game theory	Game theory is a branch of applied mathematics that provides advice about the optimal distribution of resources. In the case of a negotiation, the goal of game theory is to develop the best outcome related to the choices each person has made.
GearBi	GearBi is an online arbitration environment for the resolution of international business disputes.
genetic algorithms	Genetic algorithms are general-purpose search algorithms that use principles derived from genetics to solve problems. A population of evolving knowledge structures that evolve over time – through competition and controlled variation – is maintained. Each structure in the population represents a candidate solution to the concrete problem and has an associated fitness to determine which structures are used to form new ones in the competition. The new structures are created using genetic operators such as crossover and mutation.
hybrid reasoning	A hybrid reasoning system combines facets of one or more of the following representation schemes into a single integrated programming environment: logical, procedural, network and structured. It usually includes object orientation, rules for representing heuristic knowledge and support for a variety of search strategies.
inductive reasoning	Inductive reasoning is the process of moving from specific cases to general rules. A rule induction system is given examples of a problem where the

	outcome is known. When it has been given several examples, the rule induction system can create rules that are true from the example cases. The rules can then be used to assess other cases where the outcome is not known.
inference	Inference is the process of deriving conclusions from premises.
influence diagram	An influence diagram gives a simple visual representation of a decision problem. It provides a technique for identifying and displaying the essential elements of a decision: namely the values of issues and how they influence each other. It uses nodes to represent uncertain quantities or random variables. Lines joining the nodes represent conditional dependence/independence between the nodes.
information system	An information system is a computer system whose basic purpose is to represent/store or manipulate data, information or knowledge.
INSPIRE	The INSPIRE system uses decision theory and supports construction of utility functions. There are four main support functions in INSPIRE. One function allows the user to construct a utility function that is used to evaluate her own and her opponent's offers. The second is to present negotiation dynamics in a graph on which all offers and counter-offers are plotted. The third function is to record all messages and offers and create a negotiation history. The fourth function allows the system to verify the Pareto-optimality of the compromise (if achieved) and if a Pareto-non-optimal compromise is achieved it is used to provide negotiators with Pareto improvements that they may consider in the post-settlement stage.
Integrative negotiation	In integrative approaches to negotiation, problems are seen as having more potential solutions than are immediately obvious and the goal is to *expand the pie* before dividing it. Parties attempt to accommodate as many interests of each of the parties as possible, leading to the so-called *win–win* or *all gain* approach.

interest-based negotiation	In an interest-based orientation, the disputants attempt to reconcile their underlying interests.
issue	An issue is a legal factor that was known to be relevant to the outcome of a case.
JURIPAX	JURIPAX provides Online Dispute Resolution services including online-intake and pre-mediation solutions, online discussion-room and conference facilities and digital-document and case-management solutions.
justice-based negotiation	A rights- or justice-based orientation relies upon a determination of who is right in accordance with some accepted guidelines for behaviour.
knowledge-based system	A knowledge-based system is a computer program in which domain knowledge is explicit and contained separately from the system's other knowledge.
knowledge discovery	Knowledge discovery is the non-trivial extraction of implicit, previously unknown and potentially useful information from data.
knowledge engineering	Knowledge engineering involves the cooperation of domain experts who work with the knowledge engineer to codify and make explicit the rules or other reasoning processes that a human expert uses to solve real world problems.
knowledge engineering paradox	The knowledge engineering paradox is that the more competent domain experts become, the less able they are to describe the knowledge they use to solve problems.
knowledge engineering process	The knowledge engineering process is the process of transferring knowledge from the domain experts to the computer system. It includes the following phases: knowledge representation, knowledge acquisition, inference, explanation and justification.
knowledge representation	Knowledge representation involves structuring and encoding the knowledge in the knowledge base, so that inferences can be made by the system from the stored knowledge.

landmark case	A landmark case is one which alters our perception about knowledge in the domain – landmark cases are comparable to rules. Landmark cases are the basis of analogical reasoning.
learning	Learning is any change in a system that allows it to perform better the second time on repetition of the same task drawn from the same population.
legal positivism	Legal positivists believe that a legal system is a *closed logical system* in which correct decisions may be deduced from predetermined rules by logical means alone.
legal realism	Legal realists are jurisprudes for whom the reliance on rules is an anathema. They argue that judges make decisions for a range of reasons which cannot be articulated or at least are not apparent on the face of the judgment given.
litigation	Litigation is a contest in a court of law for the purpose of enforcing a right or seeking a remedy.
local *stare decisis*	Local *stare decisis* is the tendency of judges to be consistent with the decisions of other members of their own region (or registry).
logrolling	Logrolling is a process in which participants look collectively at multiple issues to find issues that one party considers more important than does the opposing party. Logrolling is successful if the parties concede issues to which they give low importance values.
machine learning	Machine learning is that subsection of learning in which the artificial intelligence system attempts to learn automatically.
mediation	Mediation is a process by which the participants, together with the assistance of a neutral person or persons, systematically isolate disputed issues in order to develop options, consider alternatives, and reach a consensual settlement that will accommodate their needs.
mixed legal system	A mixed legal system has principles derived in part from the civil law tradition and in part from the common law tradition. Scotland is an example of a mixed legal system.
naïve Bayesian classifiers	Naïve Bayesian classifiers assume the effect of an attribute value on a given class is independent of the other attributes. Studies comparing classification

algorithms have found the naïve Bayesian classifier to be comparable in performance with decision tree and neural network classifiers.

Nash Equilibrium | The model developed by John Nash showing that competitive behaviour among decision makers leads to a non-optimal equilibrium (known as the Nash Equilibrium).

nearest neighbour algorithm | The nearest neighbour algorithm is used in information retrieval where data that is closest to the search is retrieved. To perform this search, we need a 'metric' (distance function) between the occurrence of each piece of data. The kth nearest neighbour algorithm classifies examples in a sample by using two basic steps to classify each example: 1) find the k nearest, most similar examples in the training set to the example to be classified; 2) assign the example the same classification as the majority of k nearest retrieved neighbours.

negotiation | Negotiation is a process where the parties involved modify their demands to achieve a mutually acceptable compromise. The essence of negotiation is that there is no third party whose role is to act as facilitator or umpire.

neural networks | A neural network receives its name from the fact that it resembles a nervous system in the brain. It consists of many self-adjusting processing elements cooperating in a densely interconnected network. Each processing element generates a single output signal which is transmitted to the other processing elements. The output signal of a processing element depends on the inputs to the processing element: each input is gated by a weighting factor that determines the amount of influence that the input will have on the output. The strength of the weighting factors is adjusted autonomously by the processing element as data is processed.

neural networks in law | Neural networks are particularly useful in law because they can deal with 1) classification difficulties; 2) vague terms; 3) defeasible rules; and 4) discretionary domains.

ontology | An ontology is an explicit conceptualisation of a domain.

onus of proof	In any given scenario the onus of proof indicates the degree of certainty for a given outcome to occur. In a criminal case in common-law countries such proof must be beyond reasonable doubt, whereas in most civil cases in such countries, the proof required is by a fair preponderance of the evidence (i.e. more than 50 per cent likely to occur).
open textured legal predicate	Open textured legal predicates contain questions that cannot be structured in the form of production rules or logical propositions and which require some legal knowledge on the part of the user in order to answer.
optimistic overconfidence	People have a tendency to develop an overly optimistic view on their chances in disputes. This process is referred to as 'optimistic overconfidence', because disputants have unrealistic optimistic expectations about the validity of their judgments.
Pareto-optimal	Given a set of alternative allocations for a set of agents, a movement from one allocation to another that can make at least one agent better off without making any other agent worse off is called a Pareto improvement. An allocation is Pareto-optimal when no further Pareto improvements can be made.
power-based negotiation	A power-based orientation often takes the form of a power contest where each side strives to force the other to concede.
Principled Negotiation	Principled Negotiation promotes deciding issues on their merits rather than through a haggling process focussed on what each side says it will and will not do.
proof beyond reasonable doubt	Proof beyond reasonable doubt is such proof as precludes every reasonable hypothesis except that which it tends to support and which is wholly consistent with the defendant's guilt and inconsistent with any other rational conclusion.
proof by a fair preponderance	Proof by a fair preponderance of the evidence is the standard of proof required in

of the evidence	civil cases; a decision is made according to that evidence which as a whole is more credible and convincing to the mind and which best accords with reason and probability.
pro se litigant	A *pro se* litigant is one who represents her/himself.
ratio decidendi	*Ratio decidendi* is Latin for the 'reasons for decision', that is the legal reasons why the judge came to the conclusion that he or she did. It is the fundamental basis for the rule of law in common law systems. *Stare decisis* says that the *ratio decidendi* will apply to subsequent cases decided by courts lower in the hierarchy.
reactive devaluation	Reactive devaluation in a negotiation refers to the fact that the very offer of a particular proposal or concession – especially if the offer comes from an adversary – may diminish its apparent value or attractiveness in the eyes of the recipient.
rule base	The rule base of a legal (or indeed any) rule-based expert system is that part of the system in which the rules are stored. It is kept separate from the other part of the expert system, the inference engine.
rule-based expert systems	A rule-based expert system is a collection of rules of the form : IF <condition(s)> THEN <action>. Rule-based systems include production rule systems, and, some would argue, logic-based systems as well.
satisficing	Satisficing is a decision-making strategy of selecting the first alternative discovered that happens to be sufficient with respect to some minimal criteria.
Skype	Skype is public domain software that enables individuals and businesses to make free video and voice calls, send instant messages and share files with other Skype users.
Smartsettle	Smartsettle is an interactive computer program developed to assist those involved in negotiating agreements among parties having conflicting objectives. It can be used during the negotiation process by opposing parties or by a professional mediator. On the basis of information provided to the program, in confidence, by each party, it can help all parties identify feasible alternatives, if any exist, that should be preferred to each party's proposal. If such alternatives do not exist, the program can help parties develop counter proposals.

Split-Up	SplitUp is a hybrid rule-based/neural network system that uses textbooks, heuristics, expert advice and cases to model that part of the Family Law Act 1975 (Australia) which deals with property division. Explanation is provided through the use of Toulmin argument structures.
stare decisis	*Stare decisis* says that the *ratio decidendi* will apply to subsequent cases decided by courts lower in the hierarchy.
statutory law	Statutory law is that body of law created by acts of the legislature – in contrast to constitutional law and law generated by decisions of courts and administrative bodies.
statistical reasoning	In contrast to symbolic reasoning, statistical reasoning derives its results by checking whether or not there is a statistical correlation between two events. Examples of statistical reasoning include neural networks and rule induction systems. Whilst rule-based systems are considered to be examples of symbolic reasoning, the rules are often derived using statistical tests.
synchronous communication	Synchronous communication is direct communication, with a minimal time interval between the moment one party makes a comment in a discussion, and the other party receives this message.
Toulmin argument structure	Toulmin stated that all arguments, regardless of the domain, have a structure that consists of four basic invariants: claim, data, warrant and backing. Every argument makes an assertion. The assertion of an argument stands as the claim of the argument. A mechanism is required to act as a justification for the claim, given the data. This justification is known as the warrant. The backing supports the warrant and in a legal argument is typically a reference to a statute or precedent case.
Trust–Convenience–Expertise Triangle	The Trust–Convenience–Expertise Triangle reflects the elements that should be present in any ODR system. The parties using the system should trust it, the use of the system has to be convenient, and the system should offer expertise.
utility function	A utility function is a subjective measurement that expresses the relative value of different package by using a numerical scale.

weak discretion	According to Dworkin, weak discretion describes situations where a decision-maker must interpret standards in her own way.
WIPO	The World Intellectual Property Organization (WIPO) is a specialised agency of the United Nations. It is dedicated to developing a balanced and accessible international intellectual property system which rewards creativity, stimulates innovation and contributes to economic development while safeguarding the public interest.
zero-sum game	A zero-sum game describes a situation in which a participant's gain or loss is exactly balanced by the losses or gains of the other participant(s).
zone of possible agreement	The zone of possible agreement (ZOPA), in a negotiation, indicates the joint area or range where an agreement can be met to which both parties can agree. Within this zone, an agreement is possible. Outside of the zone, no amount of negotiation will yield an agreement.

BIBLIOGRAPHY

Abrahams, B. and Zeleznikow, J. 2008a. Asset Negotiation in Trade-Off Support with a Multi-Agent Environment. *Proceedings of First International Conference on Human Factors and Computational Models in Negotiation (HUCOM 2008)*, K. Hindriks and W. Brinkman (eds.), Delft, The Netherlands.

Abrahams, B. and Zeleznikow, J. 2008b. A Multi-Agent Architecture for Online Dispute Resolution Services. *Expanding the Horizons of ODR: Proceedings of the 5th International Workshop on Online Dispute Resolution*, M. Poblet (ed.), CEUR Workshop Proceedings Series (CEUR-WS.org), Vol. 430, Florence, Italy, 13 December 2008, pp. 51–61.

Abrahams, B. and Zeleznikow, J. 2009. Resolving Family Law Disputes with a Multi-Agent Based Negotiation Support System. *Proceedings of GDN2009, the 10th Annual Meeting INFORMS Section on Group Decision and Negotiation*, Toronto, Ontario, 14–17 June. Online, available at: http://info.wlu.ca/~wwwmath/faculty/kilgour/gdn/papers.htm (last accessed 26 August 2009).

Adelstein, R. and Miceli, T.J. 2001. Toward a Comparative Economics of Plea Bargaining. *European Journal of Law and Economics*, **11**(1): 47–67.

Alexander, R. 1997. Family Mediation: Friend or Foe for Women. *Australasian Dispute Resolution Journal*, **8**(4): 255–266.

Ashley, K. 1992. Case-Based Reasoning and its Implications for Legal Expert Systems. *Artificial Intelligence and Law*, **1**: 113–208.

Astor, H. and Chinkin, C.M. 2002. *Dispute Resolution in Australia*, 2nd edn, Sydney: LexisNexis Butterworths.

Baldwin, J. and McConville, M. 1977. *Negotiated Justice: Pressures to Plead Guilty*, London: Martin Robertson.

Ball, W.J. 1994. Using Virgil to Analyse Public Policy Arguments: A System Based on Toulmin's Informal Logic. *Social Science Computer Review*, **12**(1): 26–37.

Barendrecht, J.M. and De Vries, B.R. 2004. Fitting the Forum to the Fuss with Sticky Defaults: Failure on the Market for Dispute Resolution Services? Working Paper (SSRN 572042).

Bellucci, E. 2004. Developing Compensation Strategies for the Construction of Negotiation Decision Support Systems. PhD thesis, La Trobe University, Bundoora 3086, Victoria, Australia.

2008. AssetDivider: A New Mediation Tool in Australian Family Law. *Proceedings of the First International Working Conference on Human Factors and Computational Models in Negotiation*, Koen V. Hindriks and Willem-Paul Brinkman (eds.), Delft University of Technology, Delft, The Netherlands, pp. 11–18.

Bellucci, E. and Zeleznikow, J. 1997. Family-Negotiator: an Intelligent Decision Support System for Negotiation in Australian Family Law. *Proceedings of the Fourth Conference of the International Society for Decision Support Systems*, International Society for Decision Support Systems, Lausanne, pp. 359–373.

1998. A Comparative Study of Negotiation Decision Support Systems. *Proceedings of Thirty-First Hawaii International Conference on System Sciences*, IEEE Computer Society, Los Alamitos, California, pp. 254–262.

2001. Representations for Decision Making Support in Negotiation. *Journal of Decision Support*, **10**(3–4): 449–479.

2005a. Managing Negotiation Knowledge with the Goal of Developing Negotiation Decision Support Systems. *Proceedings of the 16th Australasian Conference on Information Systems*, Bruce Campbell, Jim Underwood and Deborah Bunker (eds.), Sydney: Australasian Chapter of the Association for Information Systems.

2005b. Managing Negotiation Knowledge: from Negotiation Support to Online Dispute Resolution. *Proceedings of Second International ODR Workshop*, Nijmegen, The Netherlands: Wolf Legal Publishers, pp. 11–22.

Bellucci, E. and Zeleznikow, J. 2006. Developing Negotiation Decision Support Systems that Support Mediators: a Case Study of the Family_Winner System. *Journal of Artificial Intelligence and Law*, **13**(2): 233–271.

Bellucci, E., Lodder, A. and Zeleznikow, J. 2004. Integrating Artificial Intelligence, Argumentation and Game Theory to Develop an Online Dispute Resolution Environment. *Proceedings of the 16th IEEE International Conference on Tools with Artificial Intelligence* ICTAI04, T.M. Khoshgoftaar (ed.), IEEE Computer Society Press, 15–17 November, Los Alamitos, California, pp. 749–754.

Bench-Capon T.J.M, Lowes, D. and McEnery, A.M. 1991. Argument-based Explanation of Logic Programs. *Knowledge Based Systems*, **4**(3): 177–183.

Bentham, J. 1988 (1789). *The Principles of Morals and Legislation*, Amherst: Prometheus Books.

Bibas, S. 2004. Plea Bargaining outside the Shadow of the Trial. *Harvard Law Review*, **117**: 2464–2547.

2006. Transparency and Participation in Criminal Procedure. *New York University Law Review*, **81**: 911–966.

Bjurulf, B. and Elgstrom, O. 2004. Negotiating Transparency, in: Elgstrom, O. and Jonsson, C. (eds.), *European Union Negotiations: Processes, Networks and Institutions*, London: Routledge.

Black, H.C. 1990. *Black's Law Dictionary*, St. Paul: West Publishing Company.

Blanchard, R.E. 1993. Situation Awareness – Transition from Theory to Practice. *Proceedings of the Human Factors and Ergonomics Society: 32nd Annual Meeting*, Santa Monica: Human Factors and Ergonomics Society, pp. 39–42.

Bol, S.H. 2005. An Analysis of the Role of Different Players in E-mediation: the (Legal) Implications. *Proceedings of the Second International Workshop on ODR*, Wolf Legal Publishers, pp. 23–29.

  2007. *Mediation en Internet, Analyse van juridische regels en noodzakelijke waarborgen voor mediation op internet*, The Hague: Sdu Uitgevers.

Brams, S.J. and Taylor, A.D. 1996. *Fair Division, from Cake Cutting to Dispute Resolution*, Cambridge University Press.

Branting, L.K. 1994. A Computational Model of Ratio Decidendi. *Artificial Intelligence and Law: an International Journal*, **2**: 1–31.

Brin, D. 2000. Disputation Arenas: Harnessing Conflict and Competitiveness for Society's Benefit. *Ohio State Journal on Dispute Resolution*, **15**: 597–617.

Brown, H.J. and Marriott, A.L. 1999. *ADR: Principles and Practice*, 2nd edn, London: Sweet & Maxwell.

Carroll, J.M., Neale, D.C., Isenhour, P.L., Rosson, M.B. and McCrickard, D.S. 2003. Notification and Awareness: Synchronizing Task-Oriented Collaborative Activity. *International Journal of Human-Computer Studies*, **58**(5): 605–632.

Chandar, S. and Zeleznikow, J. 2009. Risks to Consider when Negotiating IT Outsourcing Agreements. *Proceedings of GDN2009, the 10th Annual Meeting INFORMS section on Group Decision and Negotiation*, Toronto, Ontario, 14–17 June. Online, available at: http://info.wlu.ca/~wwwmath/faculty/kilgour/gdn/papers.htm (last accessed 26 August 2009).

Charlton, R. 2000. *Dispute Resolution Guidebook*, Sydney: LBC Information Service.

Clark, P. 1991. A Model of Argumentation and its Application in a Cooperative Expert System. PhD thesis, Turing Institute, Department of Computer Science, University of Strathclyde, Glasgow, UK.

Clegg, S. 1994. Power Relations and the Constitution of the Resistant Subject, in: Jermier, J.M., Knights, D. and Nord, W.E. (eds.), *Resistance and Power in Organizations*, London: Routledge.

Condliffe, P. 2009. Preferences and Justice in Alternative Dispute Resolution. *Proceedings of GDN2009, the 10th Annual Meeting INFORMS section on Group Decision and Negotiation*, M. Kilgour and Q. Wang (eds.), Toronto, Ontario, 14–17 June, p. 48.

Cooter, R. and Rubinfeld, D. 1994. An Economic Model of Legal Discovery. *Journal of Legal Studies*, **23**: 435–463.

Cortes Dieguez, J.P. 2008. Developing Online Dispute Resolution for Consumers in the European Union, PhD thesis, University College of Cork.

Cowdery, N. 2005. Creative Sentencing and Plea Bargaining: Does it Happen and What Are the Results?, *LawAsia Biennial Conference*: LawAsia Downunder 2.

De Vries, B., Leenes, R. and Zeleznikow, J. 2005. Fundamentals of Providing Negotiation Advice Online: the Need for Developing BATNAs. *Proceedings of Second International ODR Workshop*, Nijmegen: Wolf Legal Publishers, pp. 59–67.

Dick, J. 1987. Conceptual Retrieval and Case Law. *Proceedings of the First International Conference on Artificial Intelligence and Law*, Boston: ACM Press, pp. 106–115.

Dickey, A. 1990. *Family Law*, Sydney: The Law Book Company.

Douglas, R. and Toulson, D. 1999. WIRE Intelligent Quantum (WIRE IQ) – Tort Evaluation by Precedent instead of 'Rules'. *Proceedings of Twelfth International Conference on Legal Knowledge Based Systems*, Nijmegen: GNI, pp. 127–128.

Druckman, D. 1977. *Negotiations*, London: Sage.

   2005. *Doing Research: Methods of Inquiry for Conflict Analysis*, London: Sage.

Druckman, D. and Albin, C. 2008. *Distributive Justice and the Durability of Negotiated Agreements*, The Australian Centre for Peace and Conflict Studies, Occasional Papers Series, 10, Brisbane, Queensland.

Dufner, D., Kwon, O. and Hadidi, R. 1999. Web-CCAT: A Collaborative Learning Environment for Geographically Distributed Information Technology Students and Working Professionals. *Communications of the Association for Information Systems*, **1**(12).

Edwards, H. 1985. Alternative Dispute Resolution: Panacea or Anathema? *Harvard Law Review*, **99**: 668–684.

Eidelman, J.A. 1993. Software for Negotiations. *Law Practice Management*, **19**(7): 50–55.

Eisenberg, M.A. 1976. Private Ordering through Negotiation: Dispute Settlement and Rulemaking. *Harvard Law Review*, **89**: 637–681.

Elisha, S. and Wiltgen, T. 2006. Resolving Condominium Disputes: Mediation Works. 10 *Hawaii Bar Journal* **1**.

Endsley, M.R. 1995. Toward a Theory of Situation Awareness in Dynamic Systems. *Human Factors*, **37**(1): 32–64.

Ewing, D.W. 1989. *Justice on the Job: Resolving Grievances in the Nonunion Workplace*, Boston: Harvard Business School Press.

Fabri, M. and Contini, F. (eds.). 2001. *Justice and Technology in Europe: How ICT is Changing the Judicial Business*, The Hague: Kluwer Law International.

Fayyad, U., Piatetsky-Shapiro, G. and Smyth, P. 1996. The KDD Process for Extracting Useful Knowledge from Volumes of Data. *Communications ACM*, **39**(11): 27–41.

Finel, B. and Lord, K. 1999. The Surprising Logic of Transparency. *International Studies Quarterly*, **43**: 315–339.

Fisher, R. and Ury, W. 1981. *Getting to YES: Negotiating Agreement Without Giving In*, Boston: Houghton Mifflin.

Fisher, R., Kopelman, E. and Kupfer-Schneider, A. 1994. *Beyond Machiavelli. Tools for Coping with Conflict*, Cambridge, MA: Harvard University Press.

Fletcher, R. 2008. Mothers and Fathers Accessing Family Relationship Centres. *Family Relationships Quarterly*, **10**: 3–5.

Folberg, J. and Taylor, A. 1984. *Mediation: A Comprehensive Guide to Resolving Conflicts without Litigation*, San Francisco: Jossey-Bass.

Freeman, J.B. 1991. *Dialectics and the Macrostructure of Arguments*, Berlin: Floris Publications.

Gazal-Ayal, Oren. 2006. Partial Ban on Plea Bargains. *Cardozo Law Review*, **27**: 2295–2349.

Goldberg, S., Green, E. and Sander, F. 1985. *Dispute Resolution*, Boston: Little Brown and Company.

Goldring, J. 1976. Australian Law and International Commercial Arbitration. *Columbia Journal of Transnational Law*, **15**: 216–252.

Gordon, T.F. 1995. The Pleadings Game: An Exercise in Computational Dialectics. *Artificial Intelligence and Law*, **2**(4): 239–292.

Gray, P., Gray, X. and Zeleznikow, J. 2007. Decision Negotiating Logic: For Richer or Poorer. *Proceedings of Eleventh International Conference on Artificial Intelligence and Law*, R. Winkels (ed.), Palo Alto: ACM Press, pp. 247–251.

Gray, P.N., Tierney, R., Gray, X. and Treanor, L.M. 2006. eGanges: Pervasive Peacemaker. *Proceedings of the first International Symposium on Pervasive Computing and Applications*, Urumchi, China.

Grover, A. 2002. More Security is Needed For Online ADR Applications. 20 Alternatives to High Cost Litig. 135.

Gruber, T.R. 1995. Towards Principles for the Design of Ontologies used for Knowledge Sharing. *Intl J Human-Computer Studies*, **43**: 907–928.

Gutwin, C. and Greenberg, S. 1998. Effects of Awareness Support on Groupware Usability. *Proceedings of the SIGCHI Conference on Human Factors in Computing Systems*, Los Angeles, pp. 511–518.

Habermas, J. 1973. Wahrheitstheorien, in: Fahrenbach, H. (ed.), *Wirklichkeit und Reflexion*, Pfüllingen: Neske, pp. 211–265.

Hall, M.J.J., Calabro, D., Sourdin, T., Stranieri, A. and Zeleznikow, J. 2005. Supporting Discretionary Decision Making with Information Technology: A Case Study in the Criminal Sentencing Jurisdiction. *University of Ottawa Law and Technology Journal*, **2**(1): 1–36.

Heumann, Milton. 1981. *Plea Bargaining: The Experiences of Prosecutors, Judges, and Defense Attorneys*, University of Chicago Press.

Hodge, William, Harrison, Rodney and Colgan, Graeme. 2005. Plea Bargaining. *Commonwealth Law Journal*, 7: 1112.

Hofstede, G. 1989. Cultural Predictors of Negotiation Styles, in: Mautner-Markhof, F. (ed.), *Process of International Negotiations*, Boulder: Westview Press, pp. 193–201.

Hollander Blumoff, R. 1997. Getting to 'Guilty': Plea Bargaining as Negotiation. *Harvard Negotiation Law Review*, 2: 115–148.

Holsapple, C.W. and Whinston, A.B. 1996. *Decision Support Systems – a Knowledge Based Approach*, St. Paul: West Publishing Company.

Honeyman, C. 1985. Patterns of Bias in Mediation. *Missouri Journal of Dispute Resolution*, 141–150.

Hörnle, J. 2009. *Cross-border Internet Dispute Resolution*, Cambridge University Press.

Howard R.A. and Matheson, J.E. 1981. Influence Diagrams, in: Howard, R.A. and Matheson, J.E., *Readings on the Principles and Applications of Decision Analysis*, Vol. 2, Menlo Park, CA: Strategic Decision Group.

Hunt, A. and Thomas, D. 2000. *The Pragmatic Programmer*, Boston: Addison-Wesley.

Hutchinson, B., Tilman, V., Lodder, A.R., Borri, A. and Gouimenou, J. 2009. *CEN/ISS [Draft] Workshop Agreement on Standardisation of Online Dispute Resolution Tools*.

Iosif, V., Mika, P., Larsson, R. and Akkermans, H. 2003. Field Experimenting with Semantic Web Tools in a Virtual Organisation, in: Davies, J., Fensel, D. and van Harmelen, F. (eds.), *Towards the Semantic Web*, Chichester: John Wiley.

Jameson, J.K. 2001. Employee Perceptions of the Availability and Use of Interest-Based, Right-Based, and Power-Based Conflict Management Strategies. *Conflict Resolution Quarterly*, **19**(2): 163–196.

Jennings, N.R., Faratin, P., Lomuscio, A.R., Parsons, S., Sierra, C. and Wooldridge, M. 2000. Automated Haggling: Building Artificial Negotiators. *Pacific Rim International Conference on Artificial Intelligence*, p. 1.

Johnson, P.E., Zualkernan, I.A. and Tukey, D. 1993. Types of Expertise: An Invariant of Problem Solving. *International Journal of Man Machine Studies*, **39**: 641.

Kahneman, D. and Tversky, A. 1995. Conflict Resolution: A Cognitive Perspective, in: Arrow, K. *et al.* (eds.), *Barriers to Conflict Resolution*, New York: W.W. Norton & Company, pp. 44–60.

Kannai, R., Schild, U. and Zeleznikow, J. 2007. Modeling the Evolution of Legal Discretion – an Artificial Intelligence Approach. *Ratio Juris*, **20**(4): 530–558.

Katsh, E. and Rifkin, J. 2001. *Online Dispute Resolution: Resolving Conflicts in Cyberspace*, San Francisco: Jossey-Bass.

Kaufman-Kohler, G. and Schultz, T. 2004. *Online Dispute Resolution: Challenges for Contemporary Justice*, The Hague: Kluwer Law International.

Keller, W. 1996. Disparate Treatment of Spouse Murder Defendants. *S. Cal. Rev. L. & Women's Stud*, **6**: 255–280.

Kennedy, G., McMillan, J. and Benson, J. 1984. *Managing Negotiations*, 2nd edn, London: Hutchinson Business.

Kersten, G.E. 1997. Support for Group Decisions and Negotiations, in: Climaco, J. (ed.), *An Overview, in Multiple Criteria Decision Making and Support*, Heidelberg: Springer Verlag.

2001. Modeling Distributive and Integrative Negotiations. Review and Revised Characterization. *Group Decision and Negotiation*, **10**(6): 493–514.

Kersten, G.E. and Noronha, S.J. 1997. *Supporting International Negotiations with a WWW-based System*, Interim Report, IIASA, Austria.

1999. Negotiation via the World Wide Web: A Cross-Cultural Study of Decision Making. *Group Decision and Negotiation*, **8**: 251–279.

Klein, M.C.A., Steenbergen, W. van, Uijttenbroek, E.M., Lodder, A.R. and van Harmelen, F. 2006. Thesaurus-based Retrieval of Case Law, in: van Engers, T. (ed.), *JURIX 2006: The Nineteenth Annual Conference*, Berlin and Tokyo: IOS Press, pp. 61–70.

Kochan, T. 1992. Walton and McKersie's Behavioral Theory of Labor Relations: An Industrial Relations Perspective. *Journal of Organizational Behavior*, **13**: 289–295.

Kolodner, J.L. and Simpson, R.L. 1989. The Mediator: Analysis of an Early Case-Based Problem Solver. *Cognitive Science*, **13**(4): 507–549.

Korobkin, R. 2006. Psychological Impediments to Mediation Success: Theory and Practise. *Ohio State Journal on Dispute Resolution*, **21**: 281–238.

Kraus, S. 2001. *Strategic Negotiation in Multi-Agent Environments*, Cambridge, MA: MIT Press.

Kraus, S., Sycara, K. and Evenchik, A. 1998. Reaching Agreements through Argumentation: A Logical Model and Implementation. *Artificial Intelligence Journal*, **104**(1–2): 1–69.

Kraus, S., Hoz-Weiss, P., Wilkenfeld, J., Andersen, D. and Pate, A. 2008. Resolving Crises through Automated Bilateral Negotiations. *Artificial Intelligence Journal*, **172**(1): 1–18.

Kydd, A. 2003. Which Side Are You On? Bias, Credibility, and Mediation. *American Journal of Political Science*, **47**(4): 597–611.

Larson, D.A. 2006. Technology Mediated Dispute Resolution (TMDR): A New Paradigm. *Ohio State Journal of Dispute Resolution*, **629**.

Lax, D.A. and Sebenius, J. 1986. *The Manager as Negotiator*, New York: The Free Press.

Lewicki, R.J., Saunders, D.M. and Minton, J.W. 1999. *Zone of Potential Agreement in Negotiation*, 3rd edn, Burr Ridge, IL: Irwin-McGraw Hill.

Lewicki, R.J., Barry, B., Saunders, D.M. and Minton, J.W. 2003. *Negotiation*, 4th edn, New York: McGraw-Hill/Irwin.

Llewellyn, K. 1962. *Jurisprudence*, University of Chicago Press.

Lodder, A.R. 1999. *Dialaw: On Legal Justification and Dialogical Models of Argumentation*, Dordrecht: Kluwer Academic Publishers.

2002a. European Union E-Commerce Directive – Article by Article Comments. Guide to European Union Law on E-Commerce, in: Lodder, A.R. and Kaspersen, (eds.), *eDirectives*, The Hague: Kluwer Law International. Available at SSRN: http://ssrn.com/abstract=1009945.

2002b. Online Negotiation and Mediation: Is There Room for Argument Support Tools? Paper presented at the 17th BILETA Annual Conference. Online, availableat:www.bileta.ac.uk/Document%20Library/1/Online%20Negotiation%20 and%20Mediation%20-%20Is%20There%20Room%20for%20Argument%20 Support%20Tools.pdf (last accessed 9 November 2008).

2004. Man and Machine: What's the Difference. *JAVI*, **3**(1): 20–21.

2006. The Third Party and Beyond: An Analysis of the Different Parties, in Particular the Fifth, Involved in Online Dispute Resolution. *Information and Communication Technology Law*, **15**(2). Available at SSRN: http://ssrn.com/abstract=1269562.

Lodder, A.R. and Herczog, A. 1995 *DiaLaw: A Dialogical Framework for Modeling Legal Reasoning, Proceedings of Fifth International Conference on Artificial Intelligence and Law*, New York: ACM Press, pp. 146–155.

Lodder A.R. and Huygen, P. 2001. eADR: A Simple Tool to Structure the Information Exchange Between Parties in Online Alternative Dispute Resolution. *Legal Knowledge and the Information Systems JURIX 2001: The Fourteenth Annual Conference*, pp. 117–129.

Lodder, A.R. and Oskamp, A. (eds.). 2006. *Information Technology and Lawyers. Advanced Technology in the Legal Domain, from Challenges to Daily Routine*, Berlin: Springer.

Lodder, A.R. and Zeleznikow, J. 2005. Developing an Online Dispute Resolution Environment: Dialogue Tools and Negotiation Systems in a Three Step Model. *The Harvard Negotiation Law Review*, **10**: 287–338.

Loui, R.P. and Norman, J. 1995. Rationales and Argument Moves. *Artificial Intelligence & Law*, **3**: 159–189.

Loui, R.P., Norman, J., Olson, J. and Merill, A. 1993. A Design for Reasoning with Policies, Precedents and Rationales. *Proceedings of the Fourth International Conference on Artificial Intelligence and Law*, New York: ACM Press, pp. 202–211.

Loui, R.P., Norman, J., Alpeter, J., Pinkard, D., Craven, D., Linsday, J. and Foltz, M. 1997. Progress on Room 5: A Testbed for Public Interactive

Semi-Formal Legal Argumentation. *Proceedings of the Sixth International Conference of Artificial Intelligence and Law*, New York: ACM Press, pp. 207–214.

Mack, K. and Roach Anleu, S. 1995. Balancing Principle and Pragmatism: Guilty Pleas. *Journal of Judicial Administration*, **4**(4): 232–239.

1996. Guilty Pleas: Discussions and Agreements. *Journal of Judicial Administration*, **6**(8): 9.

1997. Sentence Discount for a Guilty Plea: Time for a New Look. *Flinders Journal of Law Reform*, **1**: 123.

1998. Reform of Pre-Trial Criminal Procedure: Guilty Pleas. *Criminal Law Journal*, **22**: 263.

Mackenzie, G., Vincent, A. and Zeleznikow, J. 2007. Decision Support for Criminal Sentencing and Plea Bargaining. *Proceedings of the Fifth International Conference on Law and Technology (IASTEAD)*, 24–26 September 2007, Berkeley, pp. 49–59.

2008. Negotiating about Charges and Pleas – Balancing Interests and Justice, in: Climaco, J., Kersten, G. and Costa, J.P. (eds.), *Proceedings of Group Decision and Negotiation 2008*, Portugal: INESC Coimbra, pp. 167–180.

Marshall, Catherine. 1989. Representing the Structure of Legal Argument. *Proceedings of Second International Conference on Artificial Intelligence and Law*, New York: ACM Press, pp. 121–127.

Matthijssen, L. 1999. *Interfacing between Lawyers and Computers. An Architecture for Knowledge Based Interfaces to Legal Databases*, Dordrecht: Kluwer Law International.

Matwin, S., Szpakowicz, S., Koperczak, Z., Kersten, G.E. and Michalowski, G. 1989. NEGOPLAN: An Expert System Shell for Negotiation Support. *IEEE Expert*, **4**(4): 50–62.

McEwen, C., Rogers, N. and Maiman, R. 1995. Bring in the Lawyers: Challenging the Dominant Approaches to Ensuring Fairness in Divorce Mediation. *Minnesota Law Review*, **79**: 1317–1412.

Milnor, J. 1998. John Nash and 'A Beautiful Mind'. *Notices of the American Mathematical Society*, **45**(10): 1329–1332.

Mnookin, R. 2003. When Not to Negotiate. *University of Colorado Law Review*, **74**: 1077–1107.

Mnookin, R. and Kornhauser, L. 1979. Bargaining in the Shadow of the Law: The Case of Divorce. *Yale Law Journal*, **88**: 950–997.

Mnookin, R. and Ross, L. 1995. Introduction, in: Arrow, K. *et al.* (eds.), *Barriers to Conflict Resolution*, New York: W.W. Norton & Company, pp. 17–18.

Mnookin, R., Peppet, S.R. and Tulumello, A.S. 2000. *Beyond Winning: Negotiating to Create Value in Deals and Disputes*, Cambridge, MA: The Belnap Press of Harvard University Press.

Mollen, S. 1999. Alternate Dispute Resolution of Condominium and Cooperative Conflicts. *St John's Law Journal*, **75**.

Murninghan, J.K. 1986. Organizational Coalitions: Structural Contingencies and the Formation Process, in: Lewicki, R.J., Sheppard, B.H. and Bazerman, M.H. (eds.), *Research on Negotiations in Organizations, Vol 1.*, Greenwich, CT: JAI Press.

Nakano, R. 2001. *Web Content Management: A Collaborative Approach*, Boston: Addison-Wesley.

Nasar, S. 1994. *A Beautiful Mind: A Biography of John Forbes Nash, Jr., Winner of the Nobel Prize in Economics*, New York: Simon & Schuster.

Nash, J. 1950. Non-Cooperative Games. PhD thesis, Princeton University.

    1953. Two Person Cooperative Games. *Econometrica*, **21**: 128–140.

Neale, M.A. and Bazerman, M.H. 1983. The Role of Perspective-taking Ability in Negotiating under Different Forms of Arbitration. *Industrial and Labor Relations Review*, **36**: 378–388.

    1991. *Cognition and Rationality in Negotiation*, New York: The Free Press.

Nitta, K. and Shibasaki, M. 1997. Defeasible Reasoning in Japanese Criminal Jurisprudence. *Artificial Intelligence and Law*, **5**: 139–176.

O'Malley, P. 1983. *Law, Capitalism, and Democracy: A Sociology of the Australian Legal Order*, London: George Allen and Unwin.

Oskamp, A., Lodder, A.R. and Apistola, M. (eds.). 2004. *IT Support of the Judiciary: Australia, Singapore, Venezuela, Norway, the Netherlands and Italy*, The Hague: Asser Press.

Orwell, G. 1945. *Animal Farm*, London: Secker and Warburg.

Osborne, M.J. and Rubinstein, A. 1990. *Bargaining and Markets*, San Francisco: Academic Press Inc.

Perelman, C. and Olbrechts-Tyteca, L. 1969. *The New Rhetoric*, translated by Wilkenson, J. and Weaver, P., University of Notre Dame Press. Originally published in 1958 in French as Perelman, C. and Olbrechts-Tyteca, L. 1958. *La Nouvelle Rhétorique: Traité de l'Argumentation*, Presses Universitaires de France.

Peterson, D. 2008. *What Determines Success in Negotiating? How to Improve as a Negotiator and Mediator*. Online, available at: www.sbcadre.org/articles/0027.htm (last accessed 6 September 2009).

Peterson, M. and Waterman, D.A. 1985. Evaluating Civil Claims: An Expert Systems Approach to Evaluating Liability Cases, in: Walter, C. (ed.), *Computer Power and Legal Reasoning*, St. Paul: West Publishing Company, pp. 627–659.

Phegan, R. 1995. The Family Mediation System: An Art of Distributions. *McGill Law Journal*, **40**: 365.

Pierani, Marco. 2005. ODR Developments under a Consumer Perspective: The Italian Case. *Proceedings of Second International ODR Workshop*, Nijmegen: Wolf Legal Publishers, pp. 43–45.

Pruitt, D.G. 1981. *Negotiation Behavior*, New York: Academic Press.

Pruitt, D.G and Carnevale, P.J. 1993. *Negotiation in Social Conflict*, Maidenhead and Philadelphia: Open University Press.

Pryles, M.C. 2002. *Dispute Resolution in Asia*, 2nd edn, The Hague: Kluwer Law International.

Quirchmayr, G. 2006. Internet, WWW and beyond, in: Lodder, A.R. and A. Oskamp (eds.), *Information Technology and Lawyers*, Dordrecht: Springer, pp. 137–163.

Raiffa, H. 1968. *Decision Analysis: Introductory Lectures on Choice under Uncertainty*, Cambridge, MA: The Belknap Press.

1982. *The Art and Science of Negotiation: How to Resolve Conflicts and Get the Best Out of Bargaining*, Cambridge, MA: The Belknap Press.

Raiffa, H., Richardson, J. and Metcalfe, D. 2002. *Negotiation Analysis: The Science and Art of Collaborative Decision Making*, Reading, MA: Addison Wesley.

Raines, S. and Conley Tyler, M. 2007. From eBay to Eternity: Advances in Online Dispute Resolution. University of Melbourne Legal Studies Research Paper No. 200. Online, available at: http://papers.ssrn.com/sol3/papers.cfm?abstract_id=955968 (last accessed 31 August 2009).

Raith, M.G. 2000. Fair Negotiation Procedures. *Mathematical Social Sciences*, **39**(3): 303–322.

Reimer, U., Brockhausen, P., Lau, Th. and Reich, J. 2003. Ontology-based Knowledge Management at Work: The Swiss Life Case Studies, in: Davies, J., Fensel, D. and van Harmelen, F. (eds.), *Towards the Semantic Web*, Chichester: John Wiley.

Riskin, L. 1996. Understanding Mediators' Orientations, Strategies, and Techniques: A Grid for the Perplexed. *Harvard Negotiation Law Review*, 7: 25.

Rissland, E., Ashley, K. and Branting, L.K. 2005. Case-Based Reasoning and Law. *The Knowledge Engineering Review*, **20**(3): 293–298.

Ross, H.L. 1980. *Settled Out of Court*, New York: Aldine.

Ross, L. 1995. Reactive Devaluation in Negotiation and Conflict Resolution, in: Arrow, K.J., Mnookin, R.H., Ross, L., Tversky, A. and Wilson, R., *Barriers to Conflict Resolution*, New York: W.W. Norton & Company, pp. 26–42.

Roth, A.E. 1979. *Axiomatic Models of Bargaining*. Lecture Notes in Economics and Mathematical Systems No. 170. Berlin: Springer-Verlag.

Rubin, J.Z. and Sander, F.E. 1991. Culture, Negotiation, and the Eye of the Beholder. *Negotiation Journal*, **6**: 249–254.

Rule, C. 2002. *Online Dispute Resolution for Businesses*, San Francisco: Jossey-Bass.

Rusanow, G. 2003. *Knowledge Management and the Smarter Lawyer*, New York: ALM Publishing.

Saaty, T. 1980. *The Analytical Hierarchy Process: Planning, Priority, Allocation*, New York: McGraw-Hill.

1994. How to Make a Decision: The Analytic Hierarchy Process. *Interfaces*, **19**: 19–43.

2005. *Theory and Applications of the Analytic Network Process*, Pittsburgh: RWS Publications.

Sander, F. 1976. Varieties of Dispute Processing, 70 Federal Rules Decisions 111.

2002. Some Concluding Thoughts. *Ohio State Journal of Dispute Resolution*, **17**: 205–211.

Schelling, T.C. 1958. The Strategy of Conflict: Prospectives for a Re-orientation of Game Theory. *Journal of Conflict Resolution*, **2**(3): 203–264.

Schiavetta, S. 2008. Electronic Alternative Dispute Resolution – Increasing Access To Justice Via Procedural Protections, PhD thesis, University of Oslo.

Schild, U. 1998. Decision Support for Criminal Sentencing. *Artificial Intelligence and Law*, **6**(4): 151–202.

Schild, U. and Zeleznikow, J. 2008. The Three Laws of Robotics Revisited. *International Journal of Intelligent Systems Technologies & Applications*, **4**(3–4): 254–270.

Schlobohm, D.A. and Waterman, D.A. 1987. Explanation for an Expert System that Performs Estate Planning. *Proceedings of the First International Conference on Artificial Intelligence and Law*, Boston: ACM Press, pp. 18–27.

Schultz, T. 2005. *Réguler le commerce électronique par la résolution des litiges en ligne*, Brussels: Bruylant.

Scott, R. and Stuntz, W. 1992. Plea Bargaining as Contract. *The Yale Law Journal*, **101**(8): 1909–1968.

Sebenius, J.K. 2007. Negotiation Analysis: Between Decisions and Games, in: Edwards, W., Miles, R. and von Winterfeldt, D. (eds.), *Advances in Decision Analysis*, Cambridge University Press, pp. 469–488.

Seifman, R.S. and Freiberg, A. 2001. Plea Bargaining in Victoria: The Role of Counsel. *Criminal Law Journal*, **25**(2): 63–74.

Senger, J. 2004. Decision Analysis in Negotiation. *Marquette Law Review*, **87**: 723–735.

Shapiro, D.L. and Brett, J.M. 1993. Comparing Three Processes Underlying Judgments of Procedural Justice: A Field Study of Mediation and Arbitration. *Journal of Personality and Social Psychology*, **65**(6): 1167–1177.

Shavell, S. 2003. Economic Analysis of Litigation and the Legal Process. Discussion Paper No. 404, John M. Olin Center for Law, Economics, and Business, Harvard University, Cambridge, MA.

Simon, H.A. 1957. *Models of Man*, New York: John Wiley.

Simpson, R. 1985. A Computer Model of Case-Based Reasoning in Problem Solving. Doctoral dissertation, School of Information and Computer Science, Georgia Institute of Technology, Atlanta, Georgia.

Solovay, N. and Reed, C.K. 2003. *The Internet and Dispute Resolution Untangling the Web*, New York: Law Journal Press.

Sourdin T. 2005. *Alternative Dispute Resolution*, 2nd edn, Australia: Lawbook Co, Thomsons.

Stipanowich, T.J. 2004. ADR and the 'Vanishing Trial': The Growth and Impact of 'Alternative Dispute Resolution'. *Journal of Empirical Legal Studies*, **1**(3): 843–912.

Stranieri, A. and Zeleznikow, J. 2005. *Knowledge Discovery from Legal Databases*, Vol. 69, Dordrecht: Springer.

Stranieri, A., Yearwood, J. and Meikle, T. 2000. The Dependency of Discretion and Consistency on Knowledge Representation. *International Review of Law Computers and Technology*, **14**: 325–340.

Stranieri, A., Zeleznikow, J. and Yearwood, J. 2001. Argumentation Structures that Integrate Dialectical and Monoletical Reasoning. *Knowledge Engineering Review*, **16**(4): 331–348.

Stranieri, A., Zeleznikow, J., Gawler, M. and Lewis, B. 1999. A Hybrid – Neural Approach to the Automation of Legal Reasoning in the Discretionary Domain of Family Law in Australia. *Artificial Intelligence and Law*, **7**(2–3): 153–183.

Stuckenschmidt, H., van Harmelen, F., de Waard, A., Scerri, T., Bhogal, R., van Buel, J., Crowlesmith, I., Fluit, Ch., Kampman, A., Broekstra, J. and van Mulligen, E. 2004. Exploring Large Document Repositories with RDF Technology: The DOPE Project. *IEEE Intelligent Expert*, **19**(3): 34–40.

Stulberg, J. 2000. Mediation, Democracy and Cyberspace. *Ohio State Journal on Dispute Resolution*, **15**: 619–642.

Stuntz, W. 2004. Plea Bargaining and Criminal Law's Disappearing Shadow. *Harvard Law Review*, **117**: 2548–2560.

Sycara, K. 1993. Machine Learning for Intelligent Support of Conflict Resolution. *Decision Support Systems*, **10**: 121–136.

   1998. Multiagent Systems. *AI Magazine*, **19**(2): 79–92.

Tata, C. 2000. Resolute Ambivalence: Why Judiciaries do not Institutionalise their Decision Support Systems? *International Review of Law, Computers and Technology*, **14**: 297–316.

Thian, Y.S. 2004. Singapore, in: Oskamp. A., Lodder, A.R. and Apistola, M. (eds.), *IT Support of the Judiciary: Australia, Singapore, Venezuela, Norway, the Netherlands and Italy*, The Hague: Asser Press, pp. 45–70.

Thiessen, E.M. 1993. ICANS: An Interactive Computer-Assisted Multi-party Negotiation Support System. PhD dissertation, School of Civil & Environmental Engineering, Cornell University, Ithaca, New York, Dissertation Abstracts International, 172p.

Thiessen, E.M. and McMahon, J.P. 2000. Beyond Win–Win in Cyberspace. *Ohio State Journal on Dispute Resolution*, **15**: 643.

Thiessen, E.M., Loucks, D.P. and Stedinger, J.R. 1998. Computer-Assisted Negotiations of Water Resources Conflicts. *Group Decision and Negotiation Journal*, **7**(2): 109–129.

Thompson, L. 1991. Information Exchange in Negotiation. *Journal of Experimental Social Psychology*, **27**: 161–179.

Tor, Avishalom, Gazal-Ayal, Oren and Garcia, Stephen M. 2006. *Substantive Fairness and Comparative Evaluation in Plea Bargain Decision Making*. Available at SSRN.

Toulmin, S. 1958. *The Uses of Argument*, Cambridge University Press.

Ury, W.L., Brett, J.M. and Goldberg, S.B. 1988. *Getting Disputes Resolved*, San Francisco: Jossey-Bass.

Van Boven, L., Gilovich, T. and Medvec, V. 2003. The Illusion of Transparency in Negotiations. *Negotiation Journal*, **19**(2): 117–131.

Van Laarschot, R., van Steenbergen, W., Stuckenschmidt, H., Lodder, A.R. and van Harmelen, F. 2005. The Legal Concepts and the Layman's Terms. Bridging the Gap through Ontology-Based Reasoning about Liability. *JURIX 2005*, IOS Press, pp. 115–125.

von Neumann, J. and Morgenstern, O. 1947. *The Theory of Games and Economic Behavior*, 2nd edn, Princeton University Press.

Vincent, A. and Zeleznikow, J. 2005. Toulmin-Based Computational Modelling of Judicial Discretion in Sentencing. *Proceedings of The Uses of Argument*, Ontario Society for the Study of Argumentation, 18–21 May, McMaster University, Hamilton, Ontario, Canada, pp. 465–475.

2006. Discretionary Judicial Sentencing: Decision Making and Decision Support, in: Hafner, Carole and O'Rourke, Maureen (eds.), *Law and Technology: LawTech 2006*, Calgary: ACTA Press, pp. 119–126.

2007. The De-Socialisation of the Courts, Sentencing Decision Support and Plea Bargaining. *International Review of Law Computers & Technology*, **21**(2): 157–175.

Vincent, A., Sourdin, T. and Zeleznikow, J. 2007. Criminal Sentencing, Intuition and Decision Support, in: Elleithy, K. (ed.), *Advances and Innovations in Systems, Computing Sciences and Software Engineering*, Berlin: Springer, pp. 41–46.

von Wright, G.H. 1972. The Logic of Preference Reconsidered. *Theory and Decision*, **3**(2): 140–169.

Vreeswijk, G.A.W. and Lodder, A.R. 2005. GearBi: Towards an Online Arbitration Environment Based on the Design Principles Simplicity, Awareness, Orientation, and Timeliness. *Artificial Intelligence and Law*, **13**(2): 297–321.

Walton, D. 2004. A New Dialectical Theory of Explanation. *Philosophical Explorations*, **7**: 71–89.

Walton, R.E. and McKersie, R.B. 1965. *A Behavioral Theory of Labor Negotiations*, New York: McGraw-Hill.

Wang, F.F. 2008, *Online Dispute Resolution: Technology, Management and Legal Practice from an International Perspective*, Abington: Woodhead Publishing.

Waterman, D.A. and Peterson, M. 1980. Rule-Based Models of Legal Expertise. *Proceedings of the First National Conference on Artificial Intelligence*, Stanford University, AAAI, pp. 272–275.

    1981. Models of Legal Decisionmaking, Technical Report, R-2717–1CJ, Rand Corporation, Santa Monica, California.

    1984. Evaluating Civil Claims: An Expert Systems Approach. *Expert Systems*, **1**(1): 65–76.

Waterman, D.A., Paul, J. and Peterson, M. 1986. Expert Systems for Legal Decision Making. *Expert Systems*, **3**(4): 212–226.

Wertheim, E., Love, A., Littlefield, L. and Peck, C. 1992. *I Win: You Win*, Ringwood: Penguin Books.

Wettig, S. and Zehendner, E. 2003. The Electronic Agent: A Legal Personality under German Law? in: Oskamp, A. and Weitzenböck, E. (eds.), *Proceedings of the Law and Electronic Agents Workshop* (LEA '03).

Wildeboer, Gwen R., Klein, Michel C.A. and Uijttenbroek, Elisabeth M. 2007. Explaining the Relevance of Court Decisions to Laymen, in: Lodder, A.R. and Mommers, L. (eds.), *Proceedings of JURIX 2007*, Amsterdam and Berlin: IOS Press, pp. 129–138.

Wilkenfeld, J., Kraus, S., Holley, K.M. and Harris, M.A. 1995. GENIE: A Decision Support System for Crisis Negotiations. *Decision Support Systems*, **14**(4): 369–391.

Williams, G.R. 1983. *Legal Negotiation and Settlement*, St. Paul: West Publishing Co.

Wright, R.W. 1999. Principled Adjudication: Tort Law and Beyond. *Canterbury Law Review*, **7**: 265–296.

Wright, R. and Miller, M. 2002. The Screening/Bargaining Tradeoff. *Stanford Law Review*, **55**: 29–117.

Wright, R. and Miller, M. 2003. Honesty and Opacity in Charge Bargains. *Stanford Law Review*, **55**: 1409–1417.

Zartman, I.W. 1993. Decision Support and Negotiation Research: A Researcher's Perspective. *Theory and Decision*, **34**(3): 345–351.

Zeleznikow, J. 2000. Building Judicial Decision Support Systems in Discretionary Legal Domains. *International Review of Law, Computers and Technology*, **14**(3): 341–356.

    2002a. Risk, Negotiation and Argumentation – a Decision Support System Based Approach. *Law, Probability and Risk*, **1**: 37–48.

    2002b. Using Web-based Legal Decision Support Systems to Improve Access to Justice. *Information and Communications Technology Law*, **11**(1): 15–33.

    2004. The Split-Up Project: Induction, Context and Knowledge Discovery in Law. *Law, Probability and Risk*, **3**: 147–168.

    2006a. Using Toulmin Argumentation to Support Dispute Settlement in Discretionary Domains, in: Hitchcock, D. and Verheij, B. (eds.), *Arguing* on the Toulmin Model: New Essays in Argument Analysis and Evaluation, Dordrecht: Springer, pp. 261–272.

2006b. Using an Argumentation Based Approach to Manage Legal Knowledge, in: Schwartz, D.G. (ed.), Encyclopedia of Knowledge Management, Hershey: Idea Group Inc, pp. 638–642.

2009. Beyond Interest Based Bargaining – Incorporating Interests and Justice in the Development of Negotiation Support Systems. Proceedings of GDN2009, the 10th Annual Meeting INFORMS Section on Group Decision and Negotiation, Toronto, Ontario, 14–17 June. Online, available at: http://info.wlu.ca/~wwwmath/faculty/kilgour/gdn/papers.htm (last accessed 26 August 2009).

Zeleznikow, J. and Abrahams, B. 2009. Incorporating Issues of Fairness into the Development of a Multi-agent Negotiation Support System. Proceedings of the Twelfth International Conference on Artificial Intelligence and Law, Barcelona: ACM Press, pp. 177–185.

Zeleznikow, J. and Bellucci, E. 2003. Family_Winner: Integrating Game Theory and Heuristics to Provide Negotiation Support. Proceedings of Sixteenth International Conference on Legal Knowledge Based System, Amsterdam: IOS Publications, pp. 21–30.

2006. Family_Mediator – Adding Notions of Fairness to those of Interests. Proceedings of Nineteenth International Conference on Legal Knowledge Based System, Amsterdam: IOS Publications, pp. 121–130.

Zeleznikow, J. and Hunter, D. 1994. Building Intelligent Legal Information Systems: Knowledge Representation and Reasoning in Law, Kluwer Computer/Law Series, 13.

Zeleznikow, J. and Stranieri, A. 1998. Split Up: The Use of an Argument Based Knowledge Representation to Meet Expectations of Different Users for Discretionary Decision Making. Proceedings of IAAI '98 – Tenth Annual Conference on Innovative Applications of Artificial Intelligence, AAAI/MIT Press, pp. 1146–1151.

Zeleznikow, J. and Vincent, A. 2007. Providing Decision Support for Negotiation: The Need for Adding Notions of Fairness to Those of Interests. University of Toledo Law Review, 38: 101–143.

Zeleznikow, J., Bellucci, E. and Hodgkin, J. 2002. Building Decision Support Systems to Support Legal Negotiation. Proceedings of the IASTED International Conference on Law and Technology (LawTech2002), Anaheim: ACTA Press, pp. 112–117.

Zeleznikow, J., Stranieri, A. and Gawler, M. 1996. Split-Up: A Legal Expert System which Determines Property Division upon Divorce. Artificial Intelligence and Law, 3: 267–275.

Zeleznikow, J., Bellucci, E., Schild, U. and Mackenzie, G. 2007a. Bargaining in the Shadow of the Law – Using Utility Functions to Support Legal Negotiation, in: Winkels, R. (ed.), *Proceedings of the Eleventh International Conference on Artificial Intelligence and Law*, Palo Alto.

Zeleznikow, J., Bellucci, E., Vincent, A. and Mackenzie, G, 2007b. Bargaining in the Shadow of a Trial: Adding Notions of Fairness to Interest-Based Negotiation in Legal Domains, in: Kersten, G., Rios, J. and Chen, E. (eds.), Proceedings of *Group Decision and Negotiation Meeting 2007*, Volume II, Concordia University, Montreal, Canada.

Zeleznikow, J., Meersman, R., Hunter, D. and van Helvoort, E. 1995. Computer Tools for Aiding Legal Negotiation. *ACIS95 – Sixth Australasian Conference on Information Systems*, Curtin University of Technology, Perth, Western Australia, pp. 231–251.

INDEX

ABA, *see* American Bar Association
ACCC (Australian Competition and
    Consumer Commission), 167
Adjusted Winner system, 91–94, 171
ADR, *see* Alternative Dispute
    Resolution
adversarial principle, 25
advice lines, 121–24
agreements, argument tools, 154
AHP, *see* Analytical Hierarchy
    Process
Alternative Dispute Resolution
    (ADR), 5
  advantages, 13
  fairness, 6–12
  norms, 22–23
American Bar Association (ABA), 36
analogical reasoning, 171
Analytical Hierarchy Process (AHP),
    155, 171
and/or graphs, 171
arbitration, 4–5, 172
  decisions, 24
  European Union recommendation,
    23–26
  GearBi system, 132–38
  online processes, 79, 82, 84, 132–38
  regulation of, 22
argument structures, 140–42
argument tools, 152–54, 156
argumentation, 148–54, 172
Art of Negotiating system, 89–90
artificial intelligence, negotiation
    support systems, 108–15
AssetDivider system, 118–21, 172
assets, equitable allocation, 91–94,
    97–108, 111–15, 116–21

asynchronous communication, 73–74,
    131, 172
Australia
  alternative dispute resolution, 8
  arbitration, 4
  Competition and Consumer
    Commission, 167
  Online Family Dispute Resolution
    Service, 124–25
  plea negotiation, 163
  Telephone Dispute Resolution
    Service, 121–24
awareness of other users, online
    arbitration, 134

bargaining
  in the shadow of the law, 7, 11,
    165–67
  interest-based, 115–25
  negotiation support systems, 91–108
  theories, 10
BATNAs (best alternative to a negoti-
    ated agreement), 115, 166, 172
  establishment of, 147–48
  plea negotiation, 145
  semantic web technology, 125–27
Bayes theorem, 173
Bayesian belief networks, 172
Bayesian classifiers, 173
Bayesian inference, 173
belief functions, 173
best alternative to a negotiated
    agreement, *see* BATNAs
BEST-project (BATNA Establishment
    using Semantic web Technology),
    125–27, 147, 166
biases in mediation, 166

blind-bidding, 75–76, 82, 84
bounded domains, 173
bounded rationality, 173
brainstorming, 173
burden of proof, 174

case adaptation, 174
case based reasoning, 174
case knowledge base, 174
case law, 87
cash variable payment items, 117
Chamberlain, Neville, 9
chapter overviews, 15–17
charge bargains, 163
children, 115, 165
citizens, justice access, 14
civil law, 174
    Claim Room, The, 148, 174
coin-tossing, 82
common law, 174
compensation, 98, 99, 159, 175
Competition and Consumer
    Commission (ACCC), 167
complexity, online arbitration, 134
compromises, 97, 130, 132
conciliation, 5
conferencing, 5
confidentiality, 28, 30
confirming evidence trap, 175
consensus, 157
consumer disputes resolution, 22–29
Contest Mention system, 143, 145
Cortes, Pablo, 19
courts, information technology, 72
    see also litigation; plea
        bargaining
critical legal studies, 175
Cybersettle system, 82, 83

data mining, 175
deadlines, arbitration process, 136
decision analysis, 175
decision support systems, 86–88,
    154–56
decision trees, 175
dedicated software, 80, 81
DEUS system, 90, 175

DiaLaw system, 150–51, 153
dialectical situations, 149
dialogue, 158–59
    process outcomes, 159–60
    tools, 153, 157
directives, see European Union (EU)
disclosures
    mediation, 31
    negotiation, 164–65
    online services, 36–38
discovery, negotiation, 164–65, 167
discretion, 176
dispute systems design, 2
distance selling, 33, 34–35
distributive approaches, negotiation, 6
divorce, see marital property
domain names dispute resolution,
    74–75
domestic violence, 123
DOPE browser, 126

eADR, 151–52
easy cases, 176
eBay, 14, 76
ECHR, see European Convention on
    Human Rights
e-commerce, 26, 32
effectiveness
    arbitration, 25–26
    mediation, 28
efficiency frontiers, 96
electronic commerce, see e-commerce
e-mail, 80
eResolution, 75
European Convention on Human
    Rights (ECHR), 19, 21
European Union (EU)
    alternative dispute resolution, 22
    arbitration recommendation (1998),
        23–26
    distance selling directive (97/7/EC),
        34–35
    e-commerce directive (2000/31/EC),
        32–34
    mediation directive (2008), 29–31
    mediation recommendation (2001),
        26–29

expanding the pie, 176
expert systems, 176

Fair Buy–Sell system, 94
Fair Division system, 94
fair negotiation, 161–67
Fair Outcomes Inc., 94
Fair Proposals system, 94
Fair Reputations system, 94
fair trial principle, 19–22
fairness
    alternative dispute resolution, 6–12
    mediation, 28
family disputes
    dialogues, 158–59
    mediation, 31, 117–18
    Online Family Dispute Resolution
        Service, 124–25
family law, argument tools, 152–54
Family_Mediator system, 117–18
Family Relationship Advice Line
    (FRAL), 121–23
Family Relationship Centres (FRCs),
    124
Family_Winner system, 91, 97–108,
    115–16, 118, 120, 155, 176
feature reduction/selection, 176
feed forward neural networks, 176
fifth party, online dispute resolution,
    79, 80, 81–84
fourth party, online dispute resolution,
    77–79, 81–84
FRAL, *see* Family Relationship Advice
    Line
FRCs, *see* Family Relationship Centres
free trade negotiations, 161
fundamentals, 1–2
future prospects, 168–70
fuzzy logic, 176

game theory, 6, 177
    decision-making support, 154–56
    negotiation support systems, 91–108
GearBi system, 132–38, 177
general software, 81
genetic algorithms, 177
GENIE system, 110–11

glossary, 171–85

HELIC-II system, 150
human mediators, accessibility of, 37
hybrid reasoning, 177

ICANN domain names dispute
    resolution process, 74–75
ICANS (Interactive Computer-
    Assisted Negotiation Support), 95
independence, arbitration, 24
inductive reasoning, 177
industrial relations, 109
influence diagrams, 178
information requirements, 25, 33
information security, 38
information society, 32, 33
information systems, 178
information technology, 2, 12–15
    advanced systems, 86–145
    future prospects, 168–70
    nature of, 79–81
    norms, 18–38
    process matching, 84–85
    process support, 72–85
INSPIRE system, 90, 127–32, 178
Institute of Arbitrators, 4
insurance companies, 76
integrated systems, 156–58
integrative negotiation, 6, 178
intelligent decision support systems,
    86–88
Interactive Computer-Assisted
    Negotiation Support, *see* ICANS
interest-based negotiation, 179
international disputes, 110, 162
InterNeg project, 127, 128
Internet, 32
issues, 151, 179

Jolis v *Jolis*, 100
JURIPAX system, 170, 179
jurisdiction, ODR providers, 38
justice, 91, 117

knowledge-based systems, 179
knowledge discovery, 179

knowledge engineering, 179
knowledge representation, 179

labour relations, *see* industrial
    relations
landmark cases, 180
LDS system, 109
legal negotiation, 7
legal positivism, 180
legal realism, 180
legality, arbitration, 26
liberty, arbitration, 26
linguistic variables, family dispute
    negotiation, 118
litigation, 5–6, 157, 180
    disclosures, 164–65
    tradition, 1
local *stare decisis*, 180
Lodder, Arno R., 149–52
logrolling, 180

machine learning, 87, 180
maintenance payments, 114
marital property, equitable allocation,
    91–94, 97–108, 111–15, 116–21
media, 162
mediation, 3–4, 157, 180
    European Union, 26–31
    The Mediation Room, 148
    online processes, 84
    videos, 124
Mediator system, 110
mixed legal system, 180
MP3-files, 80
Munich Treaty (1938), 9
mutual exclusiveness, family dispute
    negotiation, 99

naïve Bayesian classifiers, 180
Nash Equilibrium, 94, 181
natural language, argument
    tools, 153
nearest neighbour algorithms, 181
NEGOPLAN system, 109
negotiation, 2–3, 181
    agreements, 129
    artificial intelligence, 108–15

bargaining in the shadow of the law,
    165–67
challenges of, 96
compensation strategies, 159
disclosures, 164–65, 167
fairness, 6–12, 161–67
framework issues, 9
game theory, 91–108
Lodder's approach, 149–52
online processes, 84
Split-Up system, 114–15
stages of, 130
support systems, 13, 88–90, 114–15,
    128, 156–57
    artificial intelligence, 108–15
    game theory, 91–108
template-based support systems,
    88–90
transparency, 161–65, 166–67
Negotiator Pro system, 89, 90
neural networks, 88, 112, 176, 181
New York Convention, 5, 22

ODR, *see* Online Dispute Resolution
OFDRS, *see* Online Family Dispute
    Resolution Service
offers, negotiation, 130
One Accord system, 96
online arbitration, 35
Online Dispute Resolution (ODR), 27
    benefits, 13
    definition, 79
    distance selling directive, 34–35
    future prospects, 168–69
    information technology
        advanced systems, 86–145
        process support, 72–85
    international recommendations,
        35–38
    mediation, 29–31
    norms, 19–20
    providers, 74–77
    three-step model, 146–67
Online Family Dispute Resolution
    Service (OFDRS), 124–25
online services, legal
    requirements, 31

ontology-based searches, 126–27
onus of proof, 182
open textured legal predicates, 182
optimistic overconfidence, 182
orientation, online arbitration, 134
out of court settlements, 33–34
outcomes, 30, 159–60
overview of chapters, 15–17

pair-wise comparisons, 155
Pareto-optimality, 130, 182
PayPal, 21
pay-per-use software, 131
PERSUADER system, 109–10
plea bargaining, 10, 163–64
    criticisms, 142
    decision support systems,
        139–45
Pleadings Game, 149
power-based negotiation, 182
Pratt, Richard, 167
principled negotiation, 7, 182
procedural fairness, 21
proof, 182
property, *see* marital property
prosecutorial screening, 164

ratings, family dispute negotiation, 99,
    100–08, 120–21
ratio decidendi, 149, 183
rational communication, 148–49
reactive devaluation, 183
reasonable time concept, 21
Relationships Australia, 116, 162, 165
representation, arbitration, 26
reputation, 94
rights-based negotiation, 179
Ring, James F., 76
rule base, 87, 183
rule induction, 177

SAL system, 109
satisficing, 183
Schiavetta, Susan, 19–20
secrecy, 166
security, online processes, 38
semantic web technology, 125–27

sentencing decision support systems,
    139–45
simplicity, online arbitration, 133
Singapore, 72
Skillfinder, 126
Skype, 183
Smartsettle system, 84, 91, 97, 183
software, 79–85, 86–145
    see also individual systems
Split-Up system, 111–15, 166, 184
spousal maintenance, 114
SquareTrade, 76
stalemates, 146, 159
stare decisis, 184
statements, argument tools, 151, 152,
    153
statistical reasoning, 184
statutory law, 184
Swiss Life, 126
synchronous communication, 73–74,
    184

tabsheets, GearBi system, 135–36
TDRS, *see* Telephone Dispute
    Resolution Service
technology, *see* information
    technology
Telephone Dispute Resolution Service
    (TDRS), 121–24
template-based support systems,
    88–90
The Claim Room, 148, 174
Thiessen, Ernie, 95–97
third party, online dispute resolution,
    81–84
Tic-Tac-Toe game, 20
timeliness, online arbitration, 134
Torah, 1
Toulmin argument structures, 140–42,
    149
trade-offs, 97–108, 117, 120, 121, 159
transparency
    arbitration, 25
    negotiation, 11, 161–65, 166–67
trials, disclosures, 165
Trust–Convenience–Expertise
    Triangle, 77, 184

ultimatum bargaining, 11
United States, 5, 22
utility functions, 129, 184

Victoria Legal Aid, 140
videos, 124
virtual worlds, 168

weak discretion, 185
Web 2.0, 168

WIPO, *see* World Intellectual Property
    Organization, 75, 185
withdrawal rights, 35
World Intellectual Property
    Organization (WIPO), 75, 185
World Trade Organization, 161

zero-sum, 93, 185
zone of possible agreement (ZOPA), 40,
    127, 185